TAILS OF THE UNEXPECTED

Digressions, a Dog and Project X

JOHN DONOGHUE

New Moat Press, UK

This book is dedicated to anybody who ever knew me or my dog, Barney, and added to our story. Thank you.

Well, except for the guy who shouted at me when I was about twelve, for putting my lolly wrapper in the bin outside his shop when I had bought it from the shop next door. I still think about that. You, sir, are an asshole!

Contents

Marsupial Elvis

Somehow, Sparky and GoGo were still living with me. Susan always seemed to be in too much of a hurry to take them with her and I was seriously thinking of charging them board and rent. To be honest, I think she was just a bit fed up with them. After all, they didn't seem that exciting and had clearly outstayed their welcome at her house. I actually felt a bit sorry for them, just swimming endlessly around their little tank, past their ornamental sunken castle, until someone told me that goldfish only have a six-second memory. I felt sorry no more. What a fantastic life they must have! Every six seconds they were having a new adventure and what could be better than discovering a sunken castle?

"Look GoGo, a sunken castle!"

"Wow Sparky, that's amazing!"

"Look GoGo, a sunken castle!"

"Wow Sparky, that's amazing!"

"Look GoGo, a sunken castle!"

"Wow Sparky, that's amazing!"

Here I was, feeling bored with their apparent lack of

amusing antics, whilst they were having the time of their lives. I thought about putting a little deep sea diver man next to the castle, but they would probably overdose with the excitement, and by the time Sparky had finished telling GoGo about the castle and the diver, he would have forgotten what he had started talking about; it would be unfair.

"Look GoGo, a sunken castle ... and what's that ... Oh, my God ... a deep-sea diver! I wonder if he's dived... No, no, hang on, I've lost the thread ... what was I on about again?"

I had also been joined by Hammy the hamster. Hammy was no trouble really and spent most of the day driving about in his small toy car. He was meant to be the classroom pet at Deborah's school, but she had lent him to me in case I grew bored whilst Barney was away.

Oh, and in case I forgot to mention it, Barney was away.

⁰ ° ⁰ ° ⁰ °

Sorry, it's a bad habit of mine that I really should overcome. My thought process resembles that of a squirrel crossing the road. It can be a bit chaotic at times, but we get there in the end... most of the time. Don't worry, I'll try not to do it again. It should all become clear as we continue, but no promises though.

It's just that there's a lot to get through on this voyage of discoveries, some interesting, some funny and some bizarre... some very bizarre. This was the year that changed my life and could change yours.

I'd just got my first puppy, and I was eager to learn if there was more to having a dog than us both running after each other demanding to know what the other was eating.

And could I learn the secrets to turn this bewildered pup into a happy dog? More to the point, could I complete Project X in time? In fact, I've still got to explain to you what Project X is. Bear with me.

Add my daughter Bethan and my friend Deborah into the equation, combine this with the fact that I'd recently come out of the armed forces and entered the wilderness years and was looking for a new direction in my life, stir it up with some anecdotes, ramblings, digressions and tangents and you end up with "Tails of the Unexpected"... which actually seemed a much snappier title than "The Odyssey meets the Book of Revelations meets the Beano... and a puppy".

So, if you've got this far, buckle up and let's begin, but before we do, does anyone know dog speak for "Will you please stop weeing on the kitchen floor?"

° ° ° ° ° °

I run spasmodically and, by that, I don't mean I have a bizarre running style but that I go running two to three times a week.

It's a pleasant run, past a large park at the end of my street and then mostly through the woodland by the river's edge and, because the river is tidal, the scenery and wildlife change with the ebb and flow of the tides. At high tide, I have seen the best that nature can offer, from seals swimming upstream following the spawning salmon, through to swans swanning about on the sun-sparkling water, and dutiful ducks leading their downy ducklings in line as if off on a summer's outing.

At low tide I have seen the best that ASDA can offer in the form of shopping trolleys half sunk in the slimy brown sludge, along with various other flotsam and jetsam including a revolving clothesline that must have had an accident, a crate of empty Brown Ale bottles and a shoe – that must have been one hell of a night out!

There are not many sparrows about though. Apparently, they are becoming scarcer. I think pheasants are the new sparrows. I'm not sure what sparrows are supposed to be now. Maybe the old pheasants? Elsewhere, be it high or low tide, herons hide amongst the reeds on the riverbank, fishermen sit patiently at the water's edge, and I swear I've heard the hollow tapping of a woodpecker in the trees.

My running circuit takes me along the riverbank (with either the high or low tide views en route), over a small pedestrian bridge, then back the other way (same view – except back to front) and finally over a single road bridge back to my house. It's about two and a half miles all said, but I round it up to three in a pathetic effort to look impressive. However, if anyone dares to pour scorn on my meagre exercise, I remind them that I ran the last London Marathon, dressed as a banana (I didn't actually run the marathon at all. In fact, I think it would probably kill me but as long as the banana's identity remains a secret, I will take full advantage of his anonymity).

° ° ° ° ° °

By this stage in my life, I had lived on both land and sea, on both sides of the English/Welsh border and eventually on both sides of the aforementioned river. I had served in uniform in the British Army and the Royal Navy, been both a single and happily married man, felt like a small person in the big city, and the nearest I had got to being a big person in a small world was visiting the model village in Bourton-on-the-Water.

But a year ago, I had an ex-wife, lived on my own on the south side of the river, wore a suit to work and had no idea how the year would unfold.

My main source of amusement, apart from the pub, was my hobby – magic. Sadly, not the running around the garden naked at night in the company of some fit vestal virgins – with my luck I'd probably step barefoot on a slug anyway. Not even the chopping a woman in half type of magic. No, my magic was the close-up sort that happens in your hand or in front of your eyes so you can't deny its impossibility and is designed to impress attractive single young ladies. Well, that is if you don't tell them how it's done – otherwise you run the risk of suddenly reverting in their eyes from a mysterious and (hopefully) sexy man to a vision of a slightly sad bloke who's never properly grown up, sitting in his darkened bedroom practicing with a deck of cards while 'normal' people are out enjoying themselves in some trendy wine bar that probably used to be a bank.

Significant others in my life at that stage were the aforementioned Bethan, my ten-year old daughter, who manages to guess how all my tricks are done, and my good friend Deborah who comes complete with her seven-year-old Border Collie dog called Tess.

I regarded it as something of an achievement that I had reached my current age, bearing in mind that I had led such a reckless childhood by today's standards. Oh, my stars, the dangers I faced when I was small - both physical and mental. It was a world devoid of pushbike helmets, children's TV on all day, friendly Russians and bottled water (water ...in a bottle ...that you pay for! Why would you need that when there was 'council pop'?). As for mobile phones, we didn't even have a full landline phone in the house – we had a 'party line' shared with next door, so that when they were on the phone you couldn't make a call (and just had to sit quietly on the stairs and listen into Mrs Davies's conversation instead). It was fixed to a wall, and you had no idea who was ringing; you just had to pick up the receiver and find out. Scary stuff! Nowadays we know who's calling and just look at our phones in horror wondering why they didn't send a text instead. And when they do, you look at your phone and say that that could have been an emoji.

In those days, you read the cereal box at breakfast, if you went for a dump, you studied the shampoo bottles to pass the time, and if you were waiting for someone at the pub you either just had to sit there like a psychopath or else pretend to find the back of a crisp packet *really* interesting.

I'm not quite sure why, but in those days, we also answered the phone quoting our own telephone number.

"Hello, Cardiff 499456". I'm not too sure why we did this as surely the caller knew the number they had just rung. I'm pretty sure we didn't open the door saying our address as well – but I'm not ruling anything out. These were odd times.

We were also one of the last generations to grow up not using computers in school. In the days before social media people had to walk for miles just to call me a bastard. Also, as scary as it may sound to children today, I didn't have an X-Box or PlayStation because they hadn't been invented, so I had to use my imagination. Even when we did get the internet, there was just Ask Jeeves and a single cat meme.

There's a boy in Bethan's class at school called Derek. Ten years old... Derek! Anyway, Derek has an iPhone. When I was ten, the closest I came to such sophistication was one of those multi-ink pens where you could slide down a part of the top to choose what colour you wanted to use.

Mind you, it wasn't just me who was a bit of a Luddite when it came to new technology. I specifically remember the larger-than-life actor and embodiment of caps lock, Brian Blessed, being introduced to the tablet size computer that was known at the time as the 'Palm Pilot'.

"SOUNDS LIKE A WANKING MACHINE!" he boomed.

So instead of high-tech gadgetry when I was growing up, we had ads for X-ray specs, the Beano and Dandy, scary supervisors in the park whose aim was to seemingly stop you having fun, and dogs wandering the streets leaving little white turds that would silently explode into a cloud of dust if you kicked them. This was a time when twenty five pence was decent pocket money and the only thing 'race issues' meant was who ran the fastest. We had big orange Space Hoppers we hopped about on and Pogo sticks we sprang up and down on. We used to do a lot of bouncing back then. Hell, we even drank squash out of communal beakers with our friends – and sometimes we didn't even know which side they had used first. The only concession we had to Health and Safety were instructions from a squirrel called Tufty about how to cross the road safely. In hindsight, I'm not sure if a squirrel was the ideal candidate for the job, as every time I've seen one going from one side to the other, they seem to cross halfway, then decide to suddenly turn around and scurry back from whence they've come before finally changing their mind yet again, turning back and making a run for it.

A few years later there was a cat called Charley on television who used to tell us things like not to fall in water, not to overload plug sockets and not to pull tablecloths off tables, which was clearly a major issue in those days. I'm not sure why people back then thought we'd be more likely to take advice from animals rather than a responsible adult, but there we have it.

They were simpler times, and we didn't seem to worry about things as much as children nowadays, either. We weren't under so much pressure to plan out our lives and instead just merrily enjoyed our childhood without thinking too far ahead. In fact, I read recently about a young sixteen-year-old who, whilst doing her homework assisted by her dad, received a text from her mum which read: "What do you want from life?"

It was quite a profound question just to come out of the blue, especially to a young girl in the middle of preparing for her exams, but father and daughter duly took up the challenge and debated the various answers – wealth, fulfilment, love, all three?

Five minutes later, she received a second message from her mum, blaming predictive text for the error and correcting it to, "What do you want from Lidl?" (for the uninitiated, a local supermarket). In this case, the not so profound answer was something along the lines of chocolate buttons, a milkshake and a welding visor. OK, maybe not the best example to use, but you get the gist?

Then, as now, we had the dreaded BCG tuberculosis injection, and for some reason we had to do physical training after it 'to get the medication moving through our system'. I'm not exactly sure that it works like that, but I am sure that, due to some sort of time zone difference or some such thing, it hurt more in my day than it does now. I can still remember the clarion call of "My BCG, my BCG!" if anyone ventured within the ten-yard exclusion zone surrounding my left arm.

Instead, we played football up at Cyncoed Park, went swimming down the Empire pool, and played 'Escape from Colditz' whenever we could. Oh, and we cycled a lot. I had a dynamo on the bike that powered the lights when it got dark, which was good, except that, when I stopped at a junction, the wheels ceased powering the dynamo, the lights went out and I was plunged into darkness, which was bad. What a rubbish invention. A palm pilot sounds a lot more fun.

I was also frankly shocked when I discovered, years later, that you didn't actually look cool at all riding a Chopper bike whilst wearing your jumper tucked into your trousers. My God, this was a dark time when some people even felt the need to tuck their shirts into their underpants too!

I was never trendy enough to do the tucking in or even to own a Chopper. In fact, I was about as cool as someone trying to chase a ping pong ball, but I was still devastated to find out that even my ideas of cool were un-cool.

Unthinkable as it may seem now, sometimes we even ran around with sharp things, despite threats from my mum and all my friends' mums. The years have passed since then and I often wonder if these mothers were actually part-time philosophers. Maybe they were right all along. Maybe I'll never really ever be *truly* happy until someone actually does lose an eye.

All these mums were additionally programmed to chorus, "You won't feel the benefit" if we dared enter the house without taking our coats off first, "No pudding until you finish your dinner," at teatime, "Who is 'she'? The cat's mother?", "If someone asked you to jump off a cliff, would you?", "I want, never gets", and my all-time favourite, "I'll give you something to cry about!" when I was actually *already* crying about something.

It seems we were also affected by a bizarre medical phenomenon back in those days that meant if you accidentally swallowed your bubble gum, apparently it wrapped itself around your heart, if you sat too close to the telly, you got square eyes, and if you made a face and the wind changed, you stayed like that.

Actually, with that sort of wisdom from our mums, I can see now why they thought we'd get better advice from the likes of Tufty and Charley.

Yes, life may have been hard for us thirty-somethings when we were children, but the one thing we did have, that children nowadays don't seem to possess, was a decent taste in music. After embarrassing my daughter sufficiently by dancing like the wallies on 'Top of the Pops', I'd retreat into the kitchen and listen to the music I liked. One of my favourites is an Australian called Nick Barker.

° ° ° ° ° °

When I first heard the song 'Thylacine', I thought it was about some dreaded hereditary disease, a new strain of penicillin or distant cousin of the BCG, but when Nick Barker sang, "You're famous; the marsupial Elvis," I knew I was way off. It turns out that a Thylacine was also known as the Tasmanian Tiger, which was a bizarre mix of different animals. Starting from the front, which is as good a place as any to start - it had the head of a large dog, followed by the front part of a wolf and the back half of a tiger, finishing off with a rigid tail. On the undercarriage, it had 'wolfy' front legs, the back legs of a hyena and, to complete this exotic mix, a pouch like a kangaroo. I say, 'was' because they were hunted into extinction in their native Australia, with the last one, named Ben, being kept in captivity until he finally succumbed to old age and, in 1938, joined the ranks of the dodo. Mortal wombat.

Since then, in true Elvis tradition, Thylacine sightings have been reported year on year, although, to my knowledge, one has never been spotted working in a chip shop in Newcastle.

Therefore, when I was asked to choose a venue for my birthday treat, there was no hesitation. Some people may say that Edinburgh is like the girl who is pretty but really boring, and Glasgow is the fatty that shows you a good time. Both appealed, after hearing about the marsupial Elvis, there was only one place on my mind – it had to be an animalarium. What other animals would I shortly only be able to see in a glass case, stuffed with mattress filling and with marbles for eyes?

Destination: Edinburgh Zoo.

2

Run For Your Lives!

Have you ever seen a Bush Dog? I suppose you could best describe it as looking like a Lakeland Terrier and, if you have never seen a Lakeland Terrier, you could best describe it as looking like a Bush Dog.

This Bush Dog, and for ease of typing he will be called Billy, lived at the zoo, in a big room with a glass wall at the front and a little door at the rear of the room that led to somewhere else; I don't know where. Billy would appear at this door, potter into the room for about four yards and then turn round and potter back, disappearing into this unknown land beyond the door. He repeated this at intervals of about a minute, although he sometimes left a gap of around five minutes as if he was a bit scared of being labelled predictable.

Bethan and I probably spent the majority of our time, and certainly longer than anyone in polite society should, standing and waiting for Billy to appear, complete his four yards, turn round and potter away. We were amused when, once in a blue moon, Billy would come right up to the glass and peer out before hurrying back, but we were even more amused when other zoo visitors would come and peer into Billy's room to see what we were looking at. Invariably, they would come when Billy wasn't on parade and, after thirty seconds or so of looking into the empty arena, they would wander off, in search of something more exciting.

At this stage, Bethan and I would shout to each other something along the lines of, "Look, look! He's balancing that ball on his head!" As the unsuspecting onlooker ran back to catch a glimpse of this feat, only to find themselves once more looking into a bare room, we would mutter sadly to each other, "Awwwww, he's just run in."

In case you ever pay a visit to Edinburgh Zoo, with the intention of seeing this 'ball on head' phenomenon and then decide to sue because it never happened when you were there, let me make it clear now that it never occurred when we were present either. And that man and the girl running out of the zoo, and down the steps shouting, "Run for your lives, they're loose!" ...that was us too. We are sorry. We didn't mean to create panic. We were just content with fooling innocent members of the public and seeing Billy potter.

° ° ° ° ° °

I suppose it was thanks to Billy that, later on in the zoo's 'pencil and rubber' shop, I felt drawn to a book on dog psychology. It looked fascinating so I bought it to read on the train home.

It appears that all modern dog breeds are descended from the wolf – yes, even the ones that resemble a large rat and those that look as if they need a good ironing. Despite the fact that dogs have been domesticated and bred to perform different roles, they still retain seventy-five per cent of the wolf pack instincts. These wolf packs can vary in size, from two to twelve wolves, but they all have a leader and a strict hierarchy or pecking order. The leader, or top dog, is known as the alpha male. Thereafter, the other dogs develop a kind of 'squash ladder' of seniority and regularly challenge each other, vying for a better position and consequently higher status, with the perks that go with it.

The stronger wolf will be the one who forces the other into submission during a confrontation and subsequently takes his place on the ladder until he, in turn, is challenged and so on. Seniority has its perks too. When a kill is made on a hunting expedition, the rest of the pack steps aside, enabling the top dog and his mate (the alpha female) to eat first. After they have had their fill, the other dogs take their turn in order of seniority, through to the lowest of the low. Wolves, it transpires, are also very social animals – playing, hunting and sleeping together, with order of seniority dictating how close you sleep to the top dog at night.

This was all new to me. The closest I had ever come to studying wolves up to that point was watching repeats of 'It's the Wolf'. For the uninitiated, this is a cartoon in which a wolf is in pursuit of a lamb-like creature. "It's the wulaff, it's the wulaff!" the cartoon lamb would shriek in a very high-pitched irritating voice, upon spotting his 'wolfish' stalker. He was so irritating that you started to wish that the wolf *would* catch the little fucker and eat him alive but, alas, it never happened.

Anyway, the point is that it hadn't helped my understanding of dog psychology at all. In fact, as a piece of scientific research, I think it was flawed on several levels. To be honest, even as a cartoon, it was pretty rubbishy – give me 'Wacky Races' and 'Hong Kong Phooey' any day.

Moreover, the bottom line is that the favourite saying

of old women, "Rover is like a furry human. He thinks he's one of the family," doesn't quite hit the nail on the head. Rather, it seems that Rover doesn't think he is one of the family at all but considers that we are all part of *his* pack.

。 ° 。 ° 。 °

As I was out running past the park, I had noticed a variety of dogs and humans who all looked like they may have been from the same pack. There were some smiling humans, taking their dogs for a stroll and there also appeared to be some dogs taking their unhappy humans for a trudge. I thought dog walks were meant to be fun all round?

Some of the humans threw tennis balls for their dogs to fetch and some of the dogs brought the ball back and dropped it at the human's feet, whilst others had to be chased all over the park in order to retrieve it. What was going on? Surely *all* dogs were pre-programmed to fetch tennis balls - in the same way that all men have an inbuilt Pavlovian response to the click-clack of high heels? We just *have* to turn around to see who is wearing them. We can't help it.

Some of the people in the park spoke in whispers to their dog, who then responded by doing what was asked – much as I would do if I was on a night out and a promotions girl in a PVC catsuit came over to me and whispered for me to do something – actually make that 'anything'.

Other people were shouting their pet's name repeatedly, growing more incensed with each yell as their dog sniffed something at the other side of the park, apparently oblivious to their owner's frenzied pleas – much as Deborah would ignore me if I was ever brave/stupid enough to tell her that I *had* chatted to a girl in a PVC catsuit on a night out.

Some owners also seemed to have a bizarre hobby which looked as if it consisted of saving up all of their dog's poo and taking it home in a bag. Me? I've no need for a poop bag. I normally just find that my running shoes have special in-built dog poop magnets that the salesperson obviously didn't think they needed to tell me about when I bought them. I take my helping of dog poop home with me, wedged in the intricate patterns on the sole. Incidentally, as an aside, I have also found another marketing opportunity for the people who make cotton buds. Why the hell would I want to take home a whole bag of poo as well? Practice?

The book I had bought at the zoo explained it all to me (except the poo in bag stuff). The humans with the well-behaved dogs had established themselves as the top dog and their pets knew where they stood in the pack. Not being top dog wasn't humiliating for the dog either, as a dog is just content to know where it stands. As the human is usually the owner, he or she should take that top dog slot, and those people having problems were the ones who were still having their position on the squash ladder challenged. They had yet to resolve who was the top dog in their own family or pack.

Reading up on how a dog's mind operates also opened my eyes as to how I had inadvertently undermined my friend's efforts to allow her dog to know its place. At Deborah's, I found it amusing to encourage Tess to climb up onto the sofa to watch TV. In the wild, it's only the top dog that climbs up high to oversee his domain, so I was inadvertently offering Tess an invitation to be kingpin, and I've also lost count of the number of times I've literally offered a squash ladder confrontation in the form of a game of tug of war with a plastic string of sausages. I could go on, but the saving grace is that it's only with other people's animals that I have messed things up and not my own. It's funny because it wasn't my animal and my house. I wouldn't make those kinds of mistakes with my own dog.

Oh, by the way, I decided to get a dog.

3

The Dog from U.N.C.L.E.

For those of you who have never seen an 'Uncle Kenny' dog, it's a bit like the ones you used to see on wheels, being pushed around by children or senile old Majors. I'm not exactly sure if its official name is an Uncle Kenny dog but, since my Great Uncle Kenny bred them, that was the name that stuck. Urban myth has it that he once entered a dog at Crufts, but I think that is just a malicious rumour.

Incidentally, annual trips from Cardiff to Brecon to see Kenny and his dogs in my childhood were the closest I ever came to interacting with dogs unless, of course, you count the time when Matthew Quinn's dog bit me when I was in Form Three.

Since starting this chapter, I have been reliably informed that an Uncle Kenny dog is actually a Welsh Wire-Haired Terrier, so this breed appealed to me as being the ideal candidate for my first dog. There was this tenuous link in my past and, if I squinted a bit, I could almost imagine him as a large version of the Bush Dog.

o ° o ° o °

He was going to be called 'Billy' too, or even 'Billy Two'.

I suppose it was the challenge factor which instigated this. Could I think like a dog, and a top dog for that matter? Would I be able to train a dog to be obedient, based on the principles of the wolf pack? It seemed basic enough – forget modern manners and think like a canine. As an officer in the armed forces, I had been taught to ensure that the soldiers/sailors ate before I did. However, in my new pack, this was going to be turned on its head if I was to remain the top dog. I, as leader, would eat first and only then would Billy be given his food (as an officer I was also taught 'not to bleed in front of the men' and to always carry a tool for getting stones out of horse's hooves, but these nuggets of wisdom seemed less relevant to the training of the canine).

Manners normally dictated that I opened the door to let someone through but, in the wild, it's the top dog that leads the pack on their journeys. Billy would be junior to me, so I would be conveying the wrong message if I let him go through a doorway before me, up the stairs before me, or allowed him to choose where we should go on our walk. No Billy straining on the lead wrenching my arm off for me. I would be the one who decided where we would venture that day and Billy would trot obediently alongside me.

In my quest for inspiration, I even read several books on what passed as good manners for humans in this green and, with the proper social graces, hopefully pleasant land. Even pumping was covered, although they rather delicately called it 'passing wind'. The following advice was proffered:

In aristocratic circles, the correct thing to do if this happens is to carry on as if nothing has happened and the entire company should carry on as if they had not noticed.

Based on my theory of turning etiquette on its head, I deduced that if my dog farted, he should look sufficiently surprised and I in turn would point and laugh.

I was always told that I had the distasteful habit of sulking if things didn't go the way I wanted them to (school report circa baby class infants – "Donoghue is sullen and easily vexed"). Now, sulking was to be the order of the day if things didn't go my way. This was based on the principle that puppies love attention and, if you take that away, they are devastated and, in future, will seek to avoid the cause of its withdrawal. So, if Billy doesn't bring back the tennis ball in a game of fetch, my theory dictates that I should stop playing and ignore him. It seems that I would also need to master the art of actively ignoring the dog as it is no use ignoring someone unless they know they are being ignored. I would need to make it obvious that I preferred to read the paper, rather than play with a naughty puppy. Playtime wouldn't include tug of war games with strings of sausages either. Opportunities to challenge my position would be avoided if at all possible. If I let him triumph, I would be giving him the wrong message, but if I kept on winning games against my little puppy, I'd feel like a mean-spirited competitive dad. Best avoid them altogether.

My sofa also formed part of my strategy, as there would be no encouragement for Billy to oversee his domain from the comfort of my furniture. Firstly, it's my domain and, if anyone is to watch over it, it's going to be me. Secondly, I'm sure that, what may now seem like a cute puppy struggling to clamber up, won't appear so appealing when it's a dirty, wet and fully grown dog, fresh in from the muddy garden, leaping onto my armchair, even if there was an everlasting sale down at the sofa showroom. If I want Billy to be the lowest of the low in my pack, I need to keep him as the lowest of the low in the house too, and this includes preventing him from jumping up.

Mind you, neither would he be encouraged to do that dog thing where he sits on the floor, pokes his two back legs in the air and then pulls himself around with his two front legs. If I interpret this correctly, the filthy little hound is effectively using the carpet as a scratching post for his bum hole. Not nice.

Apparently though, if he knows where he stands in the pack, he will be a much happier dog and I knew that I would be a much happier owner!

. . . . . .

I soon discovered that dog ownership takes much more research than I had first thought, and this entailed learning about my potential pet's characteristics, as the only one I could recollect about an Uncle Kenny dog was that they seemed very bouncy. As I began to accost strangers, innocently walking their dogs, to enquire about temperament, training and other 'doggy-type' questions, I soon found that I needed to be careful how I phrased my questions after one awkward encounter:

Me: "Do you like Cocker Spaniels?"

Lady in park: "What an unusual thing to ask …but I'd say I probably prefer them both in equal measure."

I also discovered that if you really want to annoy someone, call their pet by the wrong gender, and that as a general rule of thumb, the smaller the dog, the crazier the girl. Perhaps the scariest moment, though, was when I asked one woman what was the worst thing about owning a dog and she informed me that, because of the slobber, it was sometimes hard to get a good grip of her dog's balls. I was therefore visibly relieved when she showed me one of those throwers that she recently purchased to solve that particular issue.

However, it was during these impromptu question and answer sessions that I encountered my first major disappointment. As bouncy as they are, Welsh Wire-Haired Terriers do not excel at off-lead training; rather, they excel at off-lead running away!

This was a devastating blow in my quest for the ideal Billy. I had made a sketchy plan of what I wanted from a dog on my daughter's whiteboard. I needed a running companion, which had to be suitable for off-lead training and also be good with children.

Billy had failed selection.

Time to seek an alternative dog. Time to seek an alternative name. Billy would forever be linked with what might have been. New name, new dog and back to the whiteboard.

° ° ° ° ° °

When I was eight, instead of having a puppy, my sister Kate arrived, and this eight-year age difference is something we have agreed to carry on for the rest of our lives – it makes things so much easier when calculating ages on birthdays and so on. I now get on very well with Kate, who also goes by the nickname of 'BooBoo'. This is worth knowing in case I lapse into lazy colloquialisms later on in the book, and it is also worth knowing that the current harmony which now exists between us was not always so.

There were six of us in the Donoghue pack. Apart from my dad and mum, I had two older brothers and a younger sister, the aforementioned Kate. Anyone who has the remotest knowledge of science, mass and volume and all that stuff, will realise that six people into one Ford

Cortina shouldn't go. But it did, and often. The car journey from Cardiff to Cwmbran takes about fifteen to twenty minutes nowadays but, in the early Seventies, the geographical make-up of South Wales must have been different because the journey would take ages.

We lived in Cardiff but my Nana and cousins, Jason and David, lived in Cwmbran; not together. Well, Jason and David did, along with Peter, Helen, my Uncle John and Aunty Eileen. What I mean is that my Nana and my cousins didn't live together in some bizarre hippy commune but, having said that, I think my Uncle John probably secretly wished that he *was* in a hippy commune. He is retired now and should be doing 'old people' stuff, like talking incessantly about his ailments and grumbling about how things are not as good as they were when he was young, but not so with Uncle John. He has grown a ponytail, plays the bongos, roller-skates, goes ceroc dancing and listens to jazz music. Listening to jazz? Now there is a sure sign of madness if ever there was one. His only concession to old age is going on like a grumpy old guy about how he finds it confusing that signs in Wales often have the English and the Welsh place name displayed together. His words, not mine, I hasten to add before I alienate a good section of potential readers from Cymru. I say Cardiff/Caerdydd – so good they named it twice.

Wales – where no man is an island… except Barry. Whilst I'm on about place names in the Principality, some towns have developed jokey second names. For example, Llantrisant, home of the Royal Mint is also known – maybe a bit unkindly - as 'The Hole with the Mint'. Other places are known because of some other interesting and unique fact: for example, did you know that Las Vegas and Merthyr are the only two places in the world where you can pay for sex with chips?

However, back to my issue with Kate; the main cause of my unhappiness with my sister was borne out of the compulsory seating arrangement in the Cortina. Mum and Dad sat in the front, while Paul and Neil, my brothers, each sat next to a window on the back seat. Kate sat between them in a baby seat while I was left to sit directly in front of her, crouched up in the foetal position, on the bump between the rear footwells, all set to be catapulted out like a human cannonball in the event of an emergency stop.

In itself, apart from just being there, it could be reasonably argued that Kate was not responsible for my unfortunate position. What Kate was responsible for, though, was pummelling my back with her feet, at every opportunity. We once travelled to France for a family holiday, and it was only when we reached Calais that anyone thought of removing her shoes. The passing years have eased both my back and any tension between us. Furthermore, the promise of seeing an 'Uncle Kenny' dog had made her reconsider her fifteen-year boycott of the North East of England where, by pure coincidence, I had been living for the last fifteen years. But there was now not going to be any 'Uncle Kenny' dog.

'Plan B' was needed.

4

Plan B

With hindsight, a dog on wheels may have been a better option, being cheaper and marginally easier to train, although, I must concede, not without its problems when going upstairs. I am certain though that, after the initial disappointment, Kate would have been fine.

However, the dog on wheels only remained a fond idea, as non-permanent marker pens were already heading for the whiteboard. Plan B entered its embryonic stage when Deborah insisted that Plan B dog should reflect its owner who, in this case, was me. I assumed she meant that being young and handsome were the qualities we now sought in my potential new pack member. The fact that she may actually have meant 'shallow and vain' was a distinct possibility, which I chose to ignore at that stage.

Dog breeds were now fed through the complex matrix selection process that combined both my wish list of dog qualities and someone else's perception of me. One breed seemed to have both the characteristics I was looking for and, according to Deborah, matched my personality.

Thankfully, I was independently assessed as not being a 'toy dog' person (I guess that ruled out wheelie dog too). A sheepherder, or cattle driving dog, it seems, did not reflect the inner me and, despite my security background, I was deemed not to be a guard dog of the Rottweiler or German Shepherd variety. Apparently, my military background did not make me eligible for a fighter like a John Bull pug either and, to me, a Shih Tzu was a zoo with no animals and, anyway, is actually another type of dog which I am not. Terriers would be no good for me either – too much running off and I am neither a large game dog nor a non-sporting one.

Apparently, I am a Labrador.

(Note to reader: I'll just wait here for a couple of minutes while you decide what breed of dog you are. Just let me know when you are ready to go on).

。 ° 。 ° 。 °

Ah, interesting choice you've made there!

Anyway, where was I? Oh yes, I remember now. Whether it had been Plan A or Plan B, nothing could have prevented the most difficult part of my whole dog-training project. I had to convince my daughter, Bethan, that having a dog was going to be a good thing and, if I failed to win her over to the cause, the whole idea would have gone the way of the pear. So much for me being top dog!

"So, are you still thinking of getting a dog?" she asked on the way to the park. I hadn't realised that Bethan even knew I was thinking about it, but I guess she realised that Billy the Bush Dog had made an impression on me.

。 ° 。 ° 。 °

My daughter's mum is a teacher, and it is easier if I just call her Susan which, as luck would have it, is actually her name. Susan is a Head Mistress no less, or Head Teacher as they are now known, and I met her when we were at high school together – Lady Mary High School to be exact (when we were both pupils I hasten to add – if she had been Head Mistress then, it would have been just wrong. Every schoolboy's dream maybe, but just wrong all the same). Her family had moved down from the North East and her father worked for a pop drink conglomerate that had a factory in Cardiff. Despite this, they were Catholic. When I was at Naval College years later, I needed a partner for the Summer Ball. I had asked Christina Stone, who used to sit in front of me in history, but she couldn't go and suggested Susan instead. I rang Susan and asked her if she wanted to come as my guest and, when she asked me where it was, I told her that the Captain held his balls in the College grounds.

Britannia Royal Naval College in Dartmouth is where all Royal Naval Officers complete their initial training and it is a magnificent venue for a ball, with its fine proud buildings, packed to the gunnels with history and overlooking the Dart River estuary. During the day, there would be rowing contests, with the Captain's wife presenting medals to the winners and shyly kissing the cox of the winning crew.

Later, in the evening, officers, resplendent in their best mess uniforms, would dance the night away with beautiful girls in ball gowns.

Susan arrived by train for the ball, and I thought I would impress her by picking her up from the station in my friend's two-seater sports car. He drove as I had yet to pass my test and, although I'm sure I looked quite dashing as I met her at the station, appeared slightly less so when we realised that there were now three of us to fit into the car. I made the journey back, laid out along the parcel shelf.

There is probably a law against that nowadays or there should be anyway. I'm not on about the laying out on the parcel shelf thing, I mean something/anything should be put in place to prevent stupid blokes like me from having the opportunity of going out with attractive, intelligent women in the first place.

But I digress, again! It's a habit that I have picked up. Still, it's free, legal, fun to do and, unlike some other habits, won't affect your eyesight.

。 ° 。 ° 。 °

I guess Bethan has inherited her love of teaching from Susan, and, with every visit to me she comes prepared to conduct a lesson. At first, these lessons were off the cuff, but now she arrives equipped with copious typed notes. She even downloads teachers' guides from the internet to see if her schoolteacher is following the lesson plan in the correct way. In her bedroom, which I have now converted into her own classroom, I sit attentively, whilst being taught by Miss Donoghue.

Interestingly, I think I have learnt more from these lessons than I did at school. In school we learnt a lot about motte and bailey castles and oxbow lakes which have not featured at all in my life since, and, if anything, I had assumed that English comprehension would have become easier in the twenty first century. I remember when I was back in Lady Mary High School, having to write long descriptive pieces about this or that character and I always gave them a Roman nose, as that seemed a great expressive feature and one that might even impress Miss Tucker. She was the really fit teacher that every school has. All the boys loved Miss Tucker and all the boys wanted to… Actually, I think for modesty's sake we'll just leave that rhyme unfinished.

With the advent of computers and Word documents, I thought the need for all that narrative would have disappeared and it would suffice to say, "Times New Roman, you know the type?" Apparently not. I had also adopted the maxim of 'If in doubt, insert a semi-colon', as no one really knows when they should be used anyway, and the reader would then accept my apparent superior knowledge of the English language. Bethan knew, though, and my reign of haphazardly using punctuation marks ended. To add insult to injury, either because I was too busy annoying Donna Herford and Katherine Kavanagh who used to sit in front of me in class at Lady Mary, daydreaming about Debbie Brown, or because I was out taking a pee at the time, but they appear to have invented a whole new stack of English grammar rules in my absence.

In my new 'school', the whole curriculum is covered in different lessons and I even receive an end of year report. Bethan has also put me on the 'Further Literacy Scheme for English', so I must be doing well (or so I thought until Deborah told me that this was the syllabus for 'children who need more support'). Despite that, I even gave her a box of sweets and a badly spelt 'thank you' card at the end of term, in the hope that I would be able to survive the six weeks of summer holidays without getting shouted at in class.

° ° ° ° ° °

Consequently, when Bethan called a conference to discuss the idea of me owning a dog, I knew this was serious. This wasn't just going to be a fun chat; this was the real thing. It was going to be a make-or-break situation, with me making my case to the chairperson (Bethan) who would then probe the arguments and ultimately give the deciding vote on whether Plan B dog would make it off the drawing board.

I therefore set about diligently preparing my rationale for having a puppy. In all fairness, Bethan is much more sensible than me and wanted to know if I had really thought about the consequences of training and looking after a demanding animal, or whether I was just doing this on a whim. She had witnessed the trouble I'd brought upon myself with her mum, when I'd returned from the fair with Bethan clutching a goldfish in a bag.

Even though she is not that keen on dogs herself, I was given a fair hearing and the conference was impressively conducted – in fact, better than most conferences I have attended in a professional capacity. Luckily, I had recently completed a substantial amount of research on dogs – reading books on their psychology, together with standard training procedures. On the basis that copying from one source was plagiarism, but blatantly copying from many was 'research', I had a file full of 'researched techniques' for training Plan B dog. I had also road tested the techniques on Tess, Deborah's seven year old collie. The answer, by the way, is, "Yes, you can teach an old dog new tricks". After my case was presented and the cross-examination was over, I waited tensely for the verdict.

I was as tense as someone in England trying to pay for goods with a Scottish five pound note. If you have ever tried that, you'll know how tense I mean!

Plan B dog was meant to complement my time with

Bethan, not to be something that detracted from her enjoyment of her visits so, if she didn't support the scheme, it would have to be forgotten. Bethan returned to the room. Drumroll…

Thumbs up!

5

Naming Baby

I phoned my dad to tell him the good news.

"Hello Dad, it's me."

"Hello Boy. How's um, how's err…?"

"Bethan?"

"How's Bethan?"

"She's fine Dad. I'll put her on in a sec. I'm going to get a dog!"

"Bloody hell boy, why do you want to do that? *We* never had a dog."

"I know we never had a dog, but I thought it would be good company. I was thinking of getting an 'Uncle Kenny' dog."

"He's bloody dead, boy!"

"I know Uncle Kenny is dead, Dad. Anyway, I'm going to get a Labrador now."

"What do you want to get a big slobbery thing like that for?"

"It's not big and slobbery Dad, it's a Labrador. I thought he could come running with me."

"He'll bloody run off, Boy."

"I'll train him not to."

"They're as thick as two short planks."

"No, they're not. Blind people have them ..." and so on.

He seemed pleased for me.

　　　᳢ ᳢ ᳢ ᳢ ᳢ ᳢

Plan B dog needed a name. 'Cerberus' was the original devil dog and Greek legend has it that he was huge – bigger than a horse, with three heads. He guarded the underworld and allowed the dead in, but not out again and, in itself, that is no bad thing otherwise we would be overrun with ghosts. The ancient Egyptians called Sirius the 'dog star' and it is visible for most of the summer. The Egyptians actually believed that Sirius was responsible for the summer heat, hence the phrase 'The dog days of summer' to describe those hot balmy summer days. 'Sparky' was the name of the Labrador in Kurt Vonnegut's 'Breakfast of Champions' (very good book - very bad film). Sparky was unable to wag his tail because of an automobile accident and had no way of showing other dogs how friendly he was so he had to fight all the time. 'Scooby Doo' (Sunday name 'Scoobert Doo') belonged to Shaggy and helped to solve mysteries as they toured around in a camper van with a serious bloke, a geeky girl and a really smart looking girl. 'Frank' on the other hand, is the black Labrador up the road. Melanie, Elvis, Mr Pork Pie, Maxine, Titch – the point is that there's an infinite number of names you can call your mangy hound or snappy bitch. Anything goes... well, except maybe 'Curiosity', in case your neighbour has cats. You'd just be setting him up as prime suspect if anything ever happened to them.

Choosing a name is one thing, but then you are stuck with it for the rest of your pooch's life. Someone I know had a dog with a striking red coat and so they called him 'Fire'. Lovely name, but you can imagine the havoc they caused when they used to yell for him to come in at the end of the evening. And what might have been acceptable for Guy Gibson of 'Dambusters' fame to call his dog, may not be so suitable today! Look it up – I'm not going to tell you in this book and risk being sacked from work! Finding the right name for anything is important.

。°。°。°

Durham has a fantastic history. It sits on the banks of the River Wear – the same one that flows past my house, on its journey to the sea. Durham is also where the Prince Bishops lived. The Normans, worried that the Northern Princes might become too powerful and threaten the King, made the Bishops of Durham into Princes and their magnificent Norman Castle dominates the skyline. The Cathedral, built in 1093, has been voted the nation's favourite building and contains the tomb of The Venerable Bede, who instigated the idea that dates should be calculated from the time of the birth of Jesus.

Thomas Wolsey, the famous Minister of King Henry VIII, who came close to becoming Pope, made his fortune from being Bishop of Durham (although he never even visited the place). The University, founded in 1832, is regarded as next in line after Oxford and Cambridge and its graduates have 'Dunelm' (the Latin name for the city) printed on their degrees. Durham even had its own Dick Whittington, Sir John Duck, who arrived in 1655 as a poor man and ended up a rich and famous mayor. He lived on

Silver Street, which is so called because that's where silver coins were made in the Middle Ages.

For the Millennium celebrations, a new state of the art theatre and performing arts complex was built to enhance this ancient city. With so much history to draw from, and so many links with prominent people from days of yore, what did the good councillors of Durham call the new magnet for the arts, this contemporary focal point?

The Gala.

It makes it sound like a bingo hall but, once again, I digress.

◦ ° ◦ ° ◦ °

The debate for a suitable name for Plan B dog raged on in the car, on the way back from a visit to Durham town. Some people advocate calling their dog the first thing that comes into their head when they see their new pup, but I thought I would take out some insurance against any lack of inspiration at the crucial time. I read that in America, there were three children christened 'Latrine' last year plus one unfortunate girl called 'Chlamydia'. At least there was no one called 'Rubella' which had made the list the previous year. Goodness knows what had inspired *their* parents.

I'm also friends with three sisters: Pixie, Treasure and Sandra. I'll let you guess the moment when their parents abandoned their happy, carefree hippy lifestyle and became accountants. I actually met Pixie a couple of years ago and told her how lovely I thought her name was, and she agreed that it certainly was great when she was eight and maybe it would have been fantastic if she had become a stripper, but now, as a forty-something manager at a funeral director's it was far from ideal. I guess she had a point.

Emlyn Hughes, the famous footballer, clearly wanted his legacy to live on and called his son Emlyn and his daughter Emma Lynn. Not to be outdone, the famous boxer and grill salesman George Foreman named *all* his five sons George.

Names can potentially be fraught with potential danger, as proved by the story an embarrassed girl once told me. It seems that at her university, everyone was allocated email addresses based on their surname and the two first letters of their first name. A very disgruntled Megan Finger disclosed that she was less than happy with the resultant Fingerme@...

Meanwhile, my friend in junior school was named Richard by his parents. All very well except his surname was Holder. Didn't they think ahead to what his name would be shortened to? The poor guy sounds like he could be one of those optional extras in a luxury car... or a hi-tech upgrade to a Palm Pilot!

More recently, I've heard of children named Moon Unit, Darth, Lucifer, Number 16 Bus Shelter, Nutella (perhaps Cinderella's crazy sister?), ABCDE, Audio Silence and Talula Does The Hula From Hawaii. I understand that in France, the government used to promulgate an official list of names that you had to choose from. Maybe that wasn't such a bad idea after all!

It seems that the old traditional dog's names had gone out of vogue. Rover, Fido, Rex, Spot, Lucky and Patch appear to have been consigned to history and human names have taken over. Maybe it's because it makes them sound more like a friend than a pet, but there is still something a little awkward when you get introduced to a dog with your child's name.

And just when you think of the ideal name, you find there's another dog with the same name just up the road, so you have to start all over again. It's no good shouting out your pet's name in the park and being surrounded the next moment by a gaggle of eager canines. But you don't want to be lumbered with the only name left, either.

Going off on a tangent slightly, I can't but help thinking that maybe our species only got its name because all the others were already taken:

God: "…oh, and remember to make sure they have the greatest knees of all time."

Angel: "OK, that's the bee eventually sorted. Next we're onto the monkey with anxiety issues."

God: mumbles something under his breath.

Angel: "Look, I know it's been a long day but you're just being silly now, and anyway, we've already named the fancy bird with all the colourful feathers that. You'll have to think of something else."

God: "Fine. How about… man?"

Meanwhile, Plan B dog names had been tossed about like a kitten in a tumble dryer and, just like the kitten, we were all getting a bit sick of it now. I know some pets don't even seem to warrant names - maybe Messrs Pavlov and Schrodinger were too preoccupied to bother to think of any. That might have resolved this particular issue for me now but wouldn't be without its difficulties calling them in at bedtime.

Then, out of the blue, Bethan suggested "Arnie".

"Barney?" came a voice from the back seat, which was probably Deborah's.

"Yes, Barney!" replied Bethan.

So, it came to pass. Plan B dog was thereafter officially referred to as Barney.

Just as finding the source of the Limpopo River was difficult, so was finding the source of a 'Barney'. Also, he had to be a black Labrador. In a dog-eat-dog world, chocolate Labradors may be delicious, but they are also the most poisonous of breeds. Observations in the high street had also caused me to believe that you have a much higher chance of going blind if you have a golden one.

He also *had* to be a 'he'.

Firstly, the name Barney lent itself to a 'he', which is important. I remember as a child, having a cat called Susie who, it was later discovered, was actually a boy cat. I'm sure that this unfortunate gender misunderstanding was one of the reasons why Susie and I never really bonded. He had to endure decades of cat calls from other felines in the street because of his name and I guess it made him grow into a tough and uncompromising puss. He was never a loving kitty and always seemed to be intent on getting one over on me.

One particularly upsetting exchange is forever etched on my brain:

Susie: "I'd like to go outside."

Me, holding open the door: "There you go, fella."

Susie: "You fool. You absolute fool."

Secondly, it was decided that Barney should be a 'he' as both Bethan and I sniggered like school children whenever Deborah mentioned the word 'bitch', although I suppose Bethan did have a kind of excuse, as she *was* still a schoolchild. Anyway, regardless of the reason, Barney was to be a boy.

Puppies sold in pet shops only seem to exist in comedy sketch shows nowadays and puppy farms are frowned upon. I accepted this boycott of puppy farms although the concept still intrigued me. What did the puppies grow on these farms, and how had they adapted the farm implements to fit their tiny paws?

It seems that the ideal time for a puppy to be taken from its mother and re-housed is when it is eight weeks old but, all in all, finding a reputable breeder with an eight-week-old black boy Labrador is no cakewalk. Then suddenly, bingo! An internet search resulted in finding black Labrador pups for sale, at great expense, down in rural Oxfordshire.

A phone call established that one of the litter still remained – a black boy Labrador puppy and, according to his owner, a handsome one at that. Young and handsome – this must have been what Deborah had meant. There was a downside, however – he would not be able to count as well as his brothers. During the birth, in her bid to free him from the birth sac, his mother had nipped one of his toes off. At least he was unique. This was going to be Barney.

Deposit dispatched, all I had to do now was wait until the appointed time.

6

A Short List of Long Demands

When I venture down to the restaurant in various hotels, I sometimes have a thin red horizontal line across my forehead, which is caused by the pressure of the elasticated rim of a shower cap. And in case you were wondering why I venture down to the restaurant rather than having room service, have you ever eaten an overly expensive burger sitting at a desk in front of a mirror? It's not much fun and certainly isn't pretty. Been there, blanked it out.

I sometimes sit watching telly in my 'home from home', wearing the free shower cap, just to feel as if I am getting my money's worth from the establishment. Furthermore, I have long believed that 'shower cap' is merely a suggestion for a place you might wear it whilst for some, over the smoke alarm in the kitchen could also fit the bill. Sometimes I bring the shower caps home in their unopened packets, along with the tiny plastic bottle of shower gel and the disproportionately large one of shampoo and conditioner. You would need a lot of hair to get through all that shampoo in one go, or maybe they are just being prepared in case you bring a pet chimp along. I do all this on what my daughter would call 'sleepovers' and the organisation I work for would describe as 'non-taxable expenses'.

Since my work, on occasions, takes me all over the UK, I realised that Barney would need to go on sleepovers too but, instead of accompanying me to a hotel and sitting in some stale, impersonal room, sporting a strangely outdated plastic cap, he would stay with friends who had 'volunteered' to look after him for the night.

° ° ° ° ° °

As Barney's arrival was some weeks away, I decided to make the best use of this time and, after much soul searching, I resolved to adopt the heavy burden of Moses to the dog world. In reality, what I was worried about was that I would be teaching my puppy one thing and then when I was away, the person kindly looking after him would inadvertently teach him the opposite - it would just confuse the young fella. I needed one set of guidelines that we would all follow and to make them sound official, I'd call them 'The Ten Commandments of Dog'.

I had toyed with the idea of using the traditional style of commandments:

"Thou shalt not sniff butt."

"Thou shalt not hump leg."

"Thou shalt not lick your own butt and then go and lick your owner's face as if you are pleased to see him."

I even thought that the 'butt' word, instead of the 'arse' word, might make it more universally acceptable but I realised I was onto a loser. I was a realist and knew that it was futile to direct orders that wouldn't be obeyed. I also realised that I had to make it seem appealing to my chosen audience.

I rather thought Abraham had spoilt the whole impact of signing up with some other religions too, by condoning that 'thing' about having to chop off the end of your 'wotsit'. Sweet Jesus! To be quite honest, I don't think it could have helped recruitment one bit and that was for the supposedly Chosen Race! God created us with a design fault that we needed to correct ourselves? Surely some mistake? Just correcting this 'minor oversight' would be fraught with its own dangers – one slip of knife and you could end up getting the sack. I know I'm a 'Cavalier' Catholic and that we decided to opt out of that one anyway, but I'm only trying to help!

I would do the job properly too and, instead of just a one liner for each Commandment, I would elaborate a bit. I can just imagine God sitting on his cloud one day, looking down aghast at what everyone was getting up to on Earth. "Those jerks are having way too much fun down there," He'd be muttering under his breath, "Well not on my watch!". Cue the hastily penned commandments.

It's quite understandable that in his desire to clean up our act down here He may have rushed the whole process a tad because that one about coveting your neighbour's ass always seemed a little vague. Don't beat around the bush; just spit it out. Are you serious about the 'donkey' thing or are you alluding to something else? You were specific enough about the 'willy' thing – why go round the houses with this one?

Not wishing to be sued for copyright or anything, I thought I would make my Commandments 'top down'. Instead, Top Dog would be in charge of implementing the commands, since this seemed safer than allowing the lowest of the low to interpret what he or she chose to understand by each decree. Also, to avoid any talk of plagiarism, the Commandments would be written 'bottom up'. That is, it would look as if it was the lowest of the low's idea all along and I would use lots of exclamation marks too, to make it look even more urgent. Genius or what?

If every dog adopted the Commandments, dogs would be interchangeable and so, arranging for Barney to be looked after for a sleepover, would be easy. I even had a personalised introduction, which I thought was a nice touch, and I also left number nine flexible so that it could be amended to fit the relevant breed. Barney would be my vehicle in the dog world to spread the word.

* * * * *

Hello, I'm Barney. Thanks for looking after me. To get the most fun out of me, it would be best if I behave like a good dog. To behave like a good dog, I need to know where I stand in the 'pack', (that's you lot by the way). Where I stand is – *you* are Top Dog, not me. If I think I'm Top Dog, I'll start to do what *I* want to do, not what you want me to. If you follow the Ten Commandments, both you and I will have a much better time together.

Playtime

Don't play rough with me, as it will only make me think that it's OK to nip or bite. Tug of war games are like a challenge to be Top Dog to me, so leave it out, Boss! I like 'fetch the ball' and games like that. If I don't give the ball back when you say 'Leave', don't wrestle it off me – just ignore me. I'll soon learn to let it go.

How Do I Learn?

I love attention – any attention. Good or bad attention!! I'll keep on doing what gets me attention. So, if I keep on barking to be let in and you come out and tell me off for barking (bad attention), then let me in. I'll think, *"Hey, barking gets attention … I like that!! And it gets me let in!!!"* And, guess what I'll do next time I'm outside when I want to get in?? Instead, ignore me and only let me in when I'm a good dog. I may jump up too. It may be cute now, but it won't be much fun when I'm a big dog! If I jump up when you come home, just turn your back and ignore me. Only turn around and praise me when I've settled down. I'll think, *"Jumping up doesn't get me attention … but if I'm settled, I get attention"* and guess what I'll do next time you come home? I'll do what gets me attention. Praise me when I'm good and I'll keep doing what earns me praise. Get the message, Boss?

School Time

I've learnt/am learning/will learn some words in Dog School to make me a good dog so I can please the Top Dog:

SIT … to sit.
DOWN … to lie down.
COME … to come back to you.
STAY … to stay put.
HEEL … to walk nicely with you when I'm out.
GET BUSY … to have a wee or poop.
FETCH … to fetch something.
LEAVE … to let go of something.
NO … what to say if I'm naughty.
BEDTIME … When it's bedtime!

I'm not that bright, so just use the words above and *no* extra ones. "Good Barney, lie down for me," or "Go to bed, you fool" just confuses me!! Word overload!! Just say, "Down" or "Bedtime".

Shouting

Don't shout at me. I have good hearing. It's just like talking to a Frenchman; you don't need to shout to make him understand – you just need to speak in words he understands. See 'School Time'.

Telling Me Off

I don't mean to be naughty but sometimes I am. Unless you catch me in the act of doing something, it's no good telling me off, as I'll have forgotten what I'm being told off for! I'll think I'm being told off just for being there! If you *do* catch me doing something I shouldn't, just say, "No", and, if need be, pull me off the furniture or correct what I'm doing. Not, "Naughty Barney", "Bad Barney" or "Why you little ...". Just say, "No" please. In fact, if truth be known, us dogs don't feel guilt. We just feel sad because you're yelling at us. Remember, I am eager to please, so I'll be disappointed to know I've upset Top Dog. No need to smack my snout either, Boss. Just be consistent or I'll get confused again!

The Lowest of the Low

I'm a dog!! I don't need to sit on the settee or lie on a comfy bed. I have fur and pads. If I'm let up on the sofa, I'll think I'm Top Dog. Climbing on things or getting up high makes me think I'm Top Dog, overseeing my domain.

Say, "No" and get me down. Keep me low and I'll behave better.

Dinner Time

The Top Dog always eats first. Please don't give me my food until after you have finished your meal. And don't feed me bits from your table or you'll never get rid of me!! While I'm on the subject, why share your chocolate bars and snacks with me? I wouldn't share my dinner with you.

Walkies!

I love 'em!! If I get too excited on our walk and start jumping up and stuff, tell me, "No", and then stop and ignore me until I calm down. It's the same if I pull on the lead or start getting ahead. Tell me, "No", and gently pull me back into line. Try walking really slowly and praising me when I'm good. You'll enjoy going for walks in future if I'm a well-behaved dog so it's worth keeping me in line. Let me sniff stuff though. That's how I 'see' the world. It's mentally and physically stimulating for me, decreases my heart rate and stress levels and makes me happy. After all, it's my walk, not yours!

I'm a Retriever

So, I'll retrieve stuff! If you find me with your slippers or best toy, don't chase me to get it back. I'll just think it's a game (and remember I like attention). It's better to tell me to, "Fetch" and then "Leave". At least you'll get it back … and remember I don't mean to be naughty … I didn't know it was important!! Keep it away from me in future.

Have Fun!

Have fun with me. That's what I'm here for! I enjoy myself better if I know where I stand … and *you* will have a better time if I know where I stand too. I'm a dog!! But *you* are Top Dog!!

Oh, and finally, please don't break treats in half and pretend you're giving me two… that's just sneaky.

Adogs.

° ° ° ° ° °

Here endeth the first lesson, but don't get me wrong, I don't expect you to follow the Dog Commandments religiously with your own dog. Hell, I've heard that some of you don't even do that for the actual Commandments!

I may not even follow the Ten Commandments of Dog to the letter either, it's just a start. I want my dog to be his own person rather than slavishly obedient to me like some canine automaton. Let's just call them the Ten Suggestions instead!

I know there'll be some leeway here and there, the occasional dog on the armchair moment, the odd tug of war, but at least it gives you an idea. I really don't mind if you want to sleep with your puppy on your bed too, that's totally up to you. After all, it's your dog, I'm not going to judge you… it's meant to ease anxiety and provide feelings of safety and security anyway. Who knows, I might even be wrong about some of the instructions. I'm not infallible. It seems no one is.

In 1631, a new version of the Bible came out with a typo. Or to be totally accurate, it had one word missing. That may not seem much, but it meant the whole print run had to be destroyed, the publishers were fined and had their printing licence taken off them as a result. What was missing was the simple word 'not'. It may not seem much, but it resulted in one of the Commandments reading, "Thou shalt commit adultery". It seems a lot of people quickly took God at his word until the error was finally rectified. It was renamed 'The Wicked Bible' and there are still a few copies of it floating about and if you happen to have one and want to sell it, it's worth about £50,000 … or you may just prefer to hang onto it and have some guilt-free shenanigans instead. Well Jesus did say love your neighbour.

Meanwhile, if you do like the idea of the Commandments, and you're into that sort of thing, as an added bonus, you can always pretend you're conducting an exorcism by shouting out, "By the power of Christ, I compel you to expel your demons!" every time your dog has a poop in the park.

7

The Abominable Showman

Dick Turpin… remember him? Is anyone else surprised at how little Dick Turpin featured in life after primary school? It may have been those motte and bailey castle and oxbow lakes in high school, but our journey into life's false expectations started off with this dandy highwayman. He seemed to crop up a lot in lessons, leading me to believe he would be a key figure in later life, but then I turned eleven and Boom! Absolutely nothing!

I must have been pretty simple as a child. From Mrs O'Leary in Baby Class Infants, through to Mr Cunliffe in Standard 4, not forgetting Mrs Cligett, Mrs Mottram and Mr Keane en route – all must either be shaking their heads in disappointment or turning in their graves. Delete where applicable.

It's not that they weren't good teachers, because they were, but rather because they failed to rid me of some very basic misconceptions that I harboured during my formative years. They have even changed the name of my Primary School, from 'Our Lady, Queen of the Universe' to 'Christ the King' in an effort to disassociate themselves from me. The misconceptions are thus:

Geography: If you go down the street where I lived in the suburbs of Cardiff, past the sweet shop, through the woods and past the field that is now a housing estate, you will come to a pipe that goes across the river. It's big enough to walk on and the supporting structure acts as handrails. We used to call it the Pipe Bridge. My mistake was that I was convinced that England was over the other side of that bridge and, naturally, in England they all wore bowler hats, carried umbrellas and skipped to the loo. I was very disappointed when I eventually found out that it was, in fact, Llanrhymney on the other side – just another bit of Cardiff and also, as it happens, home to my brother's friend, Gary.

Gary was adopted and never met his mother which, he told us, in later life made it very difficult for him to enjoy a lap dance. He was instrumental in me winning a goldfish at the fair, in that he leant over and put the ping-pong ball in the jam jar when the lady wasn't looking. In those days, we had it hard – no guaranteed prizes every time! I named the fish 'Gary', funnily enough, in honour of Gary. He (the fish, that is) lived for a record breaking fifteen years, in stark contrast to the four-hour life span of most fairground fish that make the journey home, swimming in their little plastic bag. The things that Gary the fish must have seen and forgotten in his extended lifetime! I am not sure what the life span of the human Gary is, and it's always seemed to me not the sort of thing that one should make guesses about. I wish I hadn't brought the subject up now.

I'm sure it was the very same human Gary who shocked a pleasant American family who had 'adopted' him on his trip to the States years later with his apparent revelations of the dope smoking habits of the British. They had invited him round for Sunday dinner and he sat, open mouthed, at the impressive range of meats displayed on the table.

"Isn't this like Sunday dinner back home, Gary?" they enquired politely.

"No" replied Gary. "Back in Britain we just share a joint."

Anyway, it wasn't just the Pipe Bridge that held such mystery for me. When we drove to Cwmbran, we always turned off to visit my Nana before we reached a tunnel built into the hillside. My mind boggled at what might lie beyond and, in later years, I did go through the tunnel. On the other side, there is a factory with a big sign that read something like 'Every time a monkey leaves here, it's a wrench'. They made monkey wrenches.

The other area of ignorance lay in my understanding of religion.

In my simple mind, things seemed pretty black and white. I guessed, as Catholics, we were the white and Protestants were the black. Not literally, you understand, just metaphorically. At that age, I was only aware of these two religions – you were either a Catholic or you weren't. And if you weren't a Catholic, I assumed you must therefore be a Protestant. It was nothing bad – it was just that, because I was a Catholic, I believed the things we did were the 'right' things to do. To go camping, as we did, was obviously the right thing to do whereas caravanning was therefore inherently wrong. Consequently, I logically assumed that Protestants adopted this practice. We had squash, which meant that the more glamorous drink of fizzy pop must logically be Protestant.

It was like French – everything could be classified 'Le' or 'La' except, unlike French, there was no cop out with the wishy washy 'Les'. You could name anything, and I could classify it as either Catholic or Protestant. And I mean *anything*. Not just the obvious things like cats (Catholic) and dogs (Protestant), but you name it and I could give it a religion (well, of the two I was aware existed anyway). If we use apples as an example: Golden Delicious apples (Catholic) and Granny Smiths (Protestant). Generally, it was a good guide to classification that, if something was exciting, fun or exotic, it was probably a good guess that it was Protestant. You could probably argue that a Granny Smith apple or a dog are not that exciting, fun or exotic but, if I didn't have them, that was enough to make me *think* they must be more exciting, fun or exotic than whatever I had.

BBC – Catholic, ITV – Protestant; 'Blue Peter' and 'Swap Shop' – Catholic, 'Magpie' and 'Tiswas' – Protestant.

My dad worked for the Electricity Board, so logically electricity was Catholic, therefore gas was Protestant. Tea without sugar was Catholic, tea with sugar was Protestant. Crunchy peanut butter was Catholic – so smooth peanut butter was Protestant. Quickly backtracking before I forget, I challenge you to find a Catholic who does actually takes sugar in their tea. You *may* find one but they're a rare breed. And it's not because of some new-fangled diet or health concerns, it's usually down to the fact that we all gave it up for Lent sometime in the dim and distant past because it was the laziest and easiest thing to do, rather than do anything that required any effort for forty days and nights… and we just never got back into the habit again.

Anyway, where was I? Ah yes, classifying things as Catholic and Protestant… I could go on and on, so I will.

Feeling guilty (Catholic), having a great time playing Buckaroo (Protestant); wearing everlasting nylon shirts to school (Catholic), not wearing everlasting nylon shirts to school (Protestant); vanilla ice cream (Catholic), tutti-frutti ice cream (Protestant); lace-up shoes (Catholic), slip-ons (Protestant): The Tufty Club (Catholic), Green Cross Code Man (Protestant). There was also a tantalising rumour that Protestants had things like Wagon Wheels (a biscuit ...the size of your head?!) and Kit-Kats in their biscuit barrels, instead of plain Rich Tea.

The concept of someone not wearing nylon, watching Tiswas, on a colour telly, in a caravan, whilst playing Buckaroo, feeding their dog a Granny Smith, whilst simultaneously drinking coloured pop and eating a Wagon Wheel dipped in tutti-frutti ice-cream, just blew my mind! All in all, 'Proddies' seemed to have a better time than we did.

Before we continue, just a quick apology if your own particular religion isn't on my shortlist, that's entirely down to my own ignorance rather the importance of your beliefs. I realise there are some really excellent ones out there, and some of them even have fantastic types of headwear on offer. Apologies too if a codified system of belief is not your thing. I know that many of you out there don't follow any formal faith; indeed, a friend of mine said the only thing he believed in was being a good person, although he did clarify that he wasn't currently practicing.

Anyway, I am pleased to say that I am now cured from all that and I neither expected Barney to be wearing a bowler hat nor to watch ITV.

° ° ° ° ° °

My friend Deborah is a teacher. She once told me that the best two things about teaching were July and August ...oh, and hearing that asbestos cladding had been found in the school roof – two extra weeks off - Yoohoo! She teaches in a pretty rough part of Darlington – the part that would probably be described in any Lonely Planet guide as 'a shithole'. An ASBO is probably the only qualification the kids from there would get. I'm not actually sure if Anti-Social Behaviour Orders (the aforementioned ASBO) are still a thing. If they are, Elton John might begrudgingly say, "it's a little bit funny". Otherwise, if ASBOs are not a thing anymore, just forget I mentioned it.

As a special treat, last year I performed a magic show for her class, and I was called 'The Fang' for the big event. The Fang is a character from a song, who came down to Earth from Mars, thought he was John Donoghue for a week and went home again, smiling. It was therefore deemed appropriate that this should be my name. Every day, during the month leading up to the show, various posters were displayed, such as 'Fifty Million Fang Fans Can't All Be Wrong', 'The Fang: Taking Fun Seriously', or 'Coming Soon – The Abominable Showman'.

After the show, everyone was given a special certificate plus a poster of The Fang. He looked young and handsome, or was it shallow and vain? Anyway, they were all very excited.

Deborah was excited now herself. It was two days to 'Barney Day', but I was feeling more wary than excited. I have always tried not to get too excited for fear of being disappointed.

One Christmas, when I was about twelve or thirteen, Paul, Neil, Kate and myself all trooped downstairs to find piles of presents waiting for each of us. My pile of presents was next to Paul's and, between them, was a black Panasonic tape recorder. It looked too good to be for me so I didn't want to claim it, because I knew that, if I assumed it was mine and then found out that it was really for Paul, I would have been both extremely disappointed and embarrassed (even more embarrassing than realising you've put your wheelie bin out on the wrong day).

When Paul had moved his pile to the relative safety of the settee, the black Panasonic tape recorder remained on the floor. When my dad asked me if I liked my new tape player, I was so ecstatic that I still can't find the right words to describe the feeling. I felt like someone had given me the moon on a stick. I loved Christmas but in later years I often wonder what my parents actually felt when I told them when I woke up that I'd seen Santa. They must have thought I was a right dickhead.

Anyway, I subsequently spent many happy hours in my room, taping my records or the top twenty, direct from the wireless. Those were the days, when my only stress in life was stopping the cassette before the DJ started speaking. Taping usually involved playing the record or radio very loudly and placing the tape recorder next to the speaker. However, there was also the constant risk of noise from visitors to the room, and many recordings carry the sound of my mum calling me down for tea.

My mum died a few years ago and it's at times like that when you realise those little things that were annoying then, mean everything to you now. Say the good stuff while you still can – it matters.

 ⁰ ⁰ ⁰ ⁰ ⁰

Today was 'Barney Day' minus one. Preparations to collect him were being made but, as Bethan continually reminds me, long car journeys can be boring.

Try this to liven things up a bit. Next time you're driving and need to sneeze, at the same time as you actually let rip, sneakily pull the front windscreen wash lever just as the contents of your sneeze would supposedly hit the windscreen so that there will be a torrent of water hitting the screen. For best effect, as the wipers clear your 'sneeze' off the glass, don't even look over to your passenger – just act as if nothing has happened. You may allow yourself a sly glance out of the corner of your eye to see the reaction it provokes. Mucho merriment.

Don't despair if you happen to be travelling by aeroplane on your holidays and there is no windscreen/sneeze opportunity. Instead, just get a spare oxygen mask, or Tupperware bowl with a couple of elastic ties, and wait until the person next to you has dropped off to sleep. Then, slip on the mask/bowl, nudge them awake and prepare for the belly laugh of the century as you watch their amusing little antics as they flail about, totally consumed by panic.

Alternatively, if you are not in a sneezy mood, try quickly double flashing your headlights as the car in front of you passes a speed camera. The driver will just see flashes in his mirror and be convinced he was flashed by the device and have to wait nervously for the next two weeks for a notice of intended prosecution to drop through his letterbox. Actually, come to think of it that's not very nice at all... but somehow strangely fun.

It was going to be a long return journey to Oxford and the dog books I had read all emphasised that being taken from its mother and driven to its new home could prove to be a traumatic experience for the puppy. They suggested that classical music should be played in the vehicle to relax the dog, but having searched through my CD collection, the closest I had to anything remotely classical was 'Cosi Fan Tutti Frutti' by Squeeze. Barney would have to enter his life in the North East with a different soundtrack. Two CDs by Overnight Jones, the best of Weddings Parties Anything, a Nanci Griffith album and something by Ron

Hawkins would have to do in place of Mozart and Puccini. Deborah and I set off to Cheltenham – tomorrow was Barney Day.

° ° ° ° ° °

The village we were headed for in the Oxford countryside was about an hour's drive from Cheltenham. I wasn't even sure if my puppy even existed as, since the initial chat with his owner and sending the deposit, communication had been minimal to say the least. I hadn't exactly been lying in bed at night like the agnostic dyslexic insomniac, wondering if there really was a Dog, but I did have my doubts. Deborah was confident though.

Our directions took us up a long gravel drive into a courtyard surrounded by a large farmhouse and various outbuildings and Jonathan, the owner, was there to greet us. As it is only good manners, we greeted Barney's mum first – a fine looking chocolate-coloured Labrador. Chocolate? Surely some sort of horrible mistake had occurred. I thought Barney was supposed to be black!

Apparently, Barney and the rest of the litter were in one of the outbuildings and, as the door was opened, they all looked up expectantly and started jumping around in a mini frenzy. One of this mad bunch was picked up and deposited in the courtyard. He was as black as coal – the type of coal that was extra black. Apparently, you can have chocolate, golden and black Labs mixed up in one litter. This was to be my new best friend; this was Barney.

As my puppy explored his new-found freedom, Jonathan explained about Barney's toe again. It was almost impossible to tell that he was one toe short on his left paw and it didn't seem to make the slightest difference to him anyway.

As the 'scamperee' scampered backwards and forwards, he was picked up and given to me to hold. It was as though I was a new dad who didn't know how to hold his baby properly. I dropped him on his head onto the gravel and was secretly grateful when it was suggested that we should go inside to complete the paperwork.

Barney's pedigree name is 'Hartscrest Baghdad'. Jonathan had been watching the war in Iraq when the puppies were born and, as a result, Barney's brothers and sisters had pedigree names like 'Hartscrest Basra' and 'Hartscrest Euphrates'. I was just thankful that he wasn't 'Hartscrest Weapons of Mass Destruction' or we might never find him if he ran off. Hartscrest Baghdad, or Barney as he was now to be known, could trace his family lineage back further than I could and came from very good stock, with many generations of low hip scores and high eye scores. I know – it didn't mean much to me either – but, if you just happen to be a Labrador, these are the things you would wish you had too. Someone had described this breed as being 'an eating machine on legs' and we were taken through his current feeding habits.

With the final settlement having been made, and after a promise to send photos at Christmas, we were ready to make the journey home.

Barney had been living away from his mother in the outhouse, with his brothers and sisters for a while now, so it wouldn't be such a wrench leaving her. This was no monkey. The cat box I had borrowed for the trip was deemed unnecessary, so Barney began the long journey back, sitting on Deborah's lap.

I was quite prepared to do the sneeze/windscreen trick if he appeared bored.

Barney was the perfect traveller, sitting on my passenger's lap for the entire journey. Even my choice of music was given the paws up as it obviously soothed the savage beast in him.

We had decided that it might be more reassuring for him to share his first night away from the rest of the litter with another dog. Deborah's pet, Tess, was the unwitting victim.

We had agreed that the dogs should meet on neutral territory or, at least, in Deborah's front garden. When we arrived, Barney bounded up the path as Tess padded out of her house onto the grass. Little did she know how her sedate life would be turned on its head by the arrival of this jet-black 'thing' and a rolling, barking, nipping struggle ensued whilst Tess asserted her dominance over Barney.

Barney retaliated as soon as he bounded into the house by seeking out Tess' bed in the conservatory and laying a fresh turd on it. The bed had to be ritually destroyed later as Tess would have no more to do with it after that sorry event. As if to add insult to injury, during the night, Barney climbed into the big bucket that contained Tess' food and ate his way out of it. When we came down in the morning, Barney resembled a barrel with legs.

A pool of wee and another turd on the conservatory floor completed the picture.

8

That Thin Wild Mercury

You don't have to be particularly bad to be punished; you just have to get caught. It's worthwhile bearing this in mind as, at various times as a young sailor, I had been confined to the ship, locked up in cells shoreside or given extra duties. In turn, on the rare occasions when I did something worthy, I was praised. I preferred the praise to the punishments, and I therefore decided that my technique for training Barney would be based on this concept.

If Barney did something good, like obeying an instruction, he would be praised. As an eating machine on legs, he was highly motivated by food too, so he would receive a food treat sometimes as well. Conversely, if Barney did something bad, like jumping up or biting, the praise would be taken away from him. He would be ignored. There are some excellent books on dog training, and I had compared my ideas to theirs. I seemed to be on the right track.

The only trouble with the dog manuals is that too many of them seemed to make assumptions – assumptions about the knowledge I supposedly already possessed. I was a first-time dog owner, with no previous experience and assumptions were no good to me. It may be obvious to everyone else, but I wanted to know things such as when you should start training your pup. When can you reasonably expect pup to master this or that objective? When can you move on to more advanced stuff? Am I playing with him enough? How long does the nipping stage last? Will he *ever* stop peeing in his bed? The dogs in the books only seemed to need one reprimand before mastering anything. However, I had the feeling it might be slightly different with Barney.

I compared my technique to a couple of management books too and, whilst they seemed to agree with the notion of reaping what you reward, they also warned against the dangers of inadvertently condoning inappropriate behaviour.

In 'The Greatest Management Principle in the World' by Michael LeBoeuf, there is a fable:

"A weekend fisherman looked over the side of his boat and saw a snake with a frog in its mouth. Feeling sorry for the frog, he reached down, gently removed it from the snake's mouth and let it go free. But now he felt sorry for the hungry snake. Having no food, he took out a flask of bourbon and poured a few drops into the snake's mouth. The snake swam away happy, the frog was happy, and the fisherman was happy for having performed such good deeds. He thought all was well until a few minutes passed and he heard something knock against the side of his boat. The fisherman looked down and, with stunned disbelief, saw the snake was back – this time with two frogs!"

Aha, too much warm fuzzy niceness wasn't going to do the trick and, as compassionate as I am, I realised I might need back up.

The ultimate weapon in my arsenal would be a water

spray. I had seen on TV how good they were at persuading rioters in various European Capitals to reconsider their 'scampish' activities and instead return home for a nice cup of tea. A plant spray bottle, filled with water, would be called into play when ignoring was not an option. If he was barking at three in the morning, I didn't think my neighbours would support my passive appeasement stance, and the water spray would be called into action. Neville Chamberlain I was not. I started off by purchasing two plant sprayers from the garden centre.

A couple of weeks later, a Sainsbury's store near Durham sold a super soaker…

◦ ° ◦ ° ◦ °

Meanwhile, Bethan had experienced her own 'Road to Damascus' moment. From being none too sure about the concept of Barney, she was now more than eager to spend my money on his creature comforts. Trips to the pet shop resulted in a multitude of toys and, in the main, these were made of materials that weren't to be found elsewhere in the house. The principle behind this is that a puppy doesn't know the difference between his stuff and your stuff. If you teach him that it's OK to chew a toy made from the same material as your jumper, for example, don't be surprised if your jumper is the next item to be chewed. Most toys we bought were made of rubber and I *don't* have any rubber clothes – honest! A soft squeaky toy Dalmatian in a stripy jumper, chosen by Bethan, however, did make it through this strict selection process.

She also designed and input the details into the clever machine that engraved his identity disc. Collars and leads soon followed. A soft pillow bed with funny puppy motifs was *her* choice, along with a large ceramic water bowl, which we reckoned couldn't be upturned, even by an enthusiastic pup.

I'm not sure if they were meant to be stealth bowls, but a couple of metallic food bowls were purchased that had a rubber ring around the bottom of them to muffle that 'metal on concrete' sound as a pup shuffled it along with his nose, whilst eating his food. Surely this 'nose in bowl' issue was some kind of design fault in dogs (as is the tail in air when happy, forcing you to look at its arsehole). Regardless, we bought one bowl for home use and one for his sleepover kit.

Trips to various garden centres failed to produce a kennel. We knew what we wanted – a traditional one like you find in cartoons, with a pitched roof. Nothing fancy – not one with central heating and curtains like 'Gorgeous George' the pampered Boxer dog up the street has. No, a simple kennel would be fine. If it was good enough for Snoopy, it would be good enough for Barney. An ad in the window of the corner shop eventually saved the day, and an overly large kennel was ordered based on some wrong measurements provided by my good self. Despite looking as if it was meant for a baby elephant, I kept it on the basis that Barney could have sleepovers with his new-found chums in it when I was away. And secondly, I would never ever get troubled by any Jehovah's Witnesses again as, after one look at the construction, they would assume I had the beast from hell living in my back yard. Bethan made up another disc to hang on the front of his new house. He needed to know where he stood in the pack and this would remind him. It read, 'The Lowest of the Low'.

At great expense, a new gate was erected across the back yard and I *mean* at great expense! It wasn't electric and it didn't open with a clever remote-control device but, after seeing how much I paid to have it erected, you could be forgiven for thinking it had all those features and more.

Finally, a space was needed inside the kitchen area for him to sleep at night, which meant that Jerry had to go. Jerry was a large mechanical giraffe – the sort you inserted ten pence into and had a ride on and, in this case, it was an old type ten pence piece. A former girlfriend had given it to me. Her father had a stately home and Jerry had adorned the tea shop. She had kindly restored him for me, and I had given him to Bethan one Christmas.

In the centre of the marketplace in Durham City is a statue of Charles William Vane Stewart, the third Marquis of Londonderry, seated on his war horse. A great cavalryman, in 1808 he led the Hussar Brigade and was adjutant general to the Duke of Wellington who, in turn, had nicknamed this flashing blade, 'The Bold Sabre'. If you ever have a quiz down at your local pub, you might like to know that, if a statue of a soldier on a horse has both legs in the air, the rider died in battle. If the horse has one leg in the air, the soldier died as a result of his wounds received in battle and finally, if the horse has all four legs on the ground, the person died of natural causes. The third Marquis of Londonderry's horse has just one hoof raised.

Anyway, where was I? Oh yes.

During World War II, apparently one of my ex-girlfriend's relatives had suggested that the statue should be melted down to make shells and bullets for the war effort. Londonderry may not have survived the Napoleonic War totally unscathed, but he seemed to have made it through the Second World War unmolested as he still stands, proudly looking down on the comings and goings in the marketplace. Jerry, being a comical sort of happy prancing giraffe, had all four hooves off the ground as he merrily bounced along, supported as he was by some sort of 'shaky back and forth' type mechanism under his belly. I had no idea about the significance of this particular hoof arrangement, particularly for giraffes, but I suppose you could hazard a guess that it meant he was yesterday's toy and, as such, wouldn't survive the arrival of my new and exciting playmate. Jerry was unceremoniously ridden off into the shed.

° ° ° ° ° °

Bethan came over especially early one Saturday to take Barney to have his first set of injections. After spending the first half hour helping her to search for her Easter egg that she had been saving, that I had eaten two days previously, we got the little furry one into the car. When we got to the vets the receptionist was busy apologising to someone on the phone for something.

"Once again, I'm awfully sorry I congratulated you. I thought you said babies… and I really hope they catch the fox that bit you."

Elsewhere in the waiting room was a woman with a skunk, a budgie in a cage who just looked me in the eye so that I was pretty sure he wanted to fight me, and a man who was sitting with an empty cat box, gently sobbing. Well, I'd be crying too if I had come all that way and then realised I'd forgotten to bring my pet! We sat patiently with the black one on our knees until it was our turn. When we were eventually called in, for some reason that remained unexplained, the vet was counting out seven shellfish like some kind of Babylonian tax collector. I suddenly had a flashback accompanied by a momentary panic attack in case they had changed the currency yet again without telling me.

Despite being prepared for the worst, Barney's first injections were all done without incident and on the way out, I stopped to have a chat with the receptionist about the skunk, but she replied that wasn't the most unusual thing that she's seen by a long chalk.

It was autumn time, and one day, even before the surgery had opened, a family were waiting patiently outside, carefully cradling a cardboard box. They explained that they had found a tiny hedgehog but that it wasn't responding. In the box they even had a little dish of water and some wet cat food to feed the animal. A very quick examination by the vet though had quickly established why the creature was not eating or drinking. The whole family expectantly gathered around the veterinary surgeon awaiting his diagnosis, before they all suddenly recoiled in terror, as he picked the patient up and bounced him off the wall. He then slowly explained that the hedgehog wouldn't have felt any pain because, what they had brought in was in fact a conker, still in its spikey outer casing - the fruit of the horse chestnut tree. She even showed me some of the photographs she had taken of it.

When we got back home, I tried to take some photos of Barney but he was so jet black he just came out as a black blob. I thought he looked like he was made from black mercury and, when I rang and told my brother this, he feigned confusion.

"Is he a liquid metal?" he asked and pointed out that mercury wasn't black anyway, for that matter. He was sounding like the 'comic book' guy from the Simpsons.

Meanwhile, Bethan and the thin, wild mercury played in the front garden. At the start of the day, she had been very wary of him and would jump up on his approach but, by the end of the day, she had already taught him to sit, and we were treated to a lesson entitled, "How to train your dog", with Bethan using Barney as a practical prop.

His quarantine wasn't wasted and, over the next couple of weeks, until he was ready for his final set of jabs, he grew used to wearing his collar, walking on the lead, responding to his name and still more sitting.

Most of the books I had read advocated getting up several times during the night to let the puppy out for a pee. As much as I loved my new best friend, I didn't love him *that* much. His open plan bedroom was an area in the corner of the kitchen/dining room where he slept on his little pillow bed.

This little pillow bed often adorned the roof of the kennel in the early days, as it dried in the sunshine, and I think the fact that knowing the postman knew he had wet his bed embarrassed him into learning to control his bladder pretty quickly.

The second set of injections completed, Barney was ready for the outside world.

9

Doggy Style

I had been too late to fight fascists in the Southern seas but there had still been time to take up arms against the Communists in the East. The Falklands War may have been over, but the Cold War was still as chilly as ever.

During this tense stand-off, both sides spent a great amount of money, time and effort, gathering information about each other. I had been a sailor in the Royal Navy and spent some of this time getting chilly in the Arctic on such a mission, gathering information.

I guess our assignment at the time was deemed 'secret' as we weren't even allowed to tell our families where we were going (if you happen to work for the Ministry of Defence, and the mission hasn't yet been de-classified, please skip the next few paragraphs). There were no letters sent back and forth and no phone calls. Instead, we were allowed to send a number of words to our loved ones, each month, via the 'Comms' room. We would give our twenty-word message to the Communications Officer who would then have it checked to ensure that we were not giving out any useful information that might be intercepted. This was then transmitted to a member of the Women's Royal Naval Service (Wren) in Whitehall or some such place (at that time, women didn't go to sea). From there, the message was relayed on to our wives or girlfriends (or both).

I deduced it was a Wren on the other end as one of the sailors, after being away from his young lady for four or five months, was taken to task for writing something that the Lieutenant said was unsuitable for a young girl to have to pass on. The next week, the rating had obviously mended his ways and had clearly thought deeply about his relationship and decided to commit to this young lady and use the money he had earned in the pursuit of romance, as he promised her a pearl necklace on his return. Message approved – message sent.

I always assumed that the messages came out the other end on a long thin ribbon of paper but, only ever being on the transmitting end, I never knew. You would have to ask Susan.

Luckily, I never suffered from sea sickness, unlike the hero of Trafalgar, Admiral Lord Nelson, who suffered from acute sea sickness all his life. It can't make for a happy voyage if you don't like the rolling and pitching of the ocean, as a friend and 'almost' sailor once told me. His ambitions to join the Senior Service were put on the back burner after he took the ferry from Holland to Harwich and discovered that this particular type of aquatic illness comes in two stages. He described vividly how, initially, you feel so nauseous, sweaty and queasy that you are genuinely scared you might die. Secondly, you feel even more nauseous, sweaty and queasy that you are genuinely scared you might *not* die.

He didn't actually die but didn't need nature telling him twice and joined the infantry instead. He told me he was much happier marching about on dry land and that I should try it sometime. I told him that one day I might.

Overall, I've always been lucky to serve on happy ships and not HMS Norfolk. The anti-submarine frigate had been headed for Hamburg, but for some reason, the crew weren't granted shore leave on their arrival. Whilst the official ship's motto might be 'Serving, I preserve', after their planned fun down the Reeperbahn was curtailed, the sailors gave her the new unofficial maxim, 'No Singing, No Dancing, Norfolk'.

Where *we* were actually heading for were the Russian waters beyond the Arctic Circle and I was a Sub Lieutenant on board HMS Brilliant. On 12th March 1985, at latitude 67 degrees 30 North and longitude 13 degrees East, we crossed the Circle and into the land of the Midnight Sun.

Here, the Captain stopped the ship and many of the guys climbed from the quarterdeck into the water and quickly out again, just to be able to say that they had swum in the Arctic Circle. Not exactly shore leave, but the next best thing! We stopped the ship fairly regularly in the Mediterranean for such activities but, on this occasion, the sailors didn't seem to want to linger in the water for too long. We were all awarded certificates, signed apparently by Neptune, declaring us to be loyal and trusted 'Bluenoses'. All icebergs, whales, narwhals, sea lions and other creatures of the frigid north were ordered to show us due deference and respect, under pain of his royal displeasure. So there!

We were to proceed into the Russian territorial waters and observe their naval exercises, reporting back on their warships. The stakes were quite high in that we were told that if the Cold War ever got hot, as frontline troops our life expectancy was about the same length of time as it took to boil an egg, and I don't think they were talking Ostrich eggs. The British Army Journal in February 1949 offered the following helpful advice – '*The best defence against the atom bomb is not to be there when it goes off*'. Really? Is it really??

Anyway, we were there, so we best used our preparation time by building additional structures on the deck out of old fenders and boxes in true Blue Peter style, resembling extra radar and weapon systems, to confuse the enemy. In turn, I am sure they did exactly the same.

We then spent months in defence watches, noting down every detail we could about the Soviet vessels and probably spending far too much time detailing the additional structures that seemed to have sprung up overnight on their decks.

Innocent as it may seem, they didn't like us doing this and would use larger vessels to shield their exercise activity from us. Then things started to heat up a bit when we sustained damage after being rammed. The force of the impact sent me falling through a hatch and I ended up cracking my head open. As I lay there bleeding the deck a deep vermilion, I officially became a casualty of the Cold War.

However, the whole secret affair was exposed when a Soviet plane overshot the landing area on his ship and ditched in the sea. We were first to the rescue and took the pilot back onto our vessel before handing him back over to his countrymen. This was too good an opportunity to practise discretion and, suddenly, we were all over the papers at home.

'OUR BOYS IN THE ARCTIC SAVE RUSSIAN PILOT'

I had become one of 'Our Boys'. Normally in the papers we are reported as 'drunken squaddies/sailors' but something like this happens and we suddenly become 'our boys'. Most bizarre.

Anyway, mission accomplished for this boy; time to put a candle in the window… there's a traveller coming home.

Apart from these moments of high drama, the tour was quite uneventful, and you might even say boring. As you laid in your scratcher with the safety belt on so you wouldn't get thrown out of bed as the ship tossed and pitched in the stormy seas, there was plenty of time to ponder on stuff that you wouldn't normally ponder on unless you really *did* have too much time on your hands. Did you know that, if you assume Rudolf is at the front, there are 40,320 ways to rearrange the other eight reindeer? And what were these reindeer games the other reindeer wouldn't let him play?

I had arranged a couple of 'spot the difference' competitions for the ship's crew but had to abandon this pastime in the end, after an outcry when it was found out I was sometimes posting up two identical pictures for a laugh. So, what was the perfect antidote to boredom – a beard growing contest!

I returned home with a full set. This didn't prove to be a big hit with Susan, and I was encouraged to remove it. To be honest, I think it was also a slight fire risk and, if anyone else has ever removed a similar amount of hair in one go (Whitney Houston?), I'm sure they will readily agree that it doesn't half feel cold when all that insulation has been shaved off.

My next experiment with my 'look' was to follow many years later.

❋ ❋ ❋ ❋ ❋

Spring forward and a change of service, resplendent in Army combats, with the regulation whistle chain linking into my left breast pocket, MP (Military Police) armband, red beret, weapon and moustache, I thought I was Clark Gable with a sub machine gun. A teaspoon, as it happens, had replaced the whistle, as I believed I would more likely be required to stir a brew rather than whistle for help. We were on exercise in Wales, and I had arranged to meet my best mate Tim.

Tim and I first met when we were in the Royal Anglian Regiment and he has remained my best friend ever since. He was now their recce platoon commander and, since I was now with the Military Police, we hadn't seen each other for a while before reaching Sennybridge.

I wasn't sure if we had agreed to meet at the Police Station or the Officers' Mess and neither was Tim, which resulted in me walking from the Police station to the Mess and Tim walking from the Mess to the Police Station.

At first, he walked straight past me, as he didn't recognise me at all. Maybe he really thought I *was* Clark Gable!

Actually, my period of believing I was 'Ladies' choice' was very short lived when Tim later explained that he had just thought that I looked like, "Any other bastard Military Police Corporal," and had, therefore, thought it best to keep well away, on the other side of the road.

I retained the moustache for a while, but it didn't seem to hold the same attraction for me after that. In the end, efforts to keep both sides even, constant uneven trimmings and hasty re-trimmings, left me with something resembling a Hitler-type affair so I decided to call it a day with that particular experiment and revert to the world of the clean-shaven.

My current look is morning stubble, with tired eyes,

sticky up hair as if I've just combed it with a balloon, and a tennis ball in one pocket as I get up at 'whip crack sparrow' to take Barney out for his morning constitutional. Goodness knows what the birds are so excited for at that time of the morning. Anyway, as luck would have it, apart from the tennis ball, I think this look *is* the latest fashion too.

。。。。。

I must admit that, as much as I hadn't wanted the Communists to triumph, I wasn't particularly bothered if dogs suddenly took over the world, as I had been pretty decent to Barney and I was sure that he would see me right. However, I had not bargained for his complete ambivalence to the things I did for him.

The path along the riverbank varies in distance from the water below. Sometimes, it is almost level with the river when the tide is in, and at other places it is twenty feet or so above it. On one of his very first walks, Barney was hopping about in one of his mad half-hour sessions, jumping like a spring lamb, until he made one leap too many and jumped off the path, down the near vertical bank and straight into the water.

Despite the fact that I had recently taken out full insurance on him, I leapt into action. I had no idea whether he could swim or not and the current can be quite strong in certain parts. The only place that I could scramble down was ten yards or so upstream and, as luck would have it, Barney was doggy paddling in that direction too. Grabbing the sodden dog, I wrenched him out of the water, thrust him under my left arm and struggled up the bank, cutting my hands on the brambles, whilst encrusting myself in a foul-smelling concoction of dirty river water and thick mud in the process.

On reaching the top, he just pottered off and went to sniff something new – no thanks or grateful glance at his saviour. Nothing! The sodding sodden dog.

The times I had cleaned up his stinking turds because he didn't seem to have the time; the numerous occasions I had bought him toys and the meals that I lovingly prepared every day seemed to count for nothing. Unlike Scooby Doo, he hadn't even solved any mysteries yet. I was beginning to feel that maybe I had bought a dud.

10

This Year's Model

Whitby is where Dracula came ashore when, disguised as a dog, he jumped ship and ran up the 199 steps to the old Anglo-Saxon church of St. Mary – as a black dog, so it happens! This was also to be the location for *my* black dog's first big day out.

Situated on the Yorkshire coastline, Whitby's skyline is dominated by the ruins of St. Hilda's Abbey, high on the East Cliff. Spreading below is a maze of alleyways and narrow streets, running down to the busy quayside. Captain Cook once lived there and it was, at one time, the main whaling port for the North East of England. Today, it's a combination of a quaint old fishing village and tacky holiday resort.

Don't get me wrong – I'm not knocking tacky holiday resorts. Bethan and I have spent many a happy hour on the two pence waterfall machines. We start by raiding my retirement fund (a big bowl of one and two pence pieces under the sink) and then proceed to feed all the coins into the machine's slot, including all the winnings, until there is nothing left. I've never been quite sure what we achieve but we seem to have fun doing it. In fact, whoever owns a two pence waterfall machine is onto a winner as, in all my years, I've never heard anybody say, "We're eight pence up – let's call it quits while we're ahead!"

Don't ask me how it was done but somehow Deborah had taught Barney to walk to heel. The first walk in the outside world started with about three yards' worth of sparks flying from Barney's bum as he sat down, refusing to co-operate, and had to be dragged along the street. But, thereafter, he knew the game was up and walked perfectly.

So it was that Bethan, Deborah, Barney and I arrived in the town for the first of many socialisation trips. Apparently, it's important for a puppy to be exposed to as many things as possible in the early days to prevent him developing a negative reaction when he comes across something unfamiliar in later life. It really does take a village to raise a pup.

At one point he found a stick and looked as happy as anything as he carried it along but then, he accidentally bit it in half. At first, he was devastated, but then it suddenly dawned on him that he now had two sticks… and was over the moon. Then, all thoughts of the stick vanished as we entered the town. He was like a little hoover, eating all the dropped bits of ice cream cones and sweets as he was led through the thronging streets, which made us wonder if we should have called him 'Dyson' instead. He was patted and fussed over by the whole world and his wife and even got to have a good sniff at the doorway of a kipper-smoking shed (where kippers are smoked before onward progression to the breakfast table, as opposed to some bizarre kind of club where kippers can relax and have a fag). He also learnt what it was like to feel the sand between uneven numbered toes and to climb too many steps in one go. He slept all the way home.

This expedition was followed by days at Beamish Country Park, Durham town, the Waldridge Fells and just about anywhere else where he could encounter new experiences.

。 ˚ 。 ˚ 。 ˚

One big advantage Barney did have was that he allowed me to meet a whole load of new people. Everybody wanted to meet this cute thing.

I had read about a system some years back for remembering names – all you had to do was associate the person you wanted to remember with some characteristic of theirs. Next time you wanted to recall their name, you just conjured up this image in your mind and their name would come to you in a flash. The trouble with this was that I found I was just stuck with the idea and, in the end, it was easier to remember people by the nicknames I had invented for them, rather than persevere with the next step.

On holiday in Tunisia with Deborah one year, we didn't know anyone's name. Everyone was just given a nickname based on some characteristic, something they had done or, as in one case, because I had dreamt it. One particularly attractive twenty-something girl was christened 'Flip flops and lip gloss' because she told us she was a body parts model, and both her feet and mouth had been used in adverts. During a trip to the desert, unsurprisingly our guide took a particular fancy to 'Flip flops and lip gloss', chatting her up and promising he could get her work as a hand model at his friend's jewellery shop, but I really think he just wanted to get her legs a part.

Overall, I enjoyed Tunisia... the friendly people, the scenery and fascinating places. El Jem just looks like any other small town in the middle of the desert, yet it is the home of a magnificently preserved amphitheatre that could seat sixty thousand spectators (and where much of the movie Gladiator was filmed). The next day we were in the Troglodyte village of Mamata - which was featured in the film Star Wars as Luke Skywalker's home. The Troglodytes live in caves that they dig vertically into the ground – you can actually stand on the edge and look down into them. From Mediterranean coast, through ancient cities, sun baked deserts and rugged mountains – Tunisia is a fantastic place to visit. Except for one big disappointment – sparrows. Don't get me wrong, I like sparrows. We are losing our sparrows in Britain – I miss them – but I was expecting to see something just a little more exotic when I got to foreign climes. Tunisia, however, was full of the little familiar brown fellas. I just felt like they were all taking their holiday the same time as me and that we should all feel a bit embarrassed that we had booked the same holiday resort. What happened to flocks of wild budgies and brightly coloured parakeets? I know that Deborah likes a cockatoo and I personally love any exotic bird, but sparrows? I'm sure I even recognised a few of them. It seems, however, that some of our little feathered friends couldn't afford the fare home as, when I got back to Britain, there seemed to be even fewer sparrows about than when I had left.

Back home, the names continued. The woman who knew everyone's business in the street was 'Badfinger' because she had once come to me for advice when she had cut hers. Bill, who had lived next door to me, was a Royal Marine during the Second World War and, when he died, Terry moved in. But for me, Terry would always be 'Bill's replacement'. Despite being an elderly couple, they were clearly very excited about moving into their new home because, that evening, I could hear them shagging away for what seemed like hours; lots of moaning, the headboard banging away – the whole shebang. It was only later that I found out that not all was quite as it first appeared. Bill's replacement had apparently gone to the pub, leaving his wife at home, and she had unfortunately fallen down the stairs and was banging on the wall for help. I feel guilty now about cheering her on.

As you can imagine, a lot of detailed analysis and mature thought goes into each name; for example, the skinny woman up the road is called 'Skinny woman', the weird kid down the street is 'Weird kid' and a woman I know who uses too much mascara is 'Panda'. The fat guy up the road is 'Spider-man' because he looks like he couldn't get out of the bath on his own, while the old woman three doors down is 'The Olympic Flame' because she never goes out, and so on, ad nauseum.

Apparently, even *I* was not immune from this treatment, as I was subsequently informed by Tim that, when I first appeared at the barracks, I was known as 'That Welsh Bloke'. The benefit of being Welsh in somewhere as English as Cambridge meant that my nickname was based on my nationality as opposed to some embarrassing characteristic. At school in Wales, where everybody at school was Welsh (except Susan), I was known as 'Donkey'.

I also shared a generic nickname in later life. As a Military Policeman, the other soldiers knew me, along with my fellow MPs, as a Monkey. I never really figured out why we were called this, as it was us who put *them* behind bars.

Despite having lived in the same street for seven years, the people at the park end had always seemed a bit of a mystery to me. This group of shadowy figures actually turned out to be very pleasant individuals who would stop and chat, passing the time of day with the ingrate and myself as we went on our daily meanderings.

Barney had solved his first mystery!

* ° * * ° °

There are many books available on how to train your dog, and a few excellent ones on dog psychology. There are also some very good books on how to raise your baby, with all the relevant technical information included. What I couldn't really find was a book on how to be a good dad, and how I could really develop the bond with my daughter, so I eventually decided to take matters into my own hands. I still remember a treasure hunt that I went on as a child and how much I had enjoyed it. I therefore resolved to arrange a treasure hunt for Bethan.

It was at a time when Bethan was studying the Egyptian period at school, so I decided that the hunt would have a similar theme. Drawing a map of the local area, I worked out good locations to hide each of the clues. The next task was to actually devise the rhyming clues. As it was an Egyptian affair, the clues were then converted into hieroglyphics and carefully written onto papyrus, or in this case, paper soaked in tea for several hours which was then strategically torn around the edges.

Slight detour I know, but I always find it interesting how written languages evolved. I can just imagine someone in ancient Egypt being really proud of the pyramids they'd just built.

First Egyptian: "You know, we really should write all this down, so that people in years to come will know how we build these big triangles."

Second Egyptian: "You're right. Take this down: 'Bird,

bird, snake, wavy line, something that looks like a cup, another bird, evil looking eye…"'

Based on the above, I prepared decoding books for Bethan and her friend and, on the morning of the hunt, I ran and drove to the different points, placing everything in position.

A picnic lunch of food that would have a Pharaoh-type theme (chocolate marshmallows as sphinx dung, etc.) was prepared and the scene was set. After the weeks it had taken to plan the event, it was all over in about four to five hours, but I felt that every second I had spent on it had been worth it. Bethan and her friend loved it too. Just a quick aside to clarify something here; I've actually been to Egypt when I was a sailor and, contrary to what The Bangles say, they walk just like us over there.

Anyway, the point of the tale is that if you want something to work well, it's worth putting in the effort.

Similarly, I knew that if I wanted to own an obedient dog, I would need to put in the effort with Barney. However, realising that he probably wouldn't really appreciate a treasure hunt, I enrolled my new best friend for a series of puppy socialisation classes at the local dog centre.

Sitting in a hot stuffy arena at nine on a Sunday morning was not my idea of the ideal way to spend the last day of the weekend, but I was standing by my principles and Barney, in turn, was standing by me. Bethan, Deborah and I had already spent a considerable amount of time training our pupil, so I hoped that he was already going to be ahead of most of the class.

However, I had learnt at an early stage in the military not to volunteer for anything and, with that philosophy in mind, we quietly sat back while Barney just excelled at whatever activity was called for at the appropriate time. We hadn't set ourselves up as something special so that the others would love to see us trip and fall off our pedestal. Instead, we were just one of the team who seemed to pick things up quickly. When the trainer asked the owners how they would like their pooches to walk, and one girl replied, "Like Barney!" I knew we had cracked it. At least, superficially anyway. However, his prowess in the exercise ring concealed a deep dark secret. The image of Barney as the perfect pup was as misleading as a whited sepulchre.

° ° ° ° ° °

I have a varied taste in music, which is imperative with a ten-year-old daughter. I suppose I first became interested in music generally during my last few years at school and records by Elvis Costello and The Jam initiated my collection. Forty five revolutions a minute. However, I seemed to have missed out on the 'New Romantics', and a whole swathe of the Eighties in general, because I was away at sea (I also seem to have missed out when they explained how Sudoku works and how much fun it's supposed to be). When I returned, I picked up with The Style Council, Madness, Billy Bragg, Nick Lowe and The Men They Couldn't Hang.

To Bethan, the concept of plate-sized vinyl records seems very strange, especially now that your entire music collection can be stored on a memory stick smaller than your thumb. The thing is, the quality on the records was nowhere near as good as it is nowadays, and when you listened to the songs on the computer, it was sometimes a revelation to discover what people were actually singing.

It seems that Whitney Houston was 'saving all her love for you', rather than 'shaving off her muff for you', although I still preferred my version. In 'La Isla Bonita',

Madonna was saying that 'last night, she dreamt of 'San Pedro', not 'Some Dago', and the 'trendy vicar' that Neil Diamond sung about in the Seventies never existed either – there never was a 'Reverend Blue Jeans'. Tina Turner's 1984 hit wasn't, 'What's love Dr Doolittle' and The Righteous Brothers hadn't just had their favourite cat run over either; apparently, it's not 'You've lost that lovin' feline'. I also went along with what I thought Kim Carnes was saying, but I always wondered why, in the 'Bette Davies Eyes' song, she was saying, 'All the boys think she's a spaz,' when I thought they were supposed to like her. Apparently, I now learn that they thought she was a spy (and while I'm on the subject, Sam or Dave from 'Sam and Dave' wasn't telling you he was some bizarre kind of superhero called 'Arsehole Man', but rather was eager to inform you that he was 'a soul man').

I still have my collection in a big box under the stairs, although the apparatus to play them on has long since departed. Today, my music collection is filled with the likes of The Lowest of the Low, Weddings Parties Anything, Overnight Jones and Me First and the Gimme Gimmes. I've had to keep up to date with the top ten though, via Bethan's car play list and, before that, in every Army truck, there would always be one squaddie who had brought along a ghetto blaster tuned into Radio One.

I put up with it (except for the time I threw my cabin mate's radio into the sea when I was in the navy because, well, I just like the quiet sometimes), but I do prefer songs that tell a story. I know that sounds old fashioned, but I like to hear the lyrics. However, for some inexplicable reason, when it comes down to it, I seem to like songs with lists in them best of all. And, if you are talking about list songs, the greatest must be the one hit wonder, 'You're Moving

Out Today' by Carol Bayer Sager. If you can't remember it, it's the one that goes:

> "*Pack up your rubber duck, I'd like to wish you luck.*
> *Your funny cigarettes, your sixty-one cassettes,*" etc.

There are lots of "la la la la la las" in it too, not because she has forgotten the words, but rather because she is so happy that he is moving out. I know how she feels – sometimes I would happily start singing if Barney were to pack his bag with his little food bowl and collection of toys and wander off into the sunset.

Generally, he is a great companion but, now and again, he turns into a canine version of a Nazi storm trooper. Maybe Carol could make a ditty out of some of the items he has destroyed, either of his own volition or egged on, and often assisted, by Tess.

He no longer has a bed after eating his own (twice), together with Tess' replacement bed. I also had to buy a new telephone after he bit off the connection end and Deborah has had to say goodbye to some candle holders and several ornaments. My AstroTurf doormat has now been trimmed to resemble a map of Australia, whilst the aglets on shoelaces (the plastic bit at the end of the lace, for pub quiz reference) hold a strange fascination for him.

Deborah's garden has been almost denuded of plants and replaced with deep holes. Large sections of the yard wall have had the paint scraped off them and my dining chairs have suffered bite marks on the lower reaches. Various escape attempts have resulted in my beloved new fence looking as if it has been attacked by a very large and very hungry wood eating monster. Postcards stuck onto the fridge, along with the fridge magnets that held them there, have also been unceremoniously eaten and shat out by that so-called 'man's best friend', including a postcard of the Pope (straight to hell, Barney – do not pass Go – do not collect £200 worth of dog biscuits!). Gone is my 'useful stirring stick' that is required to be kept (by law, I think) by all males over twenty one to prove they are a proper bloke, and I even think he has changed the station on my radio. A hole was chewed in a brand new fleece two hours after being bought and my notebook, containing all my ideas and things that should be invented, is now papier-mâché (how about a freezing spray so that soft turds can be frozen and more easily collected and bagged?) and I left a trail of water through the house after I filled a watering can and took it through to the garden, only to realise too late that Barney had earlier chewed a big hole in the bottom of it. I'm sure none of this was in the brochure.

Deborah told me she has had plugs chewed off two lamps and had grown so exasperated with the little demon dog that she was most upset that they weren't switched on at the time! To top it all, having checked the small print of my insurance, I don't think I'm covered for, 'Act of Dog'. All in all, Carol could write a bloody 'list' musical about him as he potters from room to room destroying things.

> *"Pack up your rubber bone, I hope you never phone,*
> *So no more walks at eight, I'll stay in bed till late,*
> *La la la la la la, la la la la la la …"*

11

Soldier 'X'

Barney was not well. I returned from work one day to be greeted by an horrendous sight.

The vilest turd imaginable adorned my yard and it was so disgusting that even the flies refused to settle on it. Barney lay half in and half out of his kennel, with his head in his paws, looking pathetic. His sad eyes looked at me the way they do best – sadly. However, I had not completed my Special Investigations course with the Royal Military Police for nothing, and I deduced that Barney was somehow the culprit in this sorry scene. He was in no condition to be interrogated though as I guessed that, in his state, the only way he could have communicated to me was by farting and I doubted that he could even do that safely.

When I'm feeling ill, I want all the sympathy that I so richly deserve as I plunder one of my hypochondriac supply kits, packed with various pills and medication. As I potter about rattling, I am also open to offers of comics and cake-like things.

Yet, Barney wasn't able to ring me at work and tell me he was feeling a bit under the weather. He probably had pains where his butterflies should have been, but he had been left alone, to suffer in silence. I felt guilty.

The warning signs had been there on his morning walk. After depositing his first poop of the day, he had sprinted off as if he wanted nothing more to do with it. He had half resembled a giraffe as he completed this exercise, stretching his neck so that his sniffing apparatus was as far away as it could possibly be from the stink-making mechanism. I had searched in vain for the deposit with my bright blue poop bag as he pretended nothing had happened.

I didn't know what I could do to ease his suffering, so I rang Deborah. She said it would pass, so I filled his bowl with fresh water, gave him a pat on the head and went in to watch telly.

Just to reassure anyone who is concerned, Barney was fine the next day; hopping around like a mad thing as if nothing had happened.

I am under the impression that there are supposed to be about seven or so dog years for every human year, so the fact that he was fully recovered the next day would be like a human taking the week off to recuperate – the canine malingerer!

∘ ∘ ∘ ∘ ∘ ∘

The next day, I read a report about Ben the Thylacine. They were thinking of cloning him with some of the DNA he had so conveniently left behind. I have never had any strong views either way on cloning but that seemed like a good idea. I missed Ben.

I once knew a girl called Joanne who laughed at all my jokes. I missed her too. She should definitely be cloned as well – a few times. She was a girl in a million, which is great really because that means that there are at least another thirty or so like her pottering about just in England and Wales alone. She was the type of girl your dad told you to marry when he was drunk and was mad at your mum. After we parted our ways, she set herself up in business whereby, for a nominal fee, she'd show up at your funeral standing in the distance, wearing dark glasses and holding a black umbrella so that people will think you've died with a dark and interesting secret. I've already put my order in so maybe I will see her again sometime.

Whilst I may be sentimentally attached to ex-partners, I was also fully aware that people became very attached to their pets. On walks with Barney, strangers would often stop us and, as they petted Barney, or tried to avoid his wee as my puppy became over excited, they would say something like, "We had a Labrador once." I knew that a sad tale was about to follow, and it would entail a story about a faithful companion who had gone to that big park in the sky, where dogs sniffed each other's bums to their hearts' content. I was at a loss as to what to say to them and wondered if I was supposed to offer, "Here, have this one." I felt like it sometimes, but more out of being sick of Barney if he had been particularly naughty, rather than in any act of compassion. Cloning a pet was something I hadn't needed to ponder on before.

As for cloning my own puppy, it all depended on which day of the week I was asked. I was going through a love/hate relationship with Barney at the time and I wondered how he would have felt if he had known this.

In turn, I wondered what Barney thought, too, sometimes. I wasn't sure, but I had a hunch. It was probably something along the lines of, *"Sleep, food, turd, food, play, sleep, food, run about like a mad thing, turd, food, sleep."*

I, on the other hand, was thinking about hosiery. We were at the camping shop searching for a length of hose for the CampinGaz gas cooker. I asked the assistant if they stocked such a thing and she replied that they sold it by the metre. As I feigned ignorance of where the meter was, to nobody's amusement, Deborah noticed something outrageous. Even more outrageous than their Christmas sale that had declared, "Now is the winter of our discount tents".

The focus of her fascination was a wildly extravagant claim being made about a tent that could be erected in *twenty* seconds. If this was the case, it was indeed miraculous. The last extravagant claim I had come across was at a furniture store called, 'The Sofa King'. They had claimed that their prices were, 'Sofa King Low'. A lot of people had been excited by this offer… I guess it's all down to the thrill of the chaise. As a Catholic, of course, I had been on camping holidays numerous times and due to the British weather, on more than one occasion, I have even had to take part in digging a mini moat around the tent. During one particularly torrential downpour, my dad had to use the axe to excavate a channel through the middle of the tent to let the water flow out the other side whilst choruses of, "Don't touch the sides! Don't touch the sides!" abounded. Curse those Protestants in their cosy caravans!

The rain was part and parcel of 'doing the right thing' but the one aspect of these holidays that I really didn't enjoy was erecting and taking down the tent. I was also normally assigned blowing up airbed duties. I have never taken any illicit drug, but I guess they must produce that same spaced out feeling that blowing continually into a rubber inflatable bed for twenty minutes creates. Hell, there were even self-inflating airbeds in this camp shop!

Stopwatch in hand, the female assistant was challenged to produce a three-berth tent in the requisite time. In its dormant state, the tent looked a bit like a collapsed spider, but the assistant grabbed the spider's body, pulled him upwards and his disjointed legs just snapped into place.

Twenty-seven seconds – what a con! Still, I was in a forgiving mood. Sold – one spider tent. This would be just the thing to impress Paul.

° ° ° ° ° °

You may recall that I have two brothers, Paul and Neil. They sat in the back seat of the car next to the windows, but time has moved on. Paul has his own car now and I believe he sits in the front.

He has had a varied life, having been a labourer and almost becoming a doctor. He has also performed experiments on people (think curing Alzheimer's rather than Joseph Mengele). A year or so was also spent as a science teacher in the roughest comprehensive in Wales before going on to sell drugs (think curing Alzheimer's again as opposed to supplying Crack and Speed to his former pupils).

His current incarnation is that of police officer in the South Wales Constabulary or 'Heddlu' as they are also known in those parts. Like the phantom banana, Paul has actually completed the London Marathon too.

His family are the living embodiment of the Simpsons and, what is more, we had planned to go camping with them in the summer.

I could just picture it now. A few practice drills and the technique would be mastered. Within twenty seconds of arriving at the campsite, Deborah and I would be sitting outside our tent, drinking beer, while Homer, Marge and the crew struggled with their pile of poles and canvas.

Paul had started off by saying that we should meet halfway, having somehow calculated this as being the Birmingham orbital ring road, although he had said that there wasn't a lot for the kids to do there. Consequently, his rather flexible notion of halfway was extended, with me going all the way down to South Wales.

Did I mention that Barney would be coming too?

。°。°。°

Meanwhile, Barney had gone deaf! My obedient pup wasn't obeying my commands anymore. Maybe I had been playing the music too loud after all. It must have driven him potty too because he seemed to prefer eating horse dung in the park to playing fetch with me (incidentally, people who buy high-end gourmet food for your dog – you know they like eating puke and shit?). However, most scary of all, he was even developing immunity to his corrective water treatment.

Don't get me wrong, I love my dog, but I love him a lot more when he's not been running me ragged misbehaving all day and it's not three in the morning and I can hear him downstairs climbing into the dustbin. "OK, eat rubbish, you asshole," I'd mutter as I turned back over and tried to get back to sleep again. I know he'd deny it when I came down in the morning, but his banana peel hat would tell a different story.

If he were a country right now, he would be planning to invade Poland. He was even committing the heinous crime of 'hanging about' while I was eating to the extent that I'd have to show my empty palms to him like some blackjack dealer afterwards just to prove that there was nothing left. I could see someone else's hand in this, or was it a paw? I suspected Tess' influence.

Whilst she was normally a perfectly well-behaved bitch (pause for sniggers to subside), she did have a few habits I'd rather she didn't pass on to my pup. The hanging round the table at mealtimes was one. Tess also seemed to have a barking problem and, if Debs went near her lead, Tess would be spinning around yelping until she got the walk she expected. The barking was the same when anyone rang the doorbell. I suspected that I knew the cause and I suspected that Deborah knew that I knew.

If this were a film and not a book, we would now hear funny, shimmery type music and the screen would go all wobbly. As we emerged on the other side, Deborah would have a different hairstyle and be wearing hot pants or something similar, and The Dukes of Hazzard would be on the telly. The whole scene would be dazzling, as if it had been sun bleached and Tess would be a puppy.

Jingle, jangle, jingle, jangle. No, it wasn't Jimmy Savile creeping up on us, it was Deborah shaking the collar and lead. "Walkies! Who wants to go on a little walkies? Tessie wants to go on a walkies," and so on, ad nauseam. Deborah would only desist when Tess was wound up into a little frenzy.

Next, Deborah would be sitting on a sofa as the doorbell goes. It is probably one that plays a tune such as Greensleeves just to help reinforce the fact that this was a long time ago. "Who's that, Tessie? Who's at the door? See who it is, good Tessie." Good Tessie, at this stage, would be barking and scrabbling at the door. More shimmery music and wobbly screen and we are back to the present day.

I hear no comment from Deborah. She knows I am right.

I preferred Barney's relative muteness. I was determined not to let him tell me what we should do together, but other factors were at work. He had been out late playing with a dog up the street and then slept the next day until eleven, and he wouldn't tell me anything about it. It seems that Barney was becoming an adolescent and my seven year to one year theory was coming back to haunt me.

I had a rebel dog on my hands, but he was a rebel without applause. He might look like a cute version of Sweep, with his big ears flapping in the wind as he darted about with his squeaky toy, but this was no ordinary Sweep... this was the arrival of Che Sweep!

。°。°。°

When we are out on our walks, if another dog is walking towards us or if we are approaching a tasty looking dump of horse manure, I usually put Barney on the lead until we pass them/it. After we pass, I let him off the lead again and it never seems to occur to him to turn round and go back to visit his new playmate/snack. Instead, he just happily dwells on what is ahead of him.

It is just this type of behaviour that has prevented dogs from taking over the world. At five months, Barney can walk, run, fetch and forage for food, whereas the baby up the street can barely sit up on his own at that age. Instead of exploiting this natural advantage, the dog just potters on, looking for more stuff to sniff – stuff that's in front of him. Admittedly, Barney always wants to sniff what is half an inch *beyond* the reach of the lead, but it's still in front of him.

Meanwhile, baby grows up, gets a dog of his very own, who in turn grows up and just potters on, looking for stuff to sniff — stuff that's in front of him. So much for evolution! It would be cruel to mock Barney's IQ level too much though, as I have known a few people in my time who would make him look like a genius.

. * . * . *

We were in Amsterdam. We seemed to have spent that whole summer either on exercise or docked in Amsterdam or Hamburg. I was on HMS Newcastle, a Destroyer, and our next tour of duty was due to be the 'Armilla patrol', keeping the Gulf open during the Iraq/Iran war.

A friend of mine, meanwhile, had spent the whole afternoon writing a letter and telling all his adventures to a female friend, who he said had an 'amazing body'. I didn't ask if it was the 'Roll up, Roll up' type of amazing or a 'perfect ten' sort of amazing. They say love is blind, but in his case, I would hazard a guess that it's probably just a bit short sighted. Anyway, as we proceeded ashore for some more adventures, he stopped underneath a big sign which seemed to read something like, 'Jesus is my friend', whereupon he posted his cherished correspondence into a large, red, metal dustbin. In hindsight, he admitted that the 'post box' had looked a bit dirty and seemed to have a rather large mouth on it. I don't think Jesus was his friend after all.

Mind you, Deborah inadvertently posted a bag of dog poo into the postbox at the end of the street the other day. I had attached a sign with Sellotape, apologising to the postie but he took the whole situation in his stride saying it happens a lot more than you'd think.

Move on a few years and the next contender was a soldier in my platoon who, in a bid to keep his breath fresh and healthy, gargled with mouthwash daily, which was good. However, not fully knowing the mechanics of the whole process, he then spat the contents back into the bottle. By the end of a few weeks, it was swimming with sediment and unidentifiable 'bits'. Of course, this was not so good, although we did all concede that it was very cost effective. It's probably down to him that we now have those warnings not to eat the contents of the little packets of Silica Gel.

After I pointed out to him the error of his ways, he started reading the instructions, but then he took them far too literally. He once came to see me after the doctor had prescribed him a suppository, or an innuendo as Italians would call it. He said that he was confused as the instructions had read *'insert in rectum'* closely followed by *'keep out of the reach of children'*. I told him that I didn't think the two statements were related, and that it was just standard procedure to print it on all tablet bottles, and nothing personal was meant by it. I explained to him that it's like when it says on adverts that four out of five people will suffer from diarrhoea, it doesn't mean that there is one crazy person who actually *enjoys* it – it's just the way they word things nowadays. He seemed happier at this explanation, but I told him that if he was still concerned about keeping things out of the reach of children, to wear a pair of high heels for a few days after taking his medication. Just to be on the safe side.

I often wondered what happened to him after he left the army. Then, recently, I read about a man who had held up a high street financial institution whilst wearing a pillowcase without eye holes, and who was subsequently arrested after fleeing 'very slowly' from the scene, after stopping to pat a dog. So, it's not beyond the realms of possibility that after the military he had a short, but rather eventful second career as a bank robber.

Finally, a fellow officer on my promotions board was telling me of his first, and nearly last, military experience.

Arriving late for his pre-Army liaison exercise, he was thrown a sleeping bag and told to get his head down. The rest of the unit had already set up camp in a clearing in the woods and were sleeping in the darkness. The standard issue sleeping bags, at the time, had a zip up the middle and toggles dotted along each edge. This was so that the bag could be folded into the middle and toggled up, before being rolled up and stored in the pocket attached to the pillow end. In the dark, Soldier 'X' unrolled the green sleeping device, felt around for the toggles and untied them. The sleeping bag was now in position to take his tired body but, in his weary state, he had overlooked the zip.

He subsequently told me that he rationalised this in his mind thus, *"There can't be a zip as this is the army and the sound of a zip might alert the enemy – hence the silent toggles."* He then lay on the bag and attempted to do up the toggles around him. He could just about tie the ones around his feet, the ones round his thighs were tight, and he could only manage the chest ones if he breathed in and continued to do so in short pant-like actions. He said he had the worst night of his life, trussed up like a hungry caterpillar, panting in shallow spurts for fear of popping open the attachments, and freezing cold as the large oblong gaps between the straining toggles were no defence against the chill night air.

In fact, stupidity has got to such epidemic proportions that the government have even started to tax it now. The stupider you are, the more tax you pay. Except instead of calling it a 'stupid tax' they called it 'The National Lottery'.

° ° ° ° ° °

Bethan was busy shining the torch around on the kitchen floor while Barney was intent on chasing the mysterious blob of light that seemed to be moving erratically around the same area.

"Dance, monkey, dance!" I shouted from the side-lines.

I had already taught Barney how to shake hands, and the thought of getting him to dance on command appealed.

Bethan is the real dancer of the family and her shelves are straining under the weight of awards and trophies. She has appeared in shows and pantomimes, and seems to have a real talent but, to be honest, she seems to excel in anything she tries.

I, on the other hand, have only ever won one trophy. It wasn't even a trophy really – it was a football medal. I had led my team to victory in an RMP inter-unit football match. My magnificent tackle was the talk of the ladies in the Officers' Mess afterwards, but I was most proud of my fantastic winning goal. I gave my medal to Bethan but, when I asked her about it recently, she said it was probably in one of her drawers somewhere. Maybe. Perhaps.

Meanwhile, Barney danced on.

I've got to admit that the sight of animals performing human-type acts has always amused me.

In Tenerife, I saw a parrot riding a pushbike – a small, parrot-sized pushbike I hasten to add. It happened in a zoo – if it had occurred in the wild, it would have been just a bit too bizarre. Incidentally, whilst I'm on about parrots, I assume the first person to ever hear a parrot speak was probably in shock for a good while afterwards. If I ever get one, the first thing I'm going to teach it to say is, "Help, they've turned me into a parrot!" just to mess with any visitors I get.

Moving on, in Tunisia, I watched guinea pigs sitting, eating at the table and, in Poland, I saw a chicken playing a guitar. I once read that, in Germany, a guy had trained his black Labrador to make a Nazi salute on command but that's just naughty.

Whilst at the zoo, I was approached by a Spanish couple who asked me to take their photo. I had been waiting for an opportunity like this for years. As they gave me their camera and posed together, I made a big show of squaring them up in the viewfinder. Then, at the last moment, I pretended to make a run for it with their camera, before stopping and taking the picture. The look on their faces was a picture, so to speak – a mixture of panic, relief and giggling, all rolled into one. It was the same type of smile you have when you see someone catch their pocket on a doorknob – you know you shouldn't find it funny, but you can't help it. I wish I could have been there when they had it developed. They laughed, I laughed, and the parrot cycled on.

° ° ° ° ° °

Dancing aside, Barney is developing into quite an agreeable little companion and, as far as Deborah is concerned, I haven't farted once since his arrival. They say that small things please small minds, and I think they must be right. I like routine, and I've started one with him. In the morning, when I come downstairs, I pretend to act shocked to see a small puppy, sitting, wagging its tail in the corner of the kitchen. In turn, Barney humours me and pretends to act equally surprised and excited to see me. Of course, when he does his morning stretch, I say to him,

"Oh, big stretch!" which, I believe, is now actually a legal requirement, as is not moving if your pet happens to fall asleep on you. All in all, I think dogs are quickly developing into my favourite morning people.

At other times, his little mind must think that I'm cold, as he will just turn up, unannounced, with a single sock or a used pair of underpants from my washing basket, in a bid to keep me warm. Charming!

He even seems to know that he has affected my finances, having to pay for all his accoutrements and those breakages at Deborah's house. Since his arrival, many is the time that Elizabeth Fry has looked up at me with those sad eyes and that lonely expression on her face as she sits, without a soul for company, in the emptiness of my wallet.

Therefore, he understands that I can only afford one tennis ball, and so very kindly goes and gets it and brings it back for me if I've been careless enough to throw it away when we've been in the park. I still think he can't quite believe that I've bought him a ball made out of carpet. It's times like those that I feel guilty for the times I've spoilt his yawn by putting my hand in his mouth or made him waste twenty-one dog minutes searching for a ball that I pretended to throw.

At other times, he just comes up and sits, leaning against me, or curls up in a ball at my feet. If he is just lying asleep on the floor, I even feel guilty if I wake him as I get up to fetch something. He'll look at me as if to say, "What is it? Do you want me to come with you?" Despite the fact that I tell him it's OK and he can stay resting, he will raise his weary little body and trot after me. Sometimes, I bet he just lies there thinking, "*I'm the luckiest dog in the world*," or probably more likely *"food, turd, sleep"*.

12

It Must be Someone's Birthday

When I was young, I harboured an ambition to become a priest or, more precisely, our local priest harboured an ambition for me to become a priest. Even then, Father Dunn seemed like he was an old guy. He spoke like a Dalek and, later on, became Canon Dunn. Maybe they wanted to fire him. I didn't know what his first name was and neither did I expect that I should know. In those days, it was, 'Father Surname', not 'Father First Name'. Anyway, Father Dunn approached my dad to see if I wanted to join up.

I thought long and hard about it. It seemed a good position and I would have a captive congregation every Sunday who would *have* to laugh at my jokes. When I was a boy, visiting priests would celebrate Mass every now and again and one or two would tell a joke during the sermon. They were rubbish, but they still managed to produce a polite chuckle from the congregation.

However, I suspected that having to look after the sick of the parish would soon make me sick of the parish, but the joke thing still had me hanging on. Also, when the

Father visited our house, it was a special event and he would normally decline the sedate cup of tea in favour of something a little stronger, and he was visiting houses all day long! For someone like me, who wasn't going to set the academic world on fire, it might be a good option. It seemed that the only real talent needed was to look sympathetic and occasionally chant something in Latin, in a sing-songy voice, which sounded rather like, "I can play dominoes better than you can."

There was also the church newspaper, the Catholic Herald. I could even write some funny tales in there. I recall flicking through an issue one day when I saw an article on birth control… I think it was a pull-out section.

Having to work at the weekend wasn't what I really wanted in a job, though, but it seemed to be par for the course for a member of the clergy.

What ultimately put me off was that I had no interest at all in golf. It seemed that every Wednesday, all the priests would gather together and play eighteen holes. I remember one visiting priest explaining during the sermon that Father 'X' had died whilst taking a putt on the fourteenth green, the previous week. He said it caused the rest of the priests much distress as they had to carry him round as they played the final four holes. There was a shuffle of feet in the congregation, and someone coughed. I don't think they were too sure how to take that. Maybe this was what they meant by 'a bridge too far'.

I decided that a career in the priesthood wasn't for me just yet; maybe later. For now, I would go for a life of sin, conveniently followed by a deathbed repentance. However, with the priesthood option temporarily out of the window, I needed to look for another career.

Unlike Bethan, who has a variety of different hobbies and interests, at her age I was just content to ride around on my bike with my mate 'Hicksey' or play football up in Cyncoed Park. Around about the time we had to choose our options at school, I realised that I didn't really have a clue what I wanted to do.

Then my dad took me to see the Military Tattoo, held in Cardiff Castle. I remember vividly to this day that there was the most fantastic re-enactment of 'The Defence of Rorke's Drift', one of the most glorious episodes in British Military history.

In a small Swedish mission station, in deepest Zululand, in January 1879, around one hundred soldiers from the 24th Regiment of Foot, The South Wales Borderers, held out against nearly four and a half thousand Zulu warriors. The rifles used were the single-shot Henry Martini type.

Twenty thousand rounds of ammunition were fired, and rifle barrels became so hot that fingers and palms were so scorched, that the soldiers had to use rags to hold them. They had been firing continuously, changing shoulders when they became too bruised and sore from the recoil. Fierce hand-to-hand combat ensued and, whilst bayonets were effective, they often snapped off in the struggle. The soldiers' clothes were ripped and stained with blood. Many could hardly speak due to the choking smoke and the heat but, against all odds, the garrison held out. Eleven Victoria Crosses, the highest award for gallantry, were won that day – the most ever to be awarded in any single action.

The Castle echoed with the sound of gunfire. This was fantastic.

Elsewhere, Sailors challenged Soldiers in field gun trials; marching bands filled the air with their music and motorcycles raced around the arena performing death-defying stunts. I also noticed that the girls seemed to look in awe at the men in their uniforms – a Venus Flytrap.

I had found my vocation. I would serve my Queen and Country, conscripted by the thought of adventure and women, rather than any ideology. Here was something to live for rather than something to die for, and something to be proud of, whichever way you looked at it.

。˚。˚。˚

We have a chequered military history in our family. Great Uncle Bert had won the Military Medal during the Great War, while during World War II Great Uncle Josh had been in the Royal Navy protecting the convoys (and sank) and Great Uncle Arthur had been a bomber pilot in the RAF (and was shot down). My Great Uncle Jeff had served in the North Africa campaign and trained as a sniper but, due to having the hiccups too much, had been transferred to a mortar platoon. I guess hiccups and being a sniper don't go that well together. According to legend, it was Great Uncle Jeff who had brought a monkey back from the war.

"He'll have to sleep in the out-house," said my Great Aunt Vera.

"He can't - he's used to the warm – he'll have to sleep in the bedroom with us," replied Jeff.

"What about the smell?"

"Well, I've put up with it for twenty years, the monkey will just have to get used to it too."

I cannot confirm if this is a true story or not, and neither can my fact checking service – i.e. Kate. However, I do remember the old adage *"never let the truth stand in the way of a good story."*

Actually, I think it was also Great Uncle Jeff who had also told me that Rommel was called the Desert Fox because he used to sneak behind the British lines and upturn all the dustbins.

Anyway, back to soldiering. My dad had also been in the army serving in the REME (Royal Electrical and Mechanical Engineers) during National Service. Paul had expressed a desire to join up several years before but had been vigorously talked out of it by my parents because of the danger. However, they must have had a change of heart as they seemed to encourage me all the way on my chosen path.

If the South Wales Borderers still existed as an entity, I am sure I would have joined them but, by then, they had amalgamated with the 41st Regiment of Foot to become 'The Royal Regiment of Wales'. So, instead, I applied to join the Senior Service – the Royal Navy. Seeing the world appealed and I looked pretty good in blue. I could always try green later.

I went through various interviews, familiarisation visits and weeks away at different Naval bases, before I found myself at the Admiralty Interview Board. This consisted of several days of intensive command exercises, psychological questioning and board interviews. We were observed at every stage of the process, to ensure we were the right calibre to join the service.

I was accepted for a short Career Commission (six years) and they asked me to join straight away. I didn't even need to complete my A-level studies. However, I had just started the Sixth Form and my parents persuaded me to stay on to complete them so that I would have something to fall back on. I agreed and my start date to commence my officer training at Dartmouth was put back until autumn 1982 which, incidentally, was the same year that Cliff Richard started dating tennis player, Sue Barker. That year, she remained unseeded. In the meantime, for me, school took a back seat as I prepared myself.

Every morning, I did a ten-mile run, followed either by rowing around Roath Park Lake or swimming, down at the Empire Pool. I also worked in the greengrocers down the road to earn some money for other activities. Byron owned the shop and was ably hindered by his father, old Mr Lewis. My dad always likes to tell the story of an unfortunate incident that occurred to me at the greengrocers.

One day, a giant of a bloke sauntered into the shop.

"I want half a lettuce."

"We don't sell half lettuces," John replied.

"My wife sent me out for half a lettuce, so I want half a lettuce."

"I told you, we only sell whole lettuces."

"You're not understanding me. I want half a lettuce and I want it NOW!"

John told him he was going into the storeroom to see the boss.

"Byron," said John, "There's a big, ugly, thick idiot who wants half a lettuce."

Byron motioned for John to look behind him and there was the big, ugly, thick idiot, standing right behind him.

"... and, luckily enough," John continued quickly, pointing to our new friend, "This gentleman would like the other half."

But I digress.

I once served one of my teachers in there – it just didn't feel right, like a spin-off series from a popular sitcom that didn't really work. I don't think either of us really enjoyed the experience.

The money I had earned at Byron's paid for me to take the bus up to North Wales, to go on a rock-climbing course but, after discovering the local beer, my money ran out and I had to hitchhike back again.

Eventually, Peggy, the Deputy Head called me in to complain that I was missing out on too much school. She only really seemed bothered about me missing my Religious Education lessons. Sister Alphonse, one of the teaching nuns, had shared Father Dunn's aspirations and was disappointed in me. I didn't feel very religious myself but maybe they saw something good, deep inside me. Very deep and very well hidden.

° ° ° ° °

Indeed, years later, after I had joined up, there were occasional multi-denominational church services held onboard ship. It was the type of service that was meant to be attended voluntarily, but you were tasked extra duties to fill your spare time if you didn't go.

The Padre would always begin his sermon with something like, "In a way, Jesus was a sailor …" and would go on to explain how, just as we were keeping the demon of communism at bay, so Jesus was holding the demon of sin at bay.

I would also attend such services when I later joined the Royal Anglians. As we stood in a semicircle in a clearing in the woods, with the smell of damp webbing in the morning breeze, the Padre would begin his sermon; this time with something along the lines of, "In a way, Jesus was an Infantry soldier ..." He would then go on to explain how Jesus led his Christian soldiers in some adventure or other against sin.

As a Military Policeman, I also attended services to hear, "In a way, Jesus was a Royal Military Policeman ..." And so on.

I never realised I had so much in common with Jesus after all.

。 ° 。 ° 。 °

What I didn't have in common with Jesus though was the fact that, due to the lucky coincidence of him being born on Christmas Day, everybody remembered *His* Birthday. Alas, not everyone remembered mine.

I suppose He had the drawback of receiving only one lot of presents – mind you, they were pretty good ones at that - although I'm not quite sure if they were supposed to be for Christmas or His birthday. The gold was fantastic, and I'm sure I'd like the Frankenstein mask, but I'm not really sure what I'd do with the myrrh. I can just hear Mary now as the Wise man proffered his gift.

"Myrrh? You bought myrrh for a baby?"

Bethan's birthday is in early January and, after all the excitement of Christmas, I didn't want her to be overlooked like me. Something had to be done.

The idea was hatched of producing a calendar with all the family's birthdays displayed and, to make it a bit more interesting, it would have pictures on each month, indicating some unusual or funny place sign from the North East.

I live close to Washington, the original Washington that is, where George's relatives came from. The districts of Philadelphia and Columbia fall within its boundaries and the villages of Quebec and Toronto are only just up the road too. I thought that one of these could provide a good photo opportunity but, in the end, it was decided to settle on the Big Apple. New York is a small village near North Shields – more like a small gooseberry really, but it would do as one of our 'months'.

Bethan had already explained to me how she had seen a funny sign on the way back from an outing to the seaside, some time back. Someone had amended the sign for Shilbottle with a horizontal piece of black masking tape, to make, 'Shitbottle'. We liked that. That was funny in our books and, in a pathetic effort to try and be original, we decided to pay a visit, equipped with a vertical piece of black masking tape, to the village of Snitter. Barney could pose next to the amended sign for added effect.

It seems that many of the places in the North East owe their names to the Norman French language. Bearpark is sadly not a place where furry mammals go to frolic, but rather a corruption of the original French name, 'Beau Repaire', meaning beautiful retreat – how times have changed. It sounded as if it would fit in as an October/November sort of month.

Maybe we should have learnt something from the Americans and just kept the original French name. Baton Rouge in America sounds a fantastic place, full of romance and mystery but if it was over here, we would have probably renamed it 'Red Stick' by now.

On the map, close to Hadrian's Wall, we found Once Brewed. I was confident that we would also find a Twice Brewed, hiding there somewhere. No one seems to have any idea what was brewed there but they would do for us. Dirt Pot was not far away but it was now in competition with Crackpot, near Richmond, in an effort to make it onto every self-respecting Donoghue's kitchen wall.

Not that far from Hadrian's Wall is a place called 'Wallish Walls' – not far from 'Stony Heap'. I'd like to think that they were maybe both called just 'Wall' long ago. One was a town full of show-offs and the other was populated by shy, insecure introverts. The show-offs would be bragging about how good their village was ... "we've not got just any old walls ...we've got Wallish Walls!"

The humble folk in the other village would then just say, "Aw fuck it, we're just a Stony Heap compared to them" – and the names would stick. I bet that's how a lot of places got their names originally... well maybe not *exactly* like that, but you get the idea.

Actually, at one time the north of England was inhabited by ancient Britons whose language closely resembled modern day Welsh. Later the north was invaded by Germanic speaking Anglo-Saxons who referred to the native Britons as Welsh, meaning foreigner. Many ancient Britons fled west to escape the Anglo-Saxons and their place of refuge became the country we know today as Wales. Some Welsh, though, made a stand, and their presence is remembered in place names containing the elements Wel or Wal.

Foggy Furze seemed to derive from the old Norse and described a piece of ploughed land where coarse grass grew, and Deaf Hill was probably the place where the guy lived who developed the idea of 'hearing dogs for the deaf'. Both were possibilities.

My favourite so far was 'No Place'. It can be found, or not as the case may be, on the road out of Durham, towards Stanley. It appears that the hamlet was located on the border of two parishes and neither parish wanted to accept responsibility for it. I guess either there were a boat load of sinners there, or more probably, they weren't that generous with their collection. Either way, it became No Place. There's No Place like home and a sign pointing to it would make a good September.

'Deborah and John only' visits were also planned to Great Cock Up, Low Bell End, Wide Open and Wetwang.

13

Last of the True Believers

Pity Me was the location for the first photo shoot. It seems very aptly named, situated on the outskirts of Durham City, between the Arndale shopping centre and the council rubbish dump. They are currently building some flats on a piece of wasteland next to the big roundabout there and a big sign tells everybody, 'This will be the place to be seen'. Yes, if you are on the way to the tip with a piss-stained mattress maybe, but otherwise I suggest not.

Some say the name Pity Me derives from 'Petit Mere', meaning small lake, but I prefer the more fanciful suggestion.

Saint Cuthbert is one of the most venerated of English saints. It was Cuthbert who converted Lindisfarne from Celtic Christianity to Roman Christianity, and after his death, the Lindisfarne Gospels were written in his honour. In 875, following Viking raids, his body was removed from Holy Island and it was eventually laid to rest on a site in a loop of the River Wear. The magnificent Durham Cathedral was built on the site and his tomb can still be seen there. It is said that the journey from Lindisfarne to

Durham took over one hundred years whilst the monks searched for a suitable place to finally lay him to rest. It seems that on their travels, the wandering monks dropped St. Cuthbert's coffin on the way. Despite being dead, Cuthbert is then supposed to have sat up in his coffin and pleaded with them to take more care and take pity on him. Hence, Pity Me. I know, I know, but he was supposed to be a miracle-working saint, wasn't he?

As an aside, when the Lindisfarne Gospels were displayed in Durham recently, in an attempt to make history more accessible, a sign on it stated that 'The Lindisfarne Gospels weigh 8.7kg, or as much as an adult badger'. Unfortunately, this wasn't much help to visitors as there was no accompanying breakdown as to how many stoats make up one badger.

Either way, I would be likely to have more pity on anyone actually living there at the current time. The sign looks more like an omen than a helpful roadside location indicator.

Bethan and I posed under the large Pity Me sign and looked sad and miserable as befits such a notice. Barney just sat there and managed a sort of grimace.

As Deborah finished taking the photo, I noticed a scary old bloke with a patch over one eye, looking out of a window at us. Bethan had already made it safely back to the car by then and when I told her of the image I'd observed, she made a detour to clock the 'thing' herself. We all then hurried away, too frightened to look back.

。 。 。 。 。 。

In military investigation, there is a term for those occasions when a particular action or reaction could reasonably be expected to happen in response to an occurrence – but did not. We call it a 'non-barking dog'.

The term comes from the case of 'Silver Blaze' in Conan Doyle's 'Memoirs of Sherlock Holmes'. Silver Blaze is a prize racehorse being protected by a stable boy and guard dogs. The night passes quietly, however the next morning the stable boy comes round from a drugged sleep. Silver Blaze is missing.

> Inspector Gregory: "Is there any point you wish to bring to my attention?"
> Holmes: "To the curious incident of the dog in the night-time."
> Inspector Gregory: "The dog did nothing in the night-time."
> Holmes: "That was the curious incident."

That is, it would reasonably be expected for the dogs to bark – but they didn't, suggesting that the thief was well known to them. Hence a 'non barking dog'.

The locals' response to Pity Me was a non-barking dog in my opinion. They just walked past the sign as if nothing was up (or looked scary and a bit put out that we had rudely imposed on their non-barking doggery). I guess in the case of places, a barking or non-barking reaction depends on familiarity with the place.

I couldn't just ask people if there was anywhere with a bizarre name locally – they wouldn't know! It just wouldn't register as bizarre to them. I looked over at Barney for any suggestions. He was scratching his head with his leg. Cheers, Barney, you're a great help.

※ ※ ※ ※ ※ ※

The rest of the calendar would need to be put on hold for the time being, as I was being abandoned. Bethan was off for a week or so, on her residential summer school. In previous years, she had attended dance and swimming schools but, this year, it was music. I think, at age ten, I was still cycling around with Hicksey, well, except for that one summer that I devoted to the humiliation of ants. We humans seem to have an odd relationship with these tiny creatures:

Ant: "Oh, I see you've dropped a few crumbs. May I take them home for my family, please?"

Humans: "No, you may fucking not!"

Anyway, there always seemed to be regular convoys of ants marching to and fro in the backyard of our house in Carisbrooke Way when I was a boy – and that's when I hatched my cunning plan. I built a small enclosure a yard or so away from a regular ant run with plasticine (Plasticine Catholic – Playdoh Protestant). I then ordered a platoon of Airfix First World War French infantry to guard it. Apart from the assorted riflemen in different poses patrolling the perimeter, there was also an officer wearing a kepi, a soldier using his entrenching tool (finishing off the barricades), a military cyclist, bugler, observer with telescope, flag-bearer and a signaller with pigeon. Finally, but most importantly for my fiendish scheme, there was a soldier carrying a sack of supplies who I made sure was clearly visible for several days making his way back and forth to the plasticine fort under military escort. Aha, the trap was complete. I then placed a spoonful of sugar inside the enclosure - but not just any spoonful of sugar – a spoonful of sugar liberally mixed with a few grains of salt!

The next step of the plan was to sit and wait. Any self-respecting soldier knows that if an advance is going well, it's probably because you are marching into an ambush.

These ants, though, seemed too cocky to ponder on basic military theorem. I seriously doubt that any of them had read The Art of War by Sun Tzu. Instead, I was confident that they would be so curious as to what the French soldier was carrying into the barricade that they couldn't help but to send out a reconnaissance party to discover what lay within. My cunning trap was complete!

My soldiers, meanwhile, had strict instructions to pretend to miss the ant recce and the inevitable column of carrying ants that would soon follow, intent on stealing the stock of sugar from the battle-hardened veterans.

Hopefully, after scaling the wall (possibly under cover of darkness) each ant would grab a white crystal from the pile within and scurry off back to the ant HQ. There they would present their takings to the Queen ant (possibly seated on a small chair fashioned out of Playdoh – we don't actually know for sure). And that is when my plan would reach its climax. One ant would present his grain of salt instead of sweet, sweet sugar and then would get a right bollocking from the Queen. The ant would be humiliated. Objective achieved.

In hindsight, I'm not very proud of myself. No one likes to be shamed. However, I am older and wiser now and realise that it would never happen like that anyway – my plan would never have actually reached fruition. There would probably be a quality control ant sorting out the salt from the sugar at the front door.

In the absence of ant humiliation classes, Bethan had departed on a course to improve her clarinet playing.

Deborah, meanwhile, had departed on her annual trip to Turkey. She had friends there and harboured thoughts of going to live and work over there, teaching English. Every now and again she would try and goad me into showing my hand by saying that she wasn't coming back. I would not be goaded though and continued to keep my cards close to my chest. There are far too many sparrows there too for my liking, anyway. I wished her a safe flight, but then remembered that I had no say in the matter.

Then, after I had said my goodbyes, I stepped on Barney's paw… by mistake. However, he didn't know it was by accident. I doubt that the concept of a mishap even existed in his little brain. He probably just wondered why I had been nasty to him. I apologised profusely and as befits such an incident occurring, I treated him like a king for the rest of the day, but maybe it was too late. After Bethan and Deborah's departure, I was too scared to check behind the sofa in case I might find a stick with a red spotted handkerchief on the end, containing Barney's toys that he planned on taking with him as he left me when I was asleep. Just to be safe, I double locked the door that night and put the bolt across. His little paws would have trouble with that if he *was* planning to escape.

Jesus wept when He felt abandoned, but I thought it would be more productive to arrange a campsite for when Deborah returned.

Bethan was due to fly out for a fortnight in Jamaica on holiday with her mum shortly after returning from music school whilst I, on the other hand, was going camping with my brother Paul, in Wales. I'll let you decide who had the best deal.

Paul had called the previous week and told me his theory about camping. He reckoned that the cheaper and more austere the campsite, the nicer the people were who used it. In turn, the more expensive and the more amenities a campsite had, indicated that it was frequented by less pleasant individuals. Therefore, I was frankly a little taken aback to take a call from him saying that he had found the ideal site. It cost quite a bit, he said, but it did have nightly entertainment, crazy golf and a heated swimming pool. The halfway point had also now migrated to a hundred miles beyond Cardiff.

As he was chatting on the phone to me, I could hear Ceri, his daughter, shouting to him that the kettle had boiled dry on the gas ring and was making a funny smell. Aha, so there is a God.

。 。 。 。 。 。

Meanwhile, I was up to my old tricks. The Fang's presence had been requested at Chloe's party. Chloe is the daughter of my mate Tim and she had asked if something magical could happen at her fifth birthday party.

Becoming five is a bit of a milestone in anyone's life – especially when you are only four.

My brother Paul had a friend called Toffo, and one day Toffo's younger brother saw my dad outside our house.

Toffo's brother: "I'm five today!"

Dad: "Five today! That's a splendid age! Just wait here."

Dad then went into the house and got some sweets and chocolates that were obviously originally meant for us and went back outside and gave them all to Toffo's brother.

Dad: "Five today! Oh my word – what an achievement! Well done – here are some sweets as a special present."

Toffo's brother: "I was five yesterday too – and a week ago – I've been five for three months now."

Dad: "Why you little......"

I'm not sure, but it's not beyond the bounds of possibility that Toffo's brother might now work for the Government.

I digress – but nevertheless, five remains a watershed

year in any small person's life, so I said I'd see what I could do.

。 。 。 。 。 。

I don't usually perform magic for children as the card and mentalist stuff I do is more intended for an adult audience (aka attractive women). So, in truth, it wasn't really my old tricks I was up to, as I had to source a whole new routine of visual effects for Chloe and her friends. However, I couldn't fail to see a friend's responsibility and so paid a visit to the magic shop in my bid to become 'Party Fang'.

Whether to impress those elusive attractive women or just to entertain children, as long as the magician isn't patronising, magic should just be fun, ('patronising', of course, means 'talking down to people').

In the event, Party Fang had a good time, Chloe had a good time, and the other kiddies had a good time; it went well. Children make a good audience. Their minds are still open to new ideas; they enjoy being entertained and I enjoy entertaining.

Many adults also retain their child-like sense of wonderment. They realise that being receptive and flexible in their thinking are good qualities to have. They are the sort of people who enjoy life and see the funny side of everything. They don't mind being silly and laughing at themselves. I like those sort of people – so does Barney.

Some adults though, (and when I say adults, I actually mean grumpy losers) think they are far too sensible to enjoy magic and they mistake *childlike* for *childish*, and I think they are missing out on a lot. Instead, they act like snobbish food critics who, if asked to taste anything different or unusual, 'poo poo' it straight away. This process with Barney normally takes three to four hours.

Have a try of this:

- Think of any number between 1 and 10
- Multiply it by 9
- If the answer is 2 digits, add the 2 numbers together
- Subtract 5 from your answer
- Convert the number into a letter 1=A, 2=B, 3=C etc
- Think of a European country that starts with the letter you have
- Think of the 2nd letter of that country
- Now pick an animal that begins with that letter
- Now think of the colour of that animal

There, now that didn't make you feel used and abused, did it? It's only a bit of fun. You are thinking of an animal and not a bird I hope too. Who except a grumpy old twerp would get themselves all bothered about that? By the way, were you thinking of a grey elephant from Denmark? Well, it works out about 80% of the time anyway. More before we left the European Union.

If it didn't work for you, try closing your eyes and act like you're shaking salt from an imaginary salt cellar into your mouth. You can actually taste the salt. If it doesn't work, try tilting your head back more, poking your tongue out, shaking the cellar harder.

Have you done it yet? Did your friends see you do it?

Anyway, the 'poo poo-er' himself hadn't actually come with me as I thought it might have been too much for him, or too much for the kiddies; I'm not sure which.

。 ° 。 ° 。 °

Barney hadn't come running with me yet either. I wanted his little bones and joints to develop properly first, and, on that basis, I never quite appreciate people's enthusiasm for running the marathon. For goodness sake, the first guy who ever did it dropped down dead at the end!

It was 490 BC and the wars between the Persians and Greeks raged. The Persians had landed a large army on the plains of Marathon, near Athens. The Athenians then sent out a smaller force in a surprise attack against the Persians. Despite being outnumbered four to one, the Athenians were victorious, and almost six and a half thousand Persians lay dead whilst less than two hundred Athenians perished. The surviving Persians then fled to the sea and south to Athens, where they hoped to attack the city before the Greek army could re-assemble there.

Phidippides, one of the Athenian soldiers, was then tasked to run the twenty six miles back to the City to deliver news of the victory and also warn of the approaching Persian ships. He followed orders, delivered his message and then dropped down dead from exhaustion.

And that's why the concept of a modern-day marathon confuses me. *"Let's find something that could kill us, and see who can do it the fastest?"*

The Athenians won, by the way, and celebrated by making posters of a female tennis player walking away from the camera scratching her bum. Years later, Mars joined in on the act and released the Snickers bar. However, I digress.

Barney still surprised himself every time he farted, for heaven's sake. Running could wait. Instead, Barney and I walked around the circuit most evenings, which we both enjoyed doing. I did, however, have to keep him on his lead when we passed the fishermen dotted around the pond, as he began to take a liking to running off and eating their bait – anything from bread to mouthfuls of maggots.

I had lost a couple of pets in unusual circumstances when I was a child, and I didn't want a tragedy to befall Barney before I had my money's worth out of him.

In case the stories below appear too shocking, disturbing or frankly unbelievable, let me assure you that I have verified all the facts with my sister Kate, prior to publication.

° ° ° ° ° °

When I was very small, I had a large rabbit. The 'very small' and 'large' aspects must be borne in mind here, as I have pictures of me riding on his back. It was an old black and white photo, but not so old that we had to hold the pose for a minute or so until the plate developed. That *would* have been difficult. Urban myth has it that once, when we went on holiday, he was sold to the butcher. In their defence, my parents said that they had asked the butcher to look after him while we were away (who, in their right mind, asks a butcher to look after a rabbit?). They said he bred rabbits, but I suspect that the only things he bred were rabbit pies. Needless to say, the bunny never returned.

I was older now, and this time in possession of two pet tortoises. In those days, you could go to the indoor market in Cardiff City centre and there would be boxes full of tortoises, all clambering over each other. Those were also the days when pet shops actually did sell puppies!

Toby and Eggbut were my tortoises' names and, apart from pottering about eating lettuce, they would sometimes double up as World War II tanks with various armaments that I constructed from my dad's old pipe cleaners, cigar tubes and matchboxes and would stick with plasticine to their shells. Now and again, my 'Action Man', assisted by copious amounts of rubber bands, would sit astride Toby or Eggbut and trundle around the garden looking for Japanese snipers, or maybe even a hiccupping Great Uncle Jeff. It seems that snipers liked to hide amongst the dandelion patch as this is where the tank usually made for. Being found so easily, I guess, was enough to bring a tear to any Jap's eye but luckily for the wily sniper, I avoided picking through the aforementioned weeds to find him for fear of weeing the bed. How was I to know that, as I had the Action Man action pilot that came in a pair of orange overalls, he probably looked less like a tank commander and more like a sad escapee from Guantanamo Bay... sitting on a tortoise.

On that basis, rather unsurprisingly, Toby and Eggbut would occasionally make a dash for freedom. I'd always check upstairs for them, but, more than likely, they had made a run for it through the hedge at the back of the garden and up the school fields to the rear, towards Cyncoed Park. Every now and again, they would be hunted down and caught by friendly people in the street who would then return the naughty pair. Unfortunately, they enjoyed this escapade once too often.

I was in the kitchen one day, when I heard a knock on the front door. My mum answered it and I could hear her talking to two girls. "Never seen them in my life before – you had better hang onto them yourselves, girls." And so it was, in that brief statement, that Toby and Eggbut ceased to be mine and instead became somebody else's playthings.

Is it any wonder that I have turned out the way I have?

I was determined that Barney would not go the same way as Toby, Eggbut and the massive un-named bunny.

14

Fear and Loathing in the Gower

Neil, my other brother, who used to sit in the back by a window, now lives in Kew with his family.

The brains in the family made their evolutionary beginnings with Paul, peaked with Neil and went rapidly downhill after that so that poor old Kate was left with virtually nothing. In a bid to comfort her, Paul once told Kate that *everyone* has talents – it was just that she concealed her light under a bushel. Sadly, he ruined this philosophy by claiming, "It's a bloody big bushel though!"

Neil is an international lawyer and is what I would classify as being very rich. I reckon that, if he had a tow bar on his car and he needed a cover for it, he would just buy a brand-new tennis ball for the job! No expense spared! He worked in Hong Kong for over a decade and even brought back his servant when he returned to the UK. She is a Filipino lady who goes by the frankly un-Filipino name of 'Tina'. He has lots of rich friends and I remember one of them telling me, most bizarrely, that his business had just floated. Do I look like a doctor? The answer, in case you were wondering, is that I do not. Still, I tried to help him out and told him that he should maybe have more fibre in his diet. I then quickly made my excuses and left, for fear he should start asking me other strange questions like, did Chewbacca have a human dick or one of those red rocket things that dogs get? Strange chap.

Despite the fact that he could probably pay somebody to walk for him, Neil likes to go walking himself. He went walking in the Himalayas once, with a goat for company, but I think they fell out with each other about halfway through the trip. To teach him a lesson, Neil ate him. Mental note to self, *"Don't fall out with Neil."*

Despite their high IQs, when they were about twelve or thirteen, Neil and Paul crushed up some poisonous berries from the garden, mixed them with water and tried to sell the concoction to strangers in the street outside the house. It doesn't seem the kind of activity that a policeman and lawyer should really be engaged in. Well, not a policeman anyway.

Neil hasn't been to visit me since I moved up here, but he promised that he would come that summer. I did feel a little isolated up in the North East and was keen for people to come to see Bethan. My dad hadn't been up to see Bethan either since my mum had died.

It seems I wasn't the only one to have been confused about geography. Despite making numerous trips to London, visiting Edinburgh, catching the ferry over to Ireland, driving to the South of France, holidays in Sri Lanka and weekend excursions to Florence, Dad seemed to believe that the journey to Durham was just *too* far. Maybe he thought it was downhill on the map from North to South and that a ten-year-old girl should sit in a stuffy car for seven or eight hours each way, to make the pilgrimage to see him instead.

I told my dad this and, by sheer coincidence, a few

days later he called to say that he was coming up in late August and would be bringing his new friend, Ann. I am not sure what her middle name actually is, but I'm pretty sure it's not 'tact'. When my Nana was ill in hospital, my dad and Ann had gone to visit her. A couple of days later, my sister Kate also went up to visit her, along with Ann and my dad who, for some reason unknown to me, is also known as Keith. The story goes that Ann had scurried into the ward ahead of them.

"Your mother looks totally different, Keith. I think she must be dying." A mixture of shock and panic swept over my dad before the nurse calmly walked over to him and informed them that the reason my Nana didn't look herself that day was probably because she wasn't herself. It was another old woman in the bed and my Nana had been moved to a different ward earlier in the day. They hurried off to her new location.

No one appears to have recorded the thoughts of the old woman lying in the bed, accused of pretending to be Nana. Well, what would *you* do if someone rushed up to your hospital bed, gave you a snap diagnosis and then scurried out again?

Note to reader: If I'm ever in hospital, no cheering up visits from Ann please.

⸰°⸰°⸰°

The black sheep son did actually return to Cardiff once in a blue moon. When there are two full moons in the month, the second one is known as the 'blue moon' and it happens about once a year.

So, I usually return to the city where I had grown up once, and sometimes even twice, a year but, when I do, it is normally just for the weekend. I have done this most years, ever since I left home to join the armed forces. I'm not exactly sure how welcome I am, as the first thing people seem to ask me when I arrive is when am I going back.

As often happens, when you meet someone far from home who comes from the same area as you, they try to establish some sort of common interest. In the transient world we now seem to live in, people appear to enjoy developing these bonds, however tenuous they may be.

Whilst the Americans I have met always seem to have known someone called 'Taffy Jones' who came from Wales and ask if I know him, exiled fellow Welshmen seem to be more specific.

Do I know this pub or that pub in Cardiff? Have I ever been to the part of town they come from? Do I know this or that person?

Unfortunately, if it has not been on my running route, in Roath Park or the Empire pool, on the Pipe Bridge or within the five mile radius of my house, where Hicksey and I used to cycle, I have no idea what they are on about. As I give disappointing, "No" answers to my potential new friend, I can see their faces drop. It seems it's not such a small world after all. I'm sure some even think I am putting on a slight Welsh accent as some bizarre sort of fashion statement. I'm also certain that some even think I'm a fake and maybe just pretending to come from Wales, to cover up the fact that I have spent the first half of my life in a mental asylum or being brought up by chimps in the wild.

When I do return to Cardiff, I seem to enter some sort of time warp. The day I left to join up has been frozen in some sort of space continuum. Somewhere, in a far-off galaxy, two aliens stare in disbelief at their monitor screens. Not just because they can't understand why Miss Universe is always won by an Earthling, but rather at the scene that is unfolding millions of light years away in a quiet suburb in South Wales.

A thirty nine-year-old man, who has a responsible job, is father to a ten-year-old daughter and who has served Her Majesty during several minor conflicts, suddenly now undergoes a metamorphosis as he pulls up outside a house in Carisbrooke Way. In a 'Quantum Leap' type scenario, even his own father apparently still sees him as a teenager and can only communicate on the level of intelligent parent to stupid boy. In another, unrelated development, the father is only able to respond to this 'teenager' in the opposite dimension. The aliens note down on their 'wahwah recorders' (a recording system whereby thoughts are visualised and then stored in image format onto a floating transparent sphere) that this apparently seems to mean that whatever the overgrown teenager says, is automatically misinterpreted and responded to in a contradictory manner by the adult.

The strength of the time warp loop varies but its influence does not seem to extend beyond Carisbrooke Way. Elsewhere, tortoises are no longer sold in cardboard boxes; the Empire pool has gone the same way as the actual Empire; the Pipe Bridge no longer leads to England and Miss Tucker no longer teaches English at Lady Mary High School.

* * * * *

The panic and excitement at the dog training school was over. The initial report of a kangaroo sighting in the field had been investigated and it transpired that it was one of the large Weimaraner dogs having a poop.

There were two Weimaraner puppies in Barney's socialisation class – tall, leggy sporting dogs, bred to spend the entire day running in the fields looking for fowl to retrieve. They are competitive, attentive and very energetic.

There were also a pair of Red Setters and, as a breed, they too have high energy levels and are supposed to run about, pointing, flushing and retrieving fowl all day. Someone had slipped up though, and hadn't given these two their job description, as they just seemed to lope around and lie down at every opportunity.

A small, bearded rat type thing made infrequent visits to the centre whilst Barney's final classmate was a small part-Labrador/part-something else cross, named Tess, who immediately rolled onto her back as soon as the three-toed one approached.

I have heard that in nearby Chester-le-Street they were breeding a cross between a Labrador and a Standard Poodle which, apparently, has the same good nature as a 'Lab' but with the benefit of not losing its hair. I think it was called a 'Labrapoo' or maybe even a 'Poudador'. This seemed like a good idea as, just from the hairs I had picked up off the carpet over the last few weeks, I could have made myself a half-scale Barney. There were no reports of a Shih Tzu/Poodle cross as I guess nobody would want a dog called a 'Shitpoo'.

As much as I wanted to be top dog in my own pack, I gently encouraged Barney to become top dog in his playgroup, with promises of games of fetch if he did well. Owner egos would be made or broken, depending on whether their pets took a dominant or submissive stance. I think Tess' mum accepted from the outset that her pooch was always going to be the lowest of the low. As it is confusing having two 'Tess' dogs in this book, small cross breed Tess will hereafter be known as 'Tess Two'.

So it was that Tess Two's mum metaphorically rolled

over onto her back in submission, as did her nubile twenty-something daughter who attended the class with her. I suppose we communicated like the parents in any playgroup, as we only seemed to know each other through our charges.

Harvey, Weimaraner No. 1, was Barney's biggest competitor for the top dog slot. Harvey's dad wanted that coveted spot for his boy, but Harvey's mum and Deborah were far too sensible to become involved. Red and Alfie, the Red Setters, didn't seem to care *who* was top dog as long as they could have a lie down. Milly, Weimaraner No. 2, had, along with her mum, missed a couple of classes and was a late entry. Nobody seemed to notice the rat-like thing and Tess Two continued to lie on her back.

Whilst Barney had the upper hand in the early classes, Harvey's confidence improved as the weeks passed. It seemed a dead heat for the top dog slot as the last class ended so I quickly put the word out that Barney was up for a rematch any time.

Barney was awarded a certificate and rosette as he finished the final class which meant that, at the age of twenty weeks, he had already drawn level with me on the prize stakes. He seemed pretty proud of his awards and I think he would have liked to display them above his sleeping area. If he had a bed, it's likely I would have granted his wish but, since he had eaten it, I refused. It's not that I was jealous of him at all – I was just worried that people might think he was some kind of show-off.

His education wasn't over though, and I decided to continue taking that thin, wild mercury thing to obedience classes as he still had a couple of habits that I wished to iron out. He didn't always come back when I called for him and there was still a tendency to jump up when he greeted people. He would bounce up and down, chase his tail in mini circles and shake his little body before taking a leap up at this long-lost, new best friend. Whilst his tiny brain was coping with all this, it forgot to tell him that he shouldn't wee all over the place. The combination of jumping up at people whilst weeing was in danger of making Barney a social outcast.

。 ° 。 ° 。 °

There had already been a strange sort of start to the day. As I was walking along the river, two thirty-something women were jogging towards me on the path. "Isn't he handsome?" one of them commented quite openly to the other, more as a statement than a question. "He's gorgeous," the other added.

I'm sure I was meant to hear their remarks and a mixture of emotions flooded over me. I was, of course, flattered but more than a little embarrassed and I also felt slightly sorry for Barney whom, in all this, they had clearly chosen to ignore. They missed out too, mind you, as normally, if an attractive woman shows any interest in him, he runs over, and licks her face and pants. (There, that's a good example: if only I had paid attention in school and really knew how to use a semi-colon properly, I could have stopped that from sounding half as smutty as it did.)

Despite feeling sympathetic towards my dog and his hurt feelings, I still made him wait for his breakfast when we returned home. As a matter of course, Barney would be made to sit for a minute in front of his dinner bowl before he was allowed to eat. On the command, he would wolf it down as if he expected me to change my mind at any moment and take the bowl away. By the way he looks at me, I'm sure he feels a bit embarrassed about how slowly I eat in comparison. He even sucks his belly in to create a vacuum to shovel the food in faster. Good things come to those who wait.

Being a much more sedate dog, Tess tends to pick at her food throughout the day so Barney has realised that there is usually plenty of dry mix in her dish. When we visit Deborah, Tess is normally pottering outside in the conservatory, so Barney goes to wait patiently by the door as if he's hoping to go and play with his mate. However, as soon as the door is opened enough, he darts through, straight past a startled Tess and into her food bowl. As I run after him, Barney's tactic is to make his nose divebomb into the bowl. He knows that the mix will explode everywhere and, even after I have snatched Tess' bowl away from him, he can leisurely hoover up the debris. Sometimes good things only come to those who wait – if they are fast enough.

Deborah might then say something like, "What goes around comes around." I have no idea what she is on about and the expression, "It will happen when you least expect it to," always puzzled me too. *What* would happen? The answer it seems is, 'it' and I was about fourteen at the time when I found out what 'it' was.

·°·°·°·°

I had gone for a day out at the beach, along with my friend Michael Leeson and his parents, whom I addressed as Mr and Mrs Leeson. Bethan seems to know all her friends' parents by their first names but, at that age, I didn't even know that my friends' parents *had* first names.

Mr Leeson, the hero of the piece, was, I guess, about fifty at the time. He was a lecturer at the university and appeared very studious. He was gangly and very quiet, and

I can't really remember having ever spoken more than a few words to him.

After a day of playing on the sand, Michael and I had climbed the footpath up from the beach to the car park and stood next to the car, waiting for Mr and Mrs Leeson to show. I could just make out the top of Mr Leeson's head bobbing up and down as he started to come into view, but then his weary little face appeared and finally the full, mild-mannered academic was revealed.

Suddenly, out of nowhere, he seemed to be possessed by the devil. His eyes widened and he threw aside the blanket and straw basket he was carrying. He started to take great strides with his long, gangly legs – strides as long as he was tall. He started shouting obscenities as he covered the ground at a lightning pace and, without slowing, a long, gangly arm scooped up a large stone from the floor and, in one fluid movement, it was thrown with considerable force and bounced off the back of a grey Hillman Imp driving out of the car park. The back of the car snaked on the ground and the wheels started to spin as the driver desperately tried to accelerate away at great speed. I could see two children with panic-stricken faces cowering in the back, looking like they were shouting at their daddy to get moving. One looked like he was crying. It was pandemonium in there.

Mr Leeson didn't end his pursuit until the car was well and truly out of sight and he had chased it a good hundred yards or so up the country lane leading away from the car park. We knew he had reached the end of his chase when the screech of tyres faded and we heard a final outburst of expletives echoing in the calm, warm evening air.

By this time, a slightly bemused Mrs Leeson had joined us while Michael and I just stood open mouthed, nervously awaiting the return of the madman. It was only when Mr

Leeson returned and saw all three of us standing by the side of his grey Hillman Imp that the horrible truth dawned on him. Michael and I *hadn't* been kidnapped and then forcibly driven off in his own car after all. His car was still parked where he left it and we were standing next to it, unharmed.

Goodness knows what the driver of the innocent car thought as he saw a swearing madman bearing down on him, throwing missiles. His heart must have been beating as if there was a hummingbird trapped inside, and the mayhem in the car must have been all consuming, as the frightened children, fearing for their very lives, jumped about weeping and shouting for their daddy to save them. What must have gone through their minds as the rock bounced off the vehicle? Nothing was said. We all got in the car and drove home in silence.

I made a mental note, *"Never buy a grey Hillman Imp."*

15

The Lambton Worm

Just as the milkman was making his rounds and dropping off an extra pint to those who had left a note out for him, Barney and I were out on our morning walk. It was a beautiful morning, and the tide was coming in, so the river was actually flowing upstream. Two swans were taking their eight cygnets out for a spot of training on the water, and the three-toed one actually stopped jumping about for a while to stare at them. I told him it was rude to do that and so, instead, he tried to surreptitiously scale the embankment on the other side of the path.

I have been climbing many times, having attended a course in North Wales, done quite a bit in the military and even gone to lessons again a few years back in a forlorn effort to impress a girl I was going out with. It was something I felt I should enjoy but I never really did. Bethan, on the other hand, seemed to love it. When we had gone to the Durham County Show, she'd resembled a little monkey, clambering up the climbing wall.

We had come back from that same County Show with an exceedingly expensive sixty pence stuffed toy panda. It had turned into one of Bethan's 'must have' weekends. To be fair, they don't happen that often but, now and again, there is a 'must have' item that, in simple terms, she must have that weekend. Recent 'must haves' include a set of red hair bobbles and a red T-shirt. Not just any red hair bobbles and red T-shirt, you understand – these are specific ones that she has pictured in her head and that I must find by trial and error. It's not that I *mind*, it's just that I would prefer a better stab at success by having a decent description up front. Comments like, "That's too red," or, "Those bobbles are too big," still echo in my ears.

It's guaranteed though, that every time we wander into Woolworths (RIP), the day suddenly transforms into a 'must have pencil case and/or folder' day. Actually, I have long suspected that Woolworths was an agency of the Chinese Government, on the basis that they appeared to have relinquished their aspiration of world domination through communism but, instead, were working towards their objective by their merciless supply of useless plastic objects.

The 'must have' at the Durham Show was a large grey teddy bear. Fifteen pounds later, we persuaded Bethan to call it quits with the pathetic small panda we had managed to win. Close, but no bear (in fact the term 'close, but no cigar' comes from the time that cigars were given out as prizes as carnivals. In hindsight, it's just as well we didn't win. Susan would have gone ape-shit with me if I brought Bethan back with a handful of smokes!). Anyway, I'm sure it was the most loved panda in the world until she got home when it was then tossed aside to become just another stuffed toy in the veritable mountain of them, living at the end of her bed. I bet he didn't even warrant a name. But she was happy.

The sunshine of the previous days had given way to a light drizzle as we set off on our morning walk. As we went into the woods, Barney was overcome by a sniffing frenzy. It was like watching a speeded-up film as he darted about in little figures of eight, his nose hovering a matter of millimetres above the ground. He would bury his head in the foliage on the side of the path, venture high up the embankment and then run down to take up precarious positions overhanging the near vertical riverbank, all in his quest for 'sniffery'. His tail, which under normal circumstances, was in a continual state of wag, was now doing a near perfect impression of car windscreen wipers in a rainstorm. I was worried it might come flying off at any moment.

The 'wag' issue had already led to a number of spillages but, thankfully, in Deborah's house, not mine. There was quite a bit of energy in that tail which only seemed to be dissipated once it had swiped a full wine glass or coffee cup. This led to the modern-day phenomenon of 'centring' whereby all potential energy dissipaters, such as wine glasses and cups, were housed in the centre of the coffee table rather than the risky exposed edges.

The sniffing had become all-consuming in Barney's little mind that morning, and he had even forgotten that the main purpose of his dad getting up and wandering out in his sticky up haired state, was for the wild four-legged one to have his dawn poo. I returned home with a still fully loaded dog.

The next day was the Saturday of my abandonment and, as the sun was beaming again, I decided to take Barney on a full circuit walk that morning.

I don't want to appear to be dwelling on the subject, but it seemed to form a big part of Barney's life and obviously meant a lot to him and, for the sake of medical research, I will therefore continue. In brief, it seemed as if Barney was making up for lost time and this morning's walk was in stark contrast to the 'no-poop' sniffing escapade.

He appeared to be testing out a new theory in his tiny mind. His thought process seemed to be that, if he deposited two poops on his normal twenty-minute morning walk, he should do two poops *every* twenty minutes. A stroll round the circuit took about an hour and I feared he might turn himself inside out in his valiant effort to keep up his quota.

My initial stab at one human year being equal to seven dog years was apparently wrong. As dogs mature much faster than us, it seemed more like fifteen dog years for each human year for the first two years and, thereafter, five dog years for each of ours. On this basis, what I initially thought was a surfeit of poops on this journey was actually, in dog years, only one poop every two and a half days, which didn't seem so excessive after all. What it did mean, though, was that I was running out of poop bags to clear up his mess. I'm not sure which is harder, splitting the atom or opening a dog poo bag, but I valiantly carried on rubbing the sides together and blowing on the tops of each bag, convinced each time, right up to the moment of opening, that they had sold me just a single sliver of plastic. And I don't know who gets more embarrassed when we make eye contact when he's having his dump, him or me, but I had to keep track of where his dirty, filthy deposits were being laid.

I managed to kick a couple of turds into the river but, in the end, had to resort to opening previously tied-up bags to make room for more of Barney's bodily rejects. At one stage I picked up a cold poo, and when I realised I had picked up some other hound's shit I felt physically sick. Why couldn't I have invested in a sloth instead of a dog – they only poop once a week!

I have often moaned about the litter that seems to be left in the countryside but, try as I might, I couldn't find any bins and the Council didn't seem to be helping themselves here. We even went off route to try and find somewhere to dump the dumps. And that's where I became confused as I reached a row of lovely cottages, just plonked along a path parallel to our normal walk when, as we approached them, the path just seemed to disappear.

It seems that some people, who are lucky enough to live in beautiful locations, want to keep the beauty all to themselves. If a right of way passes close by, they will try and put you off the scent by making it look as if you are trespassing on their land if you follow the route. The nicer people in society, who wouldn't dream of disturbing anyone else's privacy, would be deterred in case they did just that, and retreat to seek an alternative way. Meanwhile, the lucky people living in the houses are rubbing their hands together because they have managed to keep all those lovely natural views to themselves.

The Nazi and I though, have never claimed to be members of polite society, and so blundered on through. However, even we began to doubt ourselves as we walked across what seemed to be a gravelled drive, adorned with ornaments and flower displays. Eventually, we found the right of way route arrow hidden behind a couple of tubs of geraniums and continued on the path past the end of the row of houses.

The cottage owners were obviously seething inside that an 'intruder' had managed to share their fantastic vista of the woods leading down to the river. I didn't have the heart to tell them that I also posted several bags of turds in one of their postboxes too.

° ° ° ° ° °

There are three pubs over the river from me, and behind the middle one is Worm Hill. Barney and I were going to scramble up Worm Hill and perhaps visit one of the pubs on the way back.

Legend has it that, in the Middle Ages, the Lambton Worm wrapped himself around the hill, thus giving it that name. From this base, he would then venture out and terrorise the local neighbourhood. However, as much as I tried to picture a scary worm, even a very long one, I just couldn't make myself frightened. We had dragons in Wales which, I suppose, could be frightening, but a worm was just not doing it for me.

The story goes that a young member of the Lambton family was fishing one Sunday but all he caught was a small wiggling worm. Disgusted with his catch, he threw it in a well. Years later, after he had departed to fight in the Crusades, the worm emerged from the well as a huge and ferocious beast. It was like a dragon but without legs or wings. Now that was more like it! Then we have the terrorising bit.

When Lambton returned from the Holy Land, he vowed to kill the beast and, as luck would have it, a witch was on hand to offer advice on how to slaughter the worm. He was to wear a suit of armour with spikes on but, as with all good witch advice, there was a twist, and this one was that he had to kill the first living thing he saw after the worm was slain.

Lambton lured the worm into the River Wear outside my house and, as the worm tried to wrap himself around our hero, it was cut to pieces on the armour and Lambton finally chopped the beast's head off. He had planned to have his favourite hound greet him on his return so he could slay that but, in the excitement, our hero's dad was the first to welcome him. Needless to say, Lambton reneged on his promise to the witch and didn't kill his father and, as a result, the family were cursed in the process, enduring years of untimely deaths for generations.

As I regaled the tale to Barney on top of Worm Hill, I left out some of the detail. He didn't need to know about the favourite hound bit and, not wishing to frighten him, I also told him that the story had happened near Newcastle and that, afterwards, Lambton suggested that the worm's body be used as a massive sausage to feed the poor.

I finished with the Dickensian quote, "It was the Beast of Tyne, it was the Wurst of Tyne." As Barney looked up at me with a blank expression, a tumbleweed blew across the field in front of me and I swear I could hear a single church bell sounding somewhere off in the distance.

16

Doctor Shit

Snails, oysters and all that sort of food from shells, I must admit, are not my cup of tea. I was a young sailor in New Orleans at Mardi Gras time when I was given my first oyster to try. The music blared, the drink flowed, the shellfish beckoned, and I was in the mood for a little romance. The atmosphere couldn't have been more fantastic. The oyster made it half-way down my throat before it decided that it preferred the fresh air, did a U-turn and popped back up again, all over the girl in the bikini-style cowgirl outfit sitting next to me. She turned to me and, very calmly, and matter of factly, informed me what she thought of me.

"You are an idiot."

The rest of the girls looked at me as if I was thick, and I returned to the ship alone.

That was my first and only attempt at food with that type of texture.

It must have been a bit of a hit and miss affair, I suppose, working out which molluscs and shellfish were good to eat, and which weren't, and I guess that, whoever worked out that snails are good to eat, must have also tried slugs some stage. How about mushrooms? Admittedly, they're all edible, but some only once. And the guy who discovered milk – what was he doing messing with that cow in the first place? Did he look around surreptitiously first to check no one was watching? Did he drink it directly from the 'tap' or did he decant it into something first? Did he try it on with a bull later? These early food pioneers must have suffered for their art. And whilst we're on the subject, why is Old McDonald's Farm in the past tense? What tragedy unfolded there? Was he too 'experimental' with his animals and they rebelled?

Frogs' legs are another thing that I have never had a desire to try, but young Barney has. As we made our way through the woods after a heavy summer rainstorm, the mist was rising from the forest floor and I spied a large frog making his way across the path. Not having learnt from previous pointing/eating experiences, I drew Barney's attention to the amphibian. Maybe I thought he would just look and go, "Ooooh," like me but, instead, he tried to fit it all into his mouth. He immediately jumped back, spitting the frog out, and then proceeded to run around sounding like a cat trying to cough up a furball. I had once read an article about the dangers of licking a Horny Toad but had assumed it was just some sort of adult version of the popular 'kissing a frog' fairy tale. Luckily, this was just an unpleasant-tasting frog though, and Barney would live to lick another day. In fact, the next day he ate a snail.

Apparently, many snails were consumed during the Napoleonic Wars and each soldier in the French Army had to carry canned snails as emergency rations. I guess they had to carry them, otherwise they would be too slow to keep up with the marching army. Each soldier was allotted one thousand snails per week.

War in that era was much different than it is today. In battles, only three or four shots per hundred ever hit anybody. The first shot would be most accurate as the weapons were clean and there was time to load them correctly. Thereafter, accuracy diminished as the barrels became fouled and soldiers hurried to reload them in the heat of battle. A good soldier could probably fire about four rounds a minute. In the Battle of Vitoria, it is estimated that over three and a half million musket balls were fired, causing about eight thousand causalities – that works out at merely one hit per four hundred and fifty shots. I guess, after all that fighting, it might be quite nice to sit back and crack open the odd snail or two. In many ways, Napoleon was ahead of his time.

As well as being an excellent General, he was responsible for some dramatic reforms and their influence spread much further than the boundaries of France. He instigated the French Civil code or *Code Napoleon*. Under this, there were no privileges of birth and all men were equal under the law. It is still the basis of law in many countries to this day.

Whilst Paris was the sophisticated hub of reform, the North East of England in those days was a bleak place, inhabited by suspicious hunchbacks and deformed bigots. Well, at least in Hartlepool it was. As the fortunes of the different sides in the Napoleonic Wars ebbed and flowed, a French ship was once wrecked in a storm off the coast of this fishing town. The sole survivor washed up on the sands was Claude, the ship's mascot, a little monkey decked out in naval gear for the crew's amusement. The townsfolk, who had never seen a Frenchman before, seized Claude believing that he must be one of these damned foreigners, and he stood trial on the beach, accused of being a spy. His little gibberings were taken as being French. Aha! A confession. Claude was found guilty and hanged until he was dead. The end.

Well, not quite the end. After years of humiliation, being known as the place where they hanged the monkey, the good people of Hartlepool eventually made amends for their folly and, in 2002, elected a monkey as mayor of the City. And sadly enough, it's a true story.

° ° ° ° ° °

The truth about my four-legged friend was clarified one fateful morning. Any doubts I may have harboured that Barney was not a Pedigree Labrador were finally ousted when a black-clad figure burst through the toilet door as I sat there, snatched the toilet roll and ran straight off. He must have silently crept up the stairs before putting his pilfering into action. And it was only the fact that the roll was picked up in his mouth that confirmed the thief's identity. I had to improvise.

I had to improvise when I was at my RMP selection weekend as well. I had forgotten to take my towel, and after my shower, I had to dry myself on the bedroom curtains. As I stood there in the nude, liberally drying my gonads, I saw a couple of crows fighting amongst themselves on the parade ground. Instinctively, I knocked hard on the window and waved my arms about to scare them off, only to see a bemused female major who had been walking past outside, staring straight back at me. I assume that, to her, it may well have appeared that I had not only purposely stood stark naked at a window, but that I had then banged on the window specifically to get her attention, before enthusiastically shaking my junk at her. What a perfect start to the day.

The day got worse when I found that she was on the

selection panel, and I thought that would be the end of my rise to mediocrity, but somehow, I still got the transfer I wanted, so she must have seen something that impressed her that day. Anyhow, moving swiftly on.

If Kate had been at my house, things would have been different. We don't appear to have been a bright bunch in Carisbrooke Way all those years ago and checking the toilet roll holder never seemed to have crossed our minds. Every now and again a foghorn sounding, "Toilet Roll!" would emanate from an unfortunate 'sitter' who hadn't taken into account the 'supply versus demand' intricacies of such paper. It had to be loud enough to alert Kate wherever she was and, as the toilet was at the front of the house, it also probably alerted half the street to our plight. Each call was approximately six seconds long and would continue to be repeated until Kate had completed her duty and fetched a roll, either upstairs or downstairs depending on where the summons came from. In later years, the downstairs toilet was banned from such use. Stink and continued shouts of, "Toilet roll!" were not deemed the best way to greet a visitor.

Another of Kate's jobs in those days was being the remote control for the television. Actual remote controls had yet to be invented, so we made do with Kate. She would sit on the floor and, on command, like a trained monkey, she would leap into action and change the channel to see what was on the other side. It wasn't a complex task as there were only the three channels, one of which was 'Protestant' which meant that it normally had the best stuff on anyway.

She was almost made redundant after 'Blue Peter' demonstrated how to make a remote control. It was basically a stick with a rubber end on it that you could jab at the buttons. She was reinstated when this was deemed too dangerous after the telly was almost poked off the stand.

Kate is the original idiot savant and, as such, does still have her uses post invention of the modern day 'safety' remote controls. Despite going through life with little or no common sense, she does have an uncanny ability to remember details. I have now employed her as my fact-checking service, which is handy on two counts; namely accuracy of information and, if anything libellous is contained in the pages of this book, she can officially take the blame instead of me.

Whilst checking these facts, we reminisced about the time when the whole family had gone to France, when she was only an eighteen-month-old baby. As our mum lay on the beach sleeping in the sun, the rest of us played boules, the French version of bowls. As the game went on, we noticed that one of the boules was missing. Paul just happened to glance back to see Kate, standing with her feet either side of Mum's head, holding the metal boule, ready to drop it onto her face. Everyone moved swiftly and a murder in the South of France was narrowly avoided.

We both agreed that we would leave that out of the book in case it made Kate look bad.

٥ ٥ ٥ ٥ ٥ ٥

I asked Bethan a couple of years ago if she wanted me to give her pocket money. She seemed surprised and replied that she didn't need any money because, if she wanted something, she knew that she could just ask me, and I'd buy it for her. Her logic was pretty sound.

Just before she went to music school, however, she asked if she could do some jobs to earn some money to buy sweets and things while she was away. I asked if she would brush out Barney's kennel, but she said she was wearing her best clothes so I jokingly suggested that she could take over the poop scoop duties for the day, but she informed me that her mum had told her she wasn't allowed to do that. I nearly suggested that she should clean the car, but I recalled the time that she had inadvertently cleaned her mum's car with a Brillo Pad and thought better of it. She offered to do some housework for me, but it seemed a shame to waste a hot day being inside so, in the end, I paid her for getting us ice-lollies from the freezer.

Bethan seems a lot more sensible than I was at her age and I was sure she wouldn't spend all the money in one go. When we changed from old money to decimal coins, I was presented with a commemorative pack of the new coinage. The first thing I did was to prise the coins free from the display and spend them at the sweet shop. No Aztec bars, Bazooka Joes or Spangles for me that day. Instead, I bought several bags of marshmallows because they seemed to be bigger and considerably more foam-like than most other sweets clambering for my attention on that special occasion. I proceeded to eat these substitutes for my legacy until I felt sick. You can stuff a lot of marshmallows in too before you feel sick, probably enough to package up a good-sized television.

I was always a bit frightened of going on holiday after that in case they changed the currency again when I was away, and no one let me know. I thought I would look a fool, going into the sweet shop, only to have everyone laughing at me as I handed over 'old' useless money.

Of course, I had the normal children's nightmares too, like suddenly realising I was sitting in school just in my pyjamas, or even less. How I made the bus journey without noticing this fact was conveniently overlooked. The nightmare of calling a teacher, "Mum" also became reality on more than one occasion and, while the teacher smiled benignly, the rest of the class would be laughing their socks off. The memory of it still haunts me. The only thing that would be even more embarrassing would be if I were sitting, resplendent in my 'PJs', *as* I called her "Mum".

When my oldest brother Paul went off to Medical School for the first time, Kate secretly packed Bruno, his childhood teddy bear, into his case. Of course, his roommate saw Bruno emerge, blinking in the light as the case was opened and, within days, everyone knew that Paul had brought his teddy with him for comfort. I'm sure it was the shame he felt that contributed to him leaving Medical School before he could qualify; either that or the fact that he was none too bright.

When Paul returned from university three years later looking dejected, everyone was sympathetic. "At least you tried, son," my dad said as he opened the letter Paul had brought home with him, although I don't think my brother had meant to show Dad his final report. The atmosphere changed somewhat as Dad read out the tutor's final words. "You have strutted your funky stuff once too often." As Kate, Neil and I all hurried upstairs, I could hear the words echoing throughout the house. "Bloody hell, boy, Doctor? Doctor? Doctor Shit, more like!"

。°。°。°

I have never been good at waking up and, although all the signs were there that Bethan was growing up into a small adult, I suppose I really just wanted to press the snooze button and put it off a bit.

The reason I've stayed in the North East is because I wanted to be near Bethan and she only lives a few hundred yards away from me now. I wish I had been as bright and confident as she is when I was ten. Some of the best times in my life have been on our weekends together. All I have to do is think of her and I smile. We would be on one of our trips out and we'd bump into someone I knew, and I would proudly introduce my daughter to them.

"This is Beth," I'd say.

"What's Beth short for?" they would invariably ask.

"Because she's only ten," I'd respond, being jocular as was my wont, and they would stare at me as if I was stupid, as was their wont.

It's the simple things like wandering down to the park with her dressed in her Scooby Doo outfit, or going for picnics in the lazy summer countryside. We would stay out until late, and as the sun set behind us, we would allow the long shadows we cast to guide us home. I could swear that days as beautiful as that had been created just for Bethan and me. Nobody can make me feel as happy as she can. I love her very much and I suppose that was making the current situation feel worse.

I guess she was just growing up. She didn't want to hold my hand when we were out because it was supposedly embarrassing, and she was also becoming moody. *Very* moody. *Extremely* moody. At other times, she wasn't sure if she could come over as her friend might visit her instead and, anyway, even if she did come over, she didn't want to drive anywhere far in the car and so on. It was that sort of moody.

She didn't even want to play schools anymore – I was gutted because, not only did it seem like the end of an era, but I was on the verge of moving up into the next reading class too!

She was also turning into something of a 'blackcatter'. Everything I liked was rubbish and nothing seemed good enough, to the extent that if I said I had a black cat, she would have had one that was blacker. The situation was fluctuating and, in the moments when she forgot that she was supposed to act all temperamental, she held my hand again and we laughed and joked at the same old stupid stuff. When she is like that, she is the most fantastic company.

I knew it was a phase she was going through, but that didn't make it any easier. I was finding it very difficult to cope with and I couldn't even talk to my mum about it; she'd have helped me. I was feeling very awkward. I know Bethan was probably feeling even more awkward, but that was cold comfort. In fact, it made me feel worse. I just wanted it to be like the old times again.

I felt pretty awkward with Deborah sometimes too. Her husband had died and, from things she said about him, he sounded like a really nice guy. I felt like I was second best.

There was a lot of awkwardness going around; in fact, I've never seen so many 'awkwards' in one chapter. It is meant to be the most miss-spelt word in the English language, so that might explain away that fact.

The whole situation made me feel sad – sadder than when I was a child and I turned on the telly to watch the cowboy film, only to hear those dreaded words, "Except for viewers in Wales, who will have their own programme." *Much* sadder, and that's saying something. Maybe even as sad as Florence Ballard.

It was touch and go if I was even as sad as someone Kate had known at school. I can't even name the poor guy, it's that sort of sad, so let's just call him 'John Smith'. It was his eighteenth birthday, and his parents had arranged a table full of the finest finger buffet food and bought every type of drink under the sun for him to mix cocktails for his chums, and generally have a fantastic time celebrating his coming of age. They had even arranged to go out for the night to leave him to party the night away, free from the prying eyes of the adults. That's the good bit – but this is the bad bit - no one came. Not a soul, nobody, nil personages, not anyone, zero, zilch. His parents arrived back in the early hours to find him sitting like a despondent Kermit on the stairs. If that is not one of the saddest stories you've heard, I'd like to hear a sadder one! (well, I wouldn't actually). If it had been me, I would have stolen a few ornaments, spilt some wine on the floor, force fed myself half the food, made the cat sick behind the sofa, peed on the bathroom floor and maybe left a couple of condoms around the house just to at least *pretend* that some sort of wild party had just occurred (and if I *was* the poor guy who had suffered this 'I've got no mates in the entire world and people will stand and point at me and say "there's that sad bloke" till the end of time' humiliation, I would make it my solemn duty to hunt down the bastard who leaked the story and shove the entire finger buffet where the sun don't shine... but I digress).

Of course, John Smith wasn't his real name, it's actually Tony Cutmore.

Oh shit!

One of the supposedly helpful things people say is that the darkest hour is the one before dawn. It may be, but the darkest hour is also the one where it's most dark! When I was in a difficult or unpleasant situation in the military, I would get through it by mentally preparing myself. Whether it was an interrogation, sitting in a cold, wet trench, or on a particularly boring tour of duty, I would tell myself to get on with it because it would be over in a few hours, or a week, or six months, whatever the relevant timescale was. The trouble here was that I had no idea how long this would last. I suppose I would only get to know where this was going when I arrived.

A year before, Bethan and I had sat together in a coffee shop in Durham. Bethan, as usual, had ordered the largest piece of chocolate cake that money could buy, and we had belly laughed at something or other as we often did.

I now sat there alone and, as I looked out of the window in my pensive mood, I felt that it seemed like the end of the world as I knew it. A flyer propped up next to the sugar bowl informed me that today was 'The Third World Awareness Day'. Just my luck – I'd already missed the first two. As I pushed the plunger down on my cafetiere, I half expected the Renault parked in the street outside to explode.

17

Tales from the Riverbank

A wing must have fallen off a seagull, as it was now lying on the path in front of Barney and me. It must have been a terrible shock for the bird when it happened, and I suppose it must have made him fly in infinite circles afterwards. We looked up, but he wasn't circling overhead anymore, and we couldn't seem to find the rest of his body anywhere. There was just the wing. I say, 'he' but, for all I know, it could have been a 'she'.

"No!" I barked at Barney as he went to pick it up, but he picked it up just the same. I had to resort to telling him to fetch it to me to get it off him and stop him from chewing it. We didn't know if the bird was going to come back for it, and it would have been very embarrassing for all concerned if Barney had been caught eating it.

We had passed a dead mole on the path the day before. His pale hands were splayed out either side of his furry face as if he had been doing an Al Jolson impression for his woodland chums the second before he was mown down. "I'd walk a million miles for one of your smiles, my ma…" THWACK!

Barney is starting to be quite mischievous now, and I often see him chewing away at something when we are sitting in the house. I'll ask him what he's got, but that normally brings no immediate response and he'll keep on chewing. I'll get up, go over to him and prise his mouth open and shake his little head so that whatever is in there will fall out. Most of the time, there's nothing. I think it's just a game he plays with me. After I let go, he will make that sort of grimace he does in wry amusement at the situation (aha Barney, think you can beat me in a game of wits, do you? Well, you've met your equal now!). I've told him that, if that's the funniest he can be, it's rubbish. Even the visiting priests were funnier, and that's saying something.

He is funniest really when he's not trying – the way he just potters about, tilting his head to one side if he is at all puzzled by anything; the way he spends ages staring at the other dog who seems to live at the bottom of his water bowl, or the fact that he likes to walk around in a little circle before he lies down. And why does he always think that, if there's a knock on the door, it's for him? I also like the way he runs in his sleep, or just lies there with his tongue poking out. Occasionally, he sleeps on his back with his legs in the air and I thought he was dead the first time he did that. When I mentioned this to one of the assistants at the dog school, she said that when her dog was lying like that, she did a health check on his bits, but I believed that was probably a bit of a dodgy habit to fall into - and quite possibly illegal. Barney would be absolutely horrified if he woke up and found me doing that!

In fact, it was the same woman who I confided in, telling her that one morning last week, I had come down to find that Barney had done a little poop on the kitchen floor. I can scarcely believe what happened next. She had turned to me and quietly said, "Now, Mr Donoghue, *you* are really responsible for that, aren't you?". What the fuck!! Have I got this right? She was accusing *me* of sneaking down in the middle of the night and laying one down just to frame my little pup? She must be bloody sick in the head! Sick I tell you!

For someone like me, who likes things in their place, Barney is a nightmare as he leaves his toys everywhere. I for one will be quite happy when Bethan eventually puts me in an old people's home (as long as it's not one of those you hear about that leave you lying in your own piss-drenched bed for days on end). I enjoyed the routine of living both onboard ship and in barracks, and I would be quite content to pass away my twilight years just playing cards with my new old friends, and maybe once in a while sitting in front of the fire with a tartan rug on my knee; in fact, I could probably do without the rug – a tart on her own would be just fine. Maybe I would be a slightly grumpy old man by then, and spend my time making lists of what annoyed me about the world. A list of technical flaws in the dog design department would be a good place to start. I've already covered the 'nose in bowl' fault and the 'showing off arsehole too much' issue. What is it with this 'opening doors with your head' thing too? And they never shut the door after themselves, either. You would think they were born in a barn! (Well, I guess Barney has some sort of excuse in that he *was* actually born in a barn, but you get my drift). And for an animal that sleeps all night and kips most of the day, why, oh why, does he still potter about yawning all the time? And what about that couple of half-hearted kicks they do with the back legs after they've done a poop, as if they are trying to cover it up? Pathetic. Many a time have I shouted after Barney, "You're not fooling anyone!" as he scampers off. If God ever wants to do a general product recall to sort the problems, my list could prove invaluable.

Actually, if he does a recall on humans, maybe he could consider giving us our tails back so I could tell which women actually like me, although I suppose this wouldn't completely be without its other issues, such as attending a funeral of someone we don't like and feigning sadness, whilst our enthusiastic wagging is giving the game away around the back. Maybe I'll have to continue with my tried and trusted chat up line for now: Make an awkward face if you'll go out with me, or recite the alphabet backwards for no.

I never realised that dogs could snore so much either, and he has also taken to lying across doors like one of those stuffed snakes that are used to keep out the cold. I don't know if he is stupid for lying there, or if I am more stupid for not wanting to disturb him when I need to open the door. As he wakes, his one visible eye will move around in its socket as he follows my every move, and I will then hear a hollow banging sound. On investigation, I discover it's just his tail wagging onto the floor. It seems that a great deal of energy is expended when just another of those grins would suffice.

However, enough warmth – pointless nostalgia about Barney had to be a thing of the past as I had just received an important phone call from Kate and action was needed.

⁕ ⁕ ⁕

The quiet camping trip with Doctor Shit and his crew was developing into a full-blown family exercise. Kate, her husband Woody (so named because he resembles Woody from Toy Story, or was it the other way round?) and daughter Poppy were also coming down to camp for the weekend. Actually, whilst I'm on the subject, does anyone know of a tactful way to tell people that I never want to talk to their babies on the phone?

What is more, although he could afford for someone to come down in his place, Neil was also rumoured to be joining us with his clan. There would be fifteen of us altogether. This was going to be unique for me – a camping trip with the whole family, without being kicked in the back for the first three hundred miles.

I had originally planned to arrive on the Saturday but, by then, everyone else would have already claimed the best pitches. I didn't mind who had the worst pitch as long as it wasn't me. If I did arrive last, of course, everyone would be there to admire my twenty-second erection. It was a hard decision but, in the end, the pitch became paramount. I rang Deborah in Turkey and told her the change of plan, and then contacted the kennels to book Tess in a day early. Only Barney was going camping this time round.

On the last family camping holiday Neil had spent in Wales, his tent blew away in the middle of the night. I'm not sure if he said to anyone, "Toto, I've a feeling we're not in canvas anymore." In fact, I'm pretty sure he won't have, but it would have been amusing in a getting soaking wet in the middle of a storm sort of way. Actually, that sounded a lot funnier when I told it to Barney than it does now it's in print. Anyway, I thought it best not to pitch next to him if at all possible.

Paul and Neil had cycled along Offa's Dyke, or some such journey last year and, after a full day in the saddle, they had both spent the first night squeezed into Neil's tiny hiking tent. As the two of them emerged the next morning, Paul stretched out, commenting that his bum was really sore from the previous day's activities. As this drew strange looks from the surrounding campers, they decided that, rather than try and explain, it was far better to rapidly pack up their gear and make a speedy exit on their bikes.

Unfortunately, Bethan would still be on her holiday in the sun so she wouldn't be able to make it but, saying that, if you can't make a camping trip, I guess Jamaica is as good a place as any to be. It's a shame because it would also have been an opportunity for her to see all her cousins again, as she doesn't see them nearly often enough.

Meanwhile, I couldn't fail to see that this was an excellent opportunity for me to waste far too much time organising my emergency kit in preparation for the forthcoming expedition.

The laws of gravity are very, very strict – but even stricter are the laws governing male allegiance to torches, Swiss army knives, and pictures of ladies in the lingerie section of mail order catalogues.

My interest in torches had first proved useful when I was issued with my first military right-angle flashlight. It did the job well enough, but not as good as the tiny AAA torch that I had doctored by colouring the lens red with a felt-tip pen (to preserve night vision!) and tied with some parachute cord to my combats. Gradually it dawned on me that *all* of my military equipment was actually provided by the lowest bidder. In fact, it was even pretty hard to get *any* equipment from the quartermaster's stores as the store men seemed to live by the principle 'stores are for storing things' – and when they did actually issue any gear, it seemed to come in one of three sizes - too small, too big or tough shit. Sure, everything did the job more or less, so that the MOD and politicians could say that they had issued all the relevant kit to 'our boys', but it wasn't the really good kit that you needed. It was the same when I was small and all my friends had Dunlop Green Flash plimsolls, and I was still wearing the plain black 'Empire Made' daps (lace up and not even slip-on due to religious differences). They did the job but, well you know, it wasn't quite the same.

So it was that I had produced my own small, but extensively stocked, hypochondriac kit filled with bandages, plasters, safety pins and, more importantly, the world's finest tablets, capable of curing 90% of the world's commonest ailments that I could possibly suffer from whilst in the field. I also took the wise, if not anti-social, precaution of avoiding contact with anyone who could possibly have any cough or snuffle in the few weeks prior to deployment, in order to prevent cross contamination. That is, contamination of me that would make me cross. During this phase I was also vulnerable to the power of negative suggestion. So, if anyone even dared mention to me that I was perhaps looking a bit tired, I would convince myself that I must be about to come down with man flu and immediately counterattack my mutinous eco system with a barrage of assorted pills. Whoever said laughter was the best medicine obviously hasn't tried industrial strength Ibuprofen.

My survival kit, even if I say so myself, was a beauty. All incredibly small so as to fit inside an old tobacco tin (complete with shiny inside lid for signalling), and every item a winner. A condom doubles as a great water carrier (I wasn't the only one pleased when Durex started making them in different flavours), waterproof matches that I had made myself by dripping wax over the heads or ordinary matches, a small candle, garden wire and a tampon (kindling for fire-lighting). I could go on... so I will. Black shoe polish that could be used as fuel for a fire (and the smell it gives off when used this way is also good for warding off animals), hooks and line for catching fish, a snare for catching land-based animals, knife, small compass, magnifying glass and so on. You can buy them ready made now but it's not the same.

All we needed now was some decent weather. In the meantime, I decided to put my time to best use and hunted around for the Littlewoods catalogue.

18

Kevin: Angel of the North

At the top of my stairs, underneath the photo of me with some other soldiers with their faces blanked out for effect, is a picture of me with the bloke from The Cure. It's not really the bloke from The Cure, of course, but my friend Carol. It is one of those photographs where the flash was too powerful, and all you can see is a pale-looking me and someone else with wild, jet-black hair and bright red lipstick. I know it doesn't sound very flattering, but she is actually very attractive. I went out with Carol for about five years, on and off, and I am pretty sure it was she who accompanied me to the last big fun family get together.

I remember on our first date that, whilst I was happy that she didn't sneak a look in my bathroom medicine cabinet, I was also sad that I had wasted an hour setting up seventy ping pong balls in there for nothing. I haven't spoken to her for a couple of years now, but I'd love to come across her face again. I miss her company, but what I don't miss is the endless 'who is better' debate – Jesus or Father Christmas? I would tell her that it didn't really matter as most people thought they were one and the same anyway. He must be sick of people only praying to Him when they want something.

I never quite understood, as a child, the principle we had as Catholics of praying to Saints or even Mary. Surely, if you wanted something done, you went directly to the organ grinder. Maybe, the thought process behind it was that if Jesus, or God for that matter, were snowed under with prayers, a quick one to Saint 'X' would probably get through, and he would be delighted with some attention for a change. Furthermore, God would be far more likely to listen to one of the Saints coming to Him with someone's request, rather than direct from a mere mortal down on Earth – a sort of cosmic queue jumping.

₀ ° ₀ ° ₀ °

Meanwhile, in case you had forgotten, I still had my calendar project to get on with. I knew that the continuation of Project X was dependent on Bethan's continued goodwill. Therefore, the trip to Snitter would have to be meticulously planned as I wasn't sure what mood she'd be in, and I didn't want anything to go wrong and spoil the day. Briefings could then take place as to what was required in the way of equipment, such as the model (Barney) and the precise dimensions of the black masking tape to be used. Questions needed to be answered, such as, "*Would the model need to be hoisted in the air to be displayed, grimacing alongside the sign, or had the occupants of the village central to this episode already prepared defence tactics as a result of previous sign sabotage attempts?*" We would have to be in and out in a slick, well-rehearsed operation.

A reconnaissance mission was needed and, with Bethan and Debs still absent from duty, I volunteered myself for the role. I accepted that the volunteer was fit for duty and briefed myself on what was required. It was a bit rushed, but I think I understood most of what was said.

That night, I prayed to Santa for some good weather. Surely not even *he* could be busy in the height of summer.

∘ ° ∘ ° ∘ °

My journey took me past the Angel of the North, or 'Kevin', as the councillors of Durham would have probably called him. At over two hundred tonnes and twenty metres in height, with a wingspan the same as that of a Jumbo jet, it is hailed as the most viewed piece of art in Great Britain. I personally think that maybe this is just the tiniest bit misleading. From that build-up, you could be forgiven for thinking that thousands of people are flocking to some museum or other to catch a glimpse of its majesty.

In reality, it is the most viewed piece of art because you can't miss it! It's plonked at the side of the busiest road in the North East. You can't avoid seeing it unless you're blind, in which case you shouldn't be driving along the A1 anyway. If it were replaced with a big fibreglass penguin tomorrow, that in turn would then take over the mantle of the 'most viewed piece of art in the UK'. That being said, I for one would probably flock to see such an enormous 'Pingu'.

Apparently, according to the official spiel, the Angel is trying to say, "Is that all we can be?" and as I passed him on my journey, I replied, "What the hell was all that about?"

That was also the only thing I could think to put on the comments card when I visited the Baltic Arts Centre in Gateshead, recently. The Baltic, along with many other contemporary Arts Centres, seems to run along the lines of 'The Emperor's New Clothes'. If you can't understand the majesty, deep meaning and inherent aesthetic beauty of the rubbish peddled off as art on display, obviously you are not clever or artistically gifted enough.

Amongst other things, there was a sculpture made of hoover parts, and upstairs there was a monopoly board with some Rice Krispies and cocoa beans stuck on it. It was supposed to be something to do with the plight of the Third World. I thought about taking along a bag full of Barney's poops and calling it 'The Turd World Plight' just to see the reaction I would provoke. I would have probably won the Turner Prize.

I had already notched up the 'No Place' photo for the calendar when I made a quick detour on my way back from the Sainsbury's, near Durham. I had actually felt a bit self-conscious, standing taking the photo as the cars rushed past.

They all seemed to be so blasé, in a non-barking dog way, about the sign, and it made me feel a bit 'touristy', a bit like an outsider. Based on Jarvis Cocker's observation that everybody hates a tourist, I decided that I would put on my fluorescent security jacket for the next shoot and stand out so much that I would go completely full circle and fit in again. I would be Mr Council Official, viewed with suspicion, but obviously meant to be there.

Sadly, the 'Pity Me' shots were deemed unsuitable and would have to be taken again. We didn't look miserable enough and it really needed to be raining for the full effect.

I wasn't looking forward to breaking the news to Bethan.

. ° . ° . °

Sometimes you don't have the luxury of a decent recce. When we used to dock in a foreign port, for instance, we had no idea where the best places to go were. Luckily enough, the Admiralty did, and would tell us in coded form. Officially, they would promulgate a list of places that British sailors were banned from visiting and, naturally, we immediately knew these were the best ones.

Many years later, I was heading back from Poland with the two sergeants who had been looking after the border post with me. We were told that, on no account, were we to visit Berlin on our journey back, so we duly headed straight there. We parked up our vehicle, disguising the fact that it was military, and then 'demilitarised' ourselves. We only had our uniforms and the odds and sods we would wear when dossing around the barracks during the limited time off between duties, so we duly mixed and matched.

Three ragamuffins then moseyed into the City. One of the sergeants had been a paratrooper when Berlin was a city adrift in East Germany during the Cold War, and we were treated to a tour of sentry points and patrol routes. We went to Check Point Charlie and it actually did raise a smile, then we all bought bits of the old Berlin Wall. Apparently, enough 'genuine' Berlin Wall has been sold to build the wall again three times over, and mine even had a bit of graffiti on it to make it look more realistic. We saw part of the wall that was still standing, and it seemed much thinner and lower than I had imagined.

We were all starting to get a bit hungry by then and looked for somewhere to eat. We saw a Mongolian Restaurant and were tempted but decided against it, primarily because a badly translated sign in the window promised 'Special cocktails for the ladies with nuts'.

What we really wanted was cake. The old eastern bloc seemed obsessed with cake, and very soon we had also become hopeless cake junkies. We were barracked in an old Red Army camp in the former East Germany and drove daily to our post on the Polish border. Cakes would follow cold meats for breakfast, a stop off en route would be accompanied by cake and, at the morning briefing at the border itself, the Polish official would produce cakes for all the staff, us included. We liked cake. We duly stopped off at a beatnik style coffee house in Berlin and had our fix.

It seems even President Kennedy felt the same about cakes. When he gave his famous address in Berlin, he told everyone, "All free men, wherever they may live, are citizens of Berlin. And therefore, as a free man, I take pride in the words, 'Ich bin ein Berliner!' (I am a Berliner – a citizen of Berlin)". What no one had told him was that in German, a 'berliner' is a donut filled with jam.

Still hungry, we decided on a Chinese. I have always been amazed that Chinese restaurants, or takeaways, can be found everywhere you go. I imagined the family sitting somewhere in rural China, poring over a big map and wondering where to set up business next. Maybe it would be a pin in the map or perhaps they would decide to settle in the place name that sounded good. They could have no idea, as they sat cross-legged around the chart, what all these places were really like. Some would be delighted when they arrived in their new adopted home and found that Tenby, York or Winchester were such beautiful places, but others would be sick as pigs when their bus pulled up at the depot in Merthyr Tydfil. As the diesel fumes hung around inside the half lit, damp bus depot, avoiding the drizzle outside, the new arrivals would be gazing open-mouthed until one would eventually put into words what they all had been thinking. "It never looked like this in the film."

"Hey dad, are you sure it was 'Dial M for Merthyr'?"

19

A Perfectly Polite Monkey

I had no idea how to solve a particular Barney-related issue I was experiencing, and all the dog books I had read seemed to avoid the subject. If you have a boy dog, as opposed to a girl dog, you will doubtless know what I am on about. If I tell you that my only solution is to sternly tell him, "Put your lipstick away!" you can probably make an educated guess as to what I am referring to. I'd hate to think that some lady dog actually mistook it for a lip gloss. Try explaining that away to the owner. Something should be invented, and it's probably something very simple, that would end up doing the trick in the end.

Someone once told me that the Americans spent millions of dollars inventing a pen that could write in zero gravity, for the NASA space programme. It had to be able to perform upside down, not dry out in the sterile environment, and have ink that didn't freeze. The Russians saved all that money and took a pencil into space.

The other thing they don't seem to mention in all those dog manuals is why your pup finds it irresistible to eat other dog's poo. I mentioned it to the mad woman at the dog school once, and she said that she believed it was because the animal was lacking some nutrients in his food, and he obtained these by eating other dog's droppings. She added, "I don't know if there is any substance in this". I don't think substance was the right word to use to be honest.

This confirmed to me that the woman was deluded as well as sick in the head. I somehow find it hard to imagine Barney, who has a pea-sized brain to rival my sister Kate's, thinking, "Hmmm, I seem to be lacking some basic vital nutrients in my diet. If I remember the lessons correctly from puppy school, I should gain these additional vitamins and antioxidants by feasting on the excreta of other canines."

I read that there were pills that could be prescribed to make his poop taste bad, but I'm not quite sure how they tested that. They recommended that the best way to get your dog to swallow the pill was to get some cheese, eat it yourself for energy and then wrestle with your puppy to try and get them to take it. I didn't fancy that option in case I lost.

I suppose I could take him to the dog psychologist, but it would be a waste of time – he knows he's not allowed up on the couch. No, I've just come to the conclusion that he's just a dirty, greedy filth hound.

Anyway, pack your bags, we're going off on a tangent.

I was in a pub in Chichester with my friend Ruth a few years back when she spotted a guy drinking from a glass-bottomed tankard. She had asked me what the glass bottom was for, and I had replied that it was so that as he drank, he could see a life he had missed. I could be very morose sometimes. I don't know why I was then as I had met Ruth on the Military Police Investigations Course at Roussillon Barracks – a girl almost half my age and nearly twice my security clearance - and she was the most delightful company. Often, I would pop to her room in the Officers' Mess, where I would find her lounging on her bed sipping a chilled Chablis whilst I nursed warm Semillon. She also helped me improve my vocabulary as she was the one who taught me the meaning of unrequited.

Another explanation for the glass bottom is that, in the days when recruiting parties went out around the country, if you accepted the King's shilling, you could be conscripted into military service. It is said that sometimes a crafty recruiting sergeant would drop a shilling into someone's drink when they were unaware and, as the victim drank the last of his ale, the coin would slide down the tankard and touch his lips. They had then taken the King's shilling and were hauled off to serve King and Country. The glass bottom for the tankard was invented so that the drinker could check to see if there was a shilling loitering with intent in his ale. I'm not sure that's any more real than my version – I will have to check with Kate.

As far as simple inventions go, I am convinced that I invented 'Splat the Rat' – that popular game at fetes, where a furry toy rat is dropped down a five-foot or so vertical length of tubing. The aim is for the player to 'splat' the rat with a baseball bat as he pops out of the end. The clue is in the title really. To avoid copyright, it may sometimes be called 'Twat the Rat'. It is pretty hard to anticipate the right time to splat though and, if you are not careful, you can pay out a considerable sum in countless futile attempts to win a pathetic stuffed toy. A strange feeling of déjà vu has just come over me (what do French people say when *they* have déjà vu?). I am not so convinced of my invention rights that I would take the next scout pack I see using my invention at some village summer fair to every court in the land, but just convinced enough to tell Bethan, every time I see one, that it was *my* invention.

I also woke up one morning convinced that I was French and had invented the periodic table. *(Bonne occasion pour une plaisanterie française. J'ai acheté un pantalon français mais il était Toulon et Toulouse)*. I was wrong then and I may be wrong now.

I love weird inventions and quite look forward to the Betterware and Kleeneze women calling with their catalogues (are they still a thing or have JML taken over?). I can sit for literally minutes as I look through their curious pages. It is normally a good clue that, if something has a wacky spelling, it is probably quite an outlandish item. Take the Thylacine for example – that seems something straight out of a Betterware catalogue. Often in these bizarre inventions, it's the left-over letters in scrabble that are used aplenty, like the K and Z. They must be the same people who gave the names to the new republics created after the fall of the Soviet Union.

。°。°。°

I know two people called Graham. The first is the Graham at work who used to be my trusted lieutenant. When I say, 'used to be,' it isn't that he ceased to be trusted; it's just that he's not my lieutenant anymore. I moved into Security Services and Graham remained in Operations. He is an ex-Warrant Officer in the Light Infantry and does everything very efficiently at Light Infantry pace which, for the uninitiated, is quick. If he were a record player, he would be spinning at 78 rpm.

He had recently returned from an outing to Edinburgh Zoo with Mrs Graham, so I naturally enquired about Billy. It hadn't been a good trip, it transpired. They had plodded about the zoo in torrential rain and, to add insult to injury, most of the animals had wisely chosen to remain in their houses so there was very little to see. I think that is what is called a double whammy, although he said they had enjoyed the penguin parade.

The other Graham is Graham the builder. He is a serious sort of guy. Like 'work Graham', builder Graham does an excellent job, but everything is performed in slow motion. If he were spinning at 33 rpm, he would still sound as if he was being speeded up. Having two Grahams is confusing, so builder Graham will hereafter be referred to as 'Laughing Boy'.

Laughing Boy was responsible for responding to the surge in renovation fervour in my house until, one day, Barney arrived, and the money suddenly ran out. It's a bit perverse really, when I was young, I was scared on the dark, but now I'm paying for the electricity I'm scared of the light. I've got bills… they're multiplying.

Before B-Day, the Boy would estimate the number of days a particular task would take and then take twice as long, aided by Norman the (ex) foreman as his assistant. We had agreed costs up front so, apart from the occasional stomach-churning flash of builders' cleavage, I wasn't particularly worried about this over-run in the early days.

As the weeks drew on, however, I did start to dread returning home and finding the Boy pottering away, long into the night. He would chat for ages about how rushed off his feet he was, and how he never had time to see his family, and how he couldn't afford to take time off, all due to his heavy work schedule. I felt like telling him that, if he stopped chatting and just got on with the job, he might find he had all the time in the world. Even Bethan, who is very tolerant and tells me off if I make fun of the unfortunate, started to do impressions of

Laughing Boy, speaking very slowly about all sorts of rubbish.

Things were so behind schedule at one point that I had to use the ultimate sanction and threaten them with Deborah, as they both seemed a bit scared of her.

Norman was a nice chap as, indeed, was Laughing Boy but he ruined a good prop for me. I had bought an exceedingly realistic latex mask from the magic shop. I tested it for realism when Tim, who I have known for almost twenty years, came up to visit. I had waited on the bridge for him to drive past and park up outside the house when I donned the mask and, for added effect, limped down the street. As Tim wandered up the path, I followed him. "What do you want, mate?" Tim questioned. I said nothing and continued to limp towards him. Tim then started knocking furiously at the door, "John, John, let me in!" I thought he was playing along with me and took the mask off, chuckling. It was only when I could see that he was shaking like a butterfly and informed me that that was one pair of underpants that wasn't going home with him that I realised just how effective the disguise was. We agreed never to mention the incident again.

The trouble was that now the mask also made me look just like Norman, the (ex) foreman. I couldn't feel scary in it anymore; I just felt like Laughing Boy's sidekick – affable Norm.

. * . * . *

In the kitchen that Laughing Boy and Norman the (ex) foreman had built, amongst other things, are a couple of bar stools in case a lion breaks in, a drawer that will never open again because a potato masher has barricaded itself inside and a cupboard where a cooker should be. Instead, I have a very large microwave which, if you have a pacemaker fitted, is best kept at a five-yard distance. You could micro a lot of waves in there, but just don't look in there right now – it looks like a crime scene. I think it's fair to say that I'm not much of a cook.

Barney doesn't suffer though, and is properly fed twice a day. Both of these meals are 'dinner' to him. After being made to sit and patiently wait for a minute until the command to stuff his face, the concept of having to distinguish in his little mind between his 'breakfast' and 'evening meal' would just be too much. He doesn't mind what they are called as long as he gets his two square meals. Of course, in his bowl, they are actually round meals, but the term dates back from when sailors got their meals on square plates and it stuck.

I used to give lectures in the Navy about how naval sayings and customs originated, travelling around in uniform, or sometimes in 'mufti' (inspired by the practice of General Mufti, who found that sagging morale in the British Army was boosted by the policy of allowing the men to wear civilian clothing instead of uniforms on certain days of the year… and they didn't have to bring in fifty pence to do it).

I'd usually start by telling the assembled gathering that I had just come back from the local RSPCA office and it was tiny. You couldn't swing a cat in there! As the room went quiet, apart from the regulation embarrassed cough from somewhere near the back, I'd quickly try to get the audience back on side by telling them what they had come to hear.

The 'cat' in naval terms was the cat-of-nine-tails – a type of whip used to give lashings to sailors in the days of sail. Each of the nine strips of leather on the whip would be about three feet long. It would be too cramped to dispense a proper flogging below deck because, 'there wasn't room to swing a cat'. Floggings were always given up on deck where there was more space and, although the floggings have long ceased, we were left with the phrase.

Instead of a flogging, a sailor may have been made to 'run the gauntlet'. This was a form of punishment that involved forcing a matelot to make his way between two rows of men, each armed with a rope cosh with which to hit the offender. The saying now refers to running the risk of being criticised or attacked from two or more sides.

After your punishment, you may have had salt rubbed into your wound. Salt was carried on board ship as a disinfectant and was applied to wounds to prevent gangrene. This process was also very painful and to 'rub salt into wounds' has come to mean now to aggravate or to add insult to injury.

To balance things up we have 'Hunky Dory' meaning OK or satisfactory, derived from Honcho-Dori, a street in the port of Yokohama, Japan, where many a pleasure awaited visiting sailors. The crew might have imagined what adventures were 'in the offing' or about to happen when they docked. The area of sea visible from shore is known as the 'offing'. Therefore, a ship visible from land was said to be 'in the offing' – about to enter port. They might need some extra cash – and what could be easier than selling lengths of old rope? – 'Money for old rope'.

'Piping hot' and to 'pipe down' both come from the practice of the boatswain piping a signal on a whistle, or pipe, when meals were served, and alternatively, to signal the end of the day and time for lights out and silence.

'Clean sweep', meaning a complete change or nowadays also meaning an overwhelming victory, comes from the fact that in rough weather, waves washed (swept) over the decks of ships, shifting about anything that wasn't secured. It also refers to the few minutes after Barney in Che Sweep mode has had a bath and is relatively clean before getting up to his eyeballs in mud again. Barney, of course, has a bath in cold water, unlike Cleopatra who bathed in milk. It was in the film 'Carry on Cleo' where someone who is about to run her milk bath asks her, "Pasteurised?" to which she replies something along the lines of, "No, just up to my tits".

Meanwhile, back at sea, and at the Battle of Copenhagen in 1801, Nelson was signalled an order from the Admiral of the Fleet but, believing that if he followed the command his ships might have been in danger of running aground on nearby shallows, he famously put his telescope to his blind eye and didn't carry out the instruction. He might as well have held the telescope to his working brown eye – he wasn't going to act on it anyway. So, if a person ignores something nowadays, they are often said to 'turn a blind eye'.

Everybody is on their best behaviour on a date but eventually we 'show our true colours' or reveal our true intentions or personality. Early warships often carried flags from many nations on board in order to elude or deceive the enemy. The rules of civilised warfare, however, called for all ships to hoist their true national ensigns before firing a shot. Someone who finally shows his true colours is acting like a warship, which would hail another ship, flying a friendly country's flag, but then hoist their own when they were in firing range. I'm not quite sure what Cyndi Lauper was on about. And whilst I'm here, from my own personal experience, not all girls 'wanna have fun', apparently. Your flawed advice has let to many an embarrassing situation. Thanks for nothing, Cyndi!

Some say that the brass triangles that supported stacks of iron cannonballs on sailing ships were called monkeys.

In cold weather, as brass contracts more than iron, the triangles contracted sufficiently for the balls to fall off. So, it's cold enough to 'freeze the balls off a brass monkey'. There you go – not rude after all. You can say it to your Granny now.

Back in the 'brass monkey' days, women occasionally came on board ship to keep the poor lonely sailors company in port. What a nice thing to do. In the morning, the ratings had to get on with their duties whilst the women could lie in. The officers would therefore go round below deck and shout, "Show a leg!" and, if a woman's leg poked out of the hammock, its owner was allowed to rest on, while a hairy bloke's leg had to get its owner's body off to work. The Army equivalent was, 'Rise and Shine!' which the sergeants would bellow every morning as all soldiers were expected to polish their boots at the start of each day. (The early morning wake-up call 'Hands off cocks, on socks' is something totally different all together … I think it's an RAF thing).

'Sweet FA' was another naval term and actually stands for, 'Sweet Fanny Adams'. Fanny Adams was murdered in 1867 and her body dismembered. Her gravestone reads 'Here lies Sweet Fanny Adams'. At about the same time, canned corned beef was introduced to the Navy and, as the sailors thought the food looked like Fanny's mutilated corpse, they came to use the expression to refer to unpleasant meals. It subsequently came to mean nothing of value. The can, meanwhile, was used as a cup which was, in turn, referred to as a 'Fanny'. A sailor can always find a good use for a fanny.

As for the Air Force, when a Second World War fighter pilot loosed off all his ammunition – nine yards of it in one burst, he was going 'The full nine yards'.

Finally, dependant on audience reaction so far, I might

finish off by advising them never to stand behind Satan in a queue at the Post Office… 'because the Devil takes many forms'.

Cue embarrassed cough.

Meanwhile, it was Barney's relatives who brought about the phrase, 'The dog's bollocks' to mean something excellent. Apparently, it arises from the fact that licking them seems to be a particularly favourite activity of theirs. Bizarrely enough though, 'bollocks' on its own is just plain bad.

And I suppose Barney himself, after his turding activities on his long morning walk the other day, combined with the shortage of poop bags, made me into a real 'shit kicker'.

˙ ˚ ˳ ˚ ˳ ˚

As much as Barney had made me into a real shit kicker, I think I was actually becoming a soft shit kicker, as messy as that may sound.

I didn't seem to be able to hold a grudge like I used to and was feeling all the better for it. Some people seem excellent at holding grudges, allowing their stomachs to knot up whenever they hear a particular person's name mentioned, but I had concluded that life was too short for that. My mum, and my belly, would have been proud of me.

They say time flies like an arrow and fruit flies like a banana. Either way, Barney's metamorphosis into a grown-up dog was continuing at a fair pace, but was still only part way there. No longer did he lie on the floor like he had been dropped from a great height, with all four legs poking out, resembling a big letter 'H', but neither had he started to cock his leg when he had a pee. I wasn't sure if this was something instinctive or whether I would need to show him. Would I need to teach him to bury his bones too, or do dogs not do that anymore? Has bone burying been relegated to history just like cats getting stuck up trees, pianos falling out of windows and white turds?

His decision-making process still resembled that of a squirrel crossing the road, and I still don't think he entirely trusted my dry nose, but he was getting there. Everyone also seemed to comment that he was growing larger all the time but, as I was always around him, I wasn't really aware of the daily differences. I spent ages once, just staring at him but, at the end of the exercise I couldn't claim that I detected any noticeable increase in size during that test period. Other things *did* shrink however, and I was sure that Bethan and Debs would notice a big change on their return.

20

See You Next Tuesday

We all used to play a game called 'Good Dog - Bad Dog' ever since we got the thumbs up at the 'Will we, or won't we have a Plan B dog?' conference. The rules were very simple. When you saw a dog, you had to judge whether it was a good dog or a bad dog. The clue was in the title really. A good dog would be one that was neither pulling its owner's arm off, nor walking on the lead in front of said owner. It was a dog that would bring the ball back during a game of fetch, or one that didn't wee all over the person it was greeting. Aha, that's where the skill in the game was involved. A dog could be both a good dog and a bad dog, depending on the circumstances. Well, the game kept *us* happy at least.

I was looking forward to playing this some more and I felt pretty confident in assuming that Bethan and Debs would feel the same. I had read somewhere that books concerning the Third Reich, cats and golf, all sold well. I also knew that fishing was the most popular hobby in the country. If I could somehow incorporate these into a board game version of 'Good Dog - Bad Dog' and it was marketed properly, I could make my fortune. (Perhaps 'Good golfing 'n fishing dog V Bad cat-hating Nazi dog' would do the trick, with a picture of that naughty dog from Germany on the box).

When my ex-wife wasn't my ex-wife, Susan and I went to Robin's wedding years ago. We had played an embryonic version of the same game then called, 'Who is Tim?'

°°°°°°

By way of introduction, Robin had served in the Royal Anglians with Tim and me. He is a thoroughly decent chap and maybe it is unfair that he should be remembered in this way, but he is.

I couldn't be bothered to find out what we were fighting for, but our story begins with Robin and me heading off to some grid reference in order to take up our position on the edge of the killing zone, or some such place. We were up against the clock, so we decided to commit the cardinal sin of cutting across an open expanse of land, instead of skirting around the boundary where there was cover. We crouched down and sprinted across the ploughed field, weighed down with weapons and webbing, half expecting to hear shots ring out at any moment. Hopefully, if there was any shooting it would be enemy fire. Friendly fire is not actually very friendly (in the same way that 'Intelligence Corps' might confuse people by suggesting intelligence), and also seems to be uncannily more accurate than enemy fire. At least there were two of us, which meant I was only half as likely to get hit.

Robin was faster than me and had almost made it to the other side, when he slowed down considerably and ran the last ten yards in an exaggerated John Wayne style, hopping from leg to leg. I was worried that he might have been caught by some type of booby trap, but instead it transpired that he had been caught by pure over-exertion. Too much straining and effort had caused a minor 'poop discharge' incident. He undid the elastics where his combats met his boots, shook his leg to eject the 'misfire' and we set off on our way again. Now that's what I call a soldier. I'd be proud to shake his hand anytime, but not just then, you understand. We agreed never to mention the unfortunate incident again.

We hadn't seen Tim for a couple of years by the time of the wedding, and I'm not sure what we expected him to have transformed into, but guesses were made at the big fat man with the beard, the black lady with the afro, the short, balding guy with three kids, the bemused looking Chinese chap holding the battered old film poster and Times New Roman – you know the type. In his effort to prolong the game for us, Tim turned up after the wedding looking exactly the same as he always did. Six-foot-something and pretty confident. Oh, except for the time he was banging on my door like a frightened girl when I had the 'Norman' mask on. But we shan't mention that.

We had a fantastic time at the celebrations – so fantastic that I received a five-year ban from Robin's cottage in the Welsh countryside as punishment. Subsequent misdemeanours resulted in an extension to ten years and, eventually, I was banned from here to eternity. Tim seems to get off scot-free each time, by turning Queen's Evidence.

o o o o o o

Bethan was back from music school and came over early for Barney's morning walk. As we walked, we laughed at the bizarre names some dogs have been given. We once found one with a collar that said he was called '19 Sebastopol Terrace'. She pretended to beckon an imaginary dog with the long-winded name. She looked funny.

Bethan spotted what looked like a seal in the water and we watched, transfixed, as evolution happened before our very eyes and it emerged from the river as a dog. We were impressed that Barney had overnight become a mathematics genius too, and if you doubt us and think that dogs can't count, just try putting three biscuits in your pocket and only giving him two.

We also passed two suppliers of Barney's favourite snack on the riverside path that morning and all he could do as the horses trotted past was to hide behind Bethan's legs and hope they made a delivery.

Swimming at the leisure centre followed and we sniggered at some woman who must have tried to sneakily pump in the water but was given away by the bubbles (and to those people who say that 'ladies don't break wind' – I've been to a yoga class, and I know you do!). We spent longer than most people in polite society would going down the water slide, and I seriously considered a career change to become the guy at the top who just nods at people to indicate that they're free to descend.

Bethan also made it two thirds of the way across the forty-foot-long inflatable, before falling off into the water, giggling. She even belly laughed at me relating the old joke about the Native Americans, as we have to call them now.

Red Indian Number One: "Dad, how did we get our names?"

Red Indian Number Two: "All Indians are named after the first thing the mother sees when she looks out of the tepee after giving birth. Hence, your brother 'Sitting Bull' and your sister 'Rain Cloud'. Anyway, why do you ask, 'Big brown dog having a poo?'"

It's got a sort of detachable ending so you can add an appropriate punchline to suit your audience.

On the journey back from the pool, she spotted a car with an 'NL' sticker on it. I explained that I thought it came from the Netherlands, and Bethan howled at the thought of someone coming on holiday to Sunderland.

Durham was our next destination, for a trip to The Durham Light Infantry Museum. She went through the First World War tunnel system when she thought no one else was looking, and we 'tee hee'd' as she wrote a postcard from the trenches to Deborah.

Bethan had held my hand as she balanced on the wooden fence on the journey up to the market place in the centre of Durham, and even as we wandered around the town too. She said balancing on the fence was 'pympsey'. We weren't sure of the spelling, but she told me it meant that it was easy. A white evening bag was required for some event she was going to attend on holiday, and I enjoyed searching around the accessory shops until we found one. I was delighted when we discovered one that matched her requirements ideally. Naturally, as we had ventured within a hundred yards of a stationery store, Bethan also ended up taking home the requisite pencil case and folder.

As we walked into a near-empty coffee shop, she bagged the leather armchairs as I bought her the biggest piece of chocolate cake to go with her coke, whilst I had a coffee, so fresh that it narrowly missed being sent off to live with its aunt and uncle in Bel Air. It had been a great day and, all in all, we had spent most of the time just playing and laughing.

"It looks like we are putting Café Nerd back in business," said Bethan between mouthfuls. Well, the logo does look like Nerd rather than Nero. Anyway, I certainly felt like *I* was back in business.

When Bethan was picked up, Susan dropped off the two goldfish to be looked after while they were on holiday in Jamaica. In front of Bethan, I was then made to solemnly swear to replace them if they died, with either new fish or at least a sliver of carrot.

°°°°°°

I had received a postcard postmarked Turkey that morning. Deborah wrote that, one day, she wanted to take me to the library at Ephesus. I looked at the picture on the front – it didn't even look finished yet!

Debs had wanted me to go to Turkey with her on this holiday, but I was currently the casualty of a short to medium term financial downturn. Whoever said that life was like a shit sandwich was right. The more bread you have, the less shit you have to eat. Whilst Deborah was living it up in the sun abroad, I was working in the drizzle and damp that passed for a British summer, mending a split in my Wellington boots with my bicycle puncture repair kit. I had even resorted to sending a 'Get Well' card to my bank account as it was still suffering the ill effects of providing for Barney's well-being.

Her card was very chatty but, reading between the lines, I could tell that she had not been impressed about my thoughts on cloning. Specifically, she seemed to take issue with the insinuation that she didn't laugh at all my jokes and implied that she did. I was ready to counter her response on her return when I would haul out all those times she had made comments like, "I was laughing, but just quietly," or "I was chuckling in my mind," or the one that was really hurtful, "I laughed the *first* time you told it."

She couldn't deny it, it was all captured here in my quotation marks. She would have to accept that, as much as she tried to convince herself that she thought I was funny, I was actually right. I wasn't funny to her at all. She wouldn't be laughing then!

She said she was half board – I guess that's what happens if you don't take enough books with you. The food was great, apparently, and the meatballs were the dog's bollocks.

She signed off in some type of text speak that I hoped actually meant 'See you next Tuesday'.

21

The Lights of Kilgetty

The goldfishes' vacation at my house was marred by an ugly incident on day two of their stay. On hearing an almighty crash, I had rushed into the kitchen. The floor was awash with water, mixed with miniature gravel and, in the middle of it all, next to an amusing sign proclaiming 'No Fishing Allowed' were Sparky and GoGo, apparently doing sit-ups on the wood laminate surface. I quickly scooped them up and put them in a tumbler of water.

As I surveyed the scene, I could see a dog looking very sheepish in the corner, although I didn't want to jump to conclusions that it was Barney who had committed the crime. The previous day, an hour or so after the fish had been dropped off, I had received a mysterious phone call from someone who sounded suspiciously like Susan. I was told that, if the fish, "happened to die," there was no need to make any great effort to replace them as the mystery caller had grown heartily sick of cleaning them out. I suspected Susan's hand might be afoot and, of course, Barney could have just been playing his part in a contract hit. Either way, I thought it best to move the fish to the top of the fridge.

。 ° 。 ° 。 °

One Christmas, when I was a child, I had been given a 'Plasticraft' set. If I remember correctly, it contained liquid plastic and you could make your own paperweights or jewellery by placing objects inside the liquid and waiting for it to set. My mother had been ill in hospital and I had wanted to do something special for her. One of my own goldfish, called 'Spitz', had died, which provided an excellent opportunity. Out of sadness would come joy. I took it into the lean-to shed thing next to the garage and my aim was to set the fish in clear plastic as a gift for my mum. Unfortunately, the kitchen roll I used to dry the fish off also seemed to remove his orangey colour. He had been a fake all along! I pressed on regardless and was able to present my mum with a slightly mangy white 'goldfish', encased in his very own plastic tomb. You could even see down his little gulping mouth. I understand it proved to be a very popular exhibit in the hospital.

I wasn't sure if they still sold Plasticraft so hopped into the car and set off into town. If anything unfortunate did happen to the fish, I could re-discover my skills by making a lovely and very low maintenance replacement.

。 ° 。 ° 。 °

The next day dawned bright and clear. I set the alarm, locked the front door, drove to the end of the street, did a U-turn and went back to check that I had shut all the windows. I had. I set the alarm again, locked the front door, drove up to the end of the street, did a U-turn and went back to check I had turned all the taps off. I had. I set the alarm, locked the front door, drove to the end of the street, did a U-turn and went back to check if I had set the alarm and done the locking door thing. I had. I drove off again and reached the end of the street. Sparky and GoGo hadn't been fed. *"Sod 'em."*

I was off on the quiet camping trip that had been hijacked and turned into a family reunion. Deborah was back from Turkey, and I was on my way to pick her up.

We had agreed that, due to the need to make space for Barney in the back, she wouldn't take her hairdryer, tongs and other assorted hair-related products. We were in a field for goodness sake, and in the spirit of compromise, I agreed not to take my beloved emergency kit. Deborah had argued that taking the apparatus to trap and skin a rabbit was probably going a bit over the top when there was a campsite shop. I did however have an overabundance of boxer shorts. Is it just me or does everyone else pack underwear as if they're going to soil themselves at least once a day on a trip?

I did, of course, take my emergency kit, hidden in the bottom of my pants bag, and Deborah took her hair stuff, hidden in one of hers.

By the time I had packed all her stuff too, the car boot resembled a giant version of those trick mustard jars – the ones where you open them and a springy snake jumps out. The difference with this 'mustard jar' was that it was eager to eject sleeping bags and airbeds. I had told her to deflate it first. We even had to put some of the stuff on a roof rack and, as anyone knows, it is physically impossible, and possibly a legal requirement, for any man to strap down any type of load on his roof rack without saying, "That's not going anywhere!" as he tightens the straps.

"That's not going anywhere!" I said on cue as I

tightened the straps.

Naturally, as I had come to expect by now, lazy Barney stood by as I did all the hard work, just assuming that I had been good enough to pack his toys.

As we set off on our epic eight-hour journey we cursed and despised every other car on the road, until a dog stuck his head out of the window, and then we loved it. Otherwise, we entertained ourselves en route by quickly double flashing the headlights as the car in front of us passed a speed camera and sneezing on the windscreen. To add a bit of spice into the mix, I also occasionally honked my horn and enthusiastically waved at the odd random driver just so they'd spend the rest of the day wondering where they knew me from.

We were heading for the village of Amroth near Tenby, which is situated in the belt of the Pembrokeshire Coast National Park that hugs the West Wales Coast. After passing our original halfway point, then past Cardiff, then past places with names like Pantynylon and Aberbanana, we eventually entered the National Park. It was like entering a different world – pretty villages, breathtaking scenery, rugged coastlines and beautiful sandy beaches.

There were lots of sheep too and I wondered if they said, "look, a car!" every time we drove by. As well as being a strong advocate of Merino wool in my latter years, I have always been very respectful of these creatures. The human population of Wales is just over three million whereas there are about ten million sheep there. That means that if they ever rose up and turned against us, every one of us would have to fight at least three sheep and possibly a lamb. I don't know about you but I'm not sure I'm up for the task. If they knock you over with a charge, or ram raid if you will, that's potentially sixteen hooves all putting the boot in. So, best to keep on their good side.

The local newsletter seemed to neatly sum up the difference between this paradise and where we had driven from. Whilst in Newcastle, the editorial bemoaned the continued increase in violent street crime; the editor of the local publication 'Notes on the East Williamston Scene' commented, "... am I the only one who finds the crossroads at Broadmoor rather frustrating as you approach from Kilgetty? You can see the light ahead is green – but you know that, if you slow down to observe the 40mph speed limit, it will change to red just as you get there. Life is full of these little aggravations ..."

Jim Codd, the County Councillor, had written in his article that he had spotted weeds that were growing 'between the pavements and the road'. Further in, under the 'Did You Know?' section, we were reminded that, 'Keiran Head, the Milkman, will still deliver to your doorstep – you don't have to go off to the supermarket for your pinta.'

I wondered if they had changed to decimal money yet. The only thing that spoilt the enchanting image I was building in my head was the inclusion of a couple of rather tasteless Easter jokes by the local vicar.

Exhibit A:

Question: What did Jesus say to his disciples when he was on the cross?

Answer (which I'm sure is not correct): "Lay off my Easter eggs, I'll be back in a few days."

Exhibit B:

God: "LOL, they called it Good Friday."

Jesus: "They fucking WHAT?"

Anyway, even if it wasn't quite halfway between Cardiff and Newcastle, it was a pretty good choice.

. ° . ° . °

When we arrived on the campsite, the Simpsons, led by Doctor Shit, were already well established; large tent with separate accommodation pods, separate tent for food storage, well-organised kitchen/cooking area and a designated dining section. This was the tent of our leader.

Twenty yards away, a limp, creased blue rag-like thing on sticks shivered in the light breeze. This was Kate's tent. I was momentarily impressed when she showed me the inflatable double divan that she and Woody had brought along, although I was finding it hard to maintain this pretence as she introduced me to the other limited provisions she had brought on her holiday – a frying pan, two plastic plates in the shape of a flower, an antique kettle and two forty-year old fold-up nylon chairs, originally bought for Paul and Neil as five-year-olds. They had all been borrowed from Dad especially for the trip.

I am not sure what Kate expected to use the frying pan on, as there was no cooker to be seen. Believe it or not, Kate and Woody also part owned a trendy restaurant, serving trendy food in a trendy area of Cardiff. They always cease to amaze me.

I chatted to Paul and Woody while Barney got out of the car and relieved himself after the long journey and Deborah busied herself putting the tent up.

I was then approached by someone who was beautiful, small and who talked about things I didn't understand. She wasn't speaking Welsh; she was just a baby. This was Poppy, Kate and Woody's daughter. I think I speak for all, including Kate and Woody, when I say that everyone was relieved that she had not inherited Woody's looks, nor Kate's pea-sized brain.

That night, the 'Norman the (ex) foreman' mask was used to good effect, scaring the living daylights out of various family members as they made their way back from the toilet block in the dark by jumping out of the shadows pretending to be an alien, proclaiming, "I am the thing from Uranus!" The mask was later re-christened Barry. It sounded slightly scarier than Norman, but not very much. There is an old expression that goes: Give a man a mask and you will see his true face. If that's true, mine is jovial idiot.

。°。°。°

Great Britain was basking under the promised heatwave thanks, I believe, in no small part to my excessive use of deodorant spray in the late Eighties.

We had decided to go to the beach, and Barafundul Bay was truly breathtaking if the old guy wheezing at the top of the cliff path was anything to go by. A happy day was spent down on the sands, running in and out of the sea, throwing the ball for Barney to swim and fetch and, after getting that gritty noise when eating lunch, realising why they are called sandwiches. We arrived back at the campsite early evening, tired and slightly sunburnt after a full day in the sun.

Neil and his family had arrived on site by then and, after a quick shower, I emerged to greet them, pinky and perky – pinky from the sun and perky after being re-awakened in the shower. I just want to stress that I am not referring in derogatory terms to Neil and his wife Molly.

After games of cricket in the field, using the familiar 'backyard six' rule (hit a six into the boundary hedge and you are out), we were ready for a barbecue of various overcooked meat-related dishes, accompanied by beer and wine aplenty.

It was nearing sundown, but as we're not in the Wild West, we'll just say it was almost dusk. A lantern took the place of the traditional fireplace and, as everyone, including Barry, sat round in the gentle electric glow, stories were swapped.

The stars had all come out to look down on us and I randomly would point up and declare confidently, "See those stars? That's Leo the Lion," and everyone would accept my supposed superior knowledge of the night sky because I'd been a sailor. Actually, I think whoever dreamt up the names for the various constellations, based on some dubious dot to dot skills, was having a laugh. In the end it was like he wasn't even trying; take Canis Minor for example. "Those two stars over there? That's a small dog, that is." You what?

As the evening wore on, the conversation started to become more philosophical, and a general debate ensued over which Greek philosopher had the most unfortunate death. Chrysippus of Soli, said to have died of laughing after watching a donkey trying to eat his figs, or Aeschylus, who was killed by an eagle dropping a tortoise on his head.

And what about the infamous wanking man of Pompeii? Forever frozen in time looking like he was indulging in some classic 'me time' as he was covered by the volcanic ash. I can just imagine him now, forlornly protesting his innocence as he began to set like stone, "Aww, man! It's not what it looks like!"

As the chatter and banter ebbed and flowed around the lamp, Paul seemed troubled. Now that he was a policeman, he seemed to want to unburden himself of a matter that appeared to have been preying on his mind for a number of years.

It seems that when he was twelve or thirteen, he had been told by Mum to do some odd jobs for eighty-odd-year-old Mrs Davies next door but one. In turn, Mrs Davies had asked Paul to pop down to the paper shop and buy her a copy of 'Woman and Home'. He had duly popped, only to be informed by Mrs Whitehead in the shop that they had sold out.

"Is there any other magazine that you were asked to get if we were sold out?"

"Errrr, I don't know," replied Paul.

"Well how old is the lady you were getting it for?" She was eighty-odd. It was eighty-odd-year-old Mrs Davies, the one next door but one.

"Errrr, I don't know," replied Paul, insipidly.

Mrs Whitehead duly packed Paul off with the latest issue of 'Cosmopolitan', which he then trotted back with, reading open-mouthed at the blatant tales of rumpy pumpy and female experimentation.

He posted it through Mrs Davies' letterbox and went home to play on his bike.

Mrs Davies was found dead the next day. 'Death by misadventure' was recorded.

Paul confessed to us that he somehow felt guilty. We all agreed that he probably was.

We looked to Neil, our legal expert, for advice. Neil thought for a bit in silence and then, addressing us all, regaled us with a limerick he had learnt.

> *There was a young man from Newcastle,*
> *Who opened a brown paper parcel.*
> *In it was shit,*
> *And on it was writ,*
> *'A present from somebody's arsehole'.*

It was getting a bit late in the day to get philosophical, but someone asked the question as to whether Neil's profound piece was poetry or prose, which reminded me of a story about the Irish writer Brendan Behan. He was once invited to Oxford to take part in a debate about the distinction between the two. His opponent had spoken for almost two hours on the subject when Behan rose to his feet and promised to be brief. He then recited an old Dublin rhyme.

> *There was a young fella named Rollocks,*
> *Who worked for Ferrier Pollocks,*
> *As he walked on the strand,*
> *With a girl by the hand,*
> *The water came up to his ankles.*

"That," declared Behan, "is prose. But if the tide had been in it would have been poetry."

Later in the evening, after everyone had gone to bed, I took Barney out for his evening constitutional and waited patiently as he carefully selected the ideal spot for his deposit. It was a lovely balmy night, and the moon was out, bathing the whole campsite in its gentle glow. Everything was perfect with the world and, as I stood there, even Barney's poop seemed to remind me of something classically Shakespearean as it was ejected out of his hot little body and met the cool night air before it piled up on the ground.

A Midsummer Shite's Steam.

. . . . . .

I was right and Deborah was wrong. My emergency kit *was* needed. The next morning, I was called out of my tent to see if there was anything in my extensive hypochondriacs' kit to treat a sting. Molly and Neil had got up early to play a quick round of crazy golf and a bee had stung her between the first and second holes.

A quick rummage around produced a tube of sting relief stuff. We also spared a quiet thought for the bee that had to fly off home without his sting and with half his bottom missing. How would he explain that away to the Queen?

Burn relief plasters were also needed later for 'a leg burnt on car exhaust incident' and my special tablets also cured a case of excessive farting for an anonymous sufferer. However, no rabbits were skinned in the completion of this chapter.

Deborah was also right, to be fair. Her haircare products were needed – desperately needed, looking at the state of her bonce.

We all went in convoy to Bosherton lily ponds for a final trip before Neil, Kate and their respective hangers-on departed for their weekday homes. It was a sad moment, made even sadder when an enthusiastic Poppy presented me with a drawing that she had done of me. Surely my head's not that big. Pathetic… do it again!

The next day, Paul and Co. also left and, as it wouldn't be the same any more on our own at the site, Debs and I searched for a new campsite to spend the rest of our holiday.

We had had a fantastic time and the only element missing was Bethan who, by all accounts, was swimming in the crystal-clear waters off Jamaica as we played our 'backyard six' cricket.

As we drove to pastures new, we cursed the lights at Broadmoor as we approached from the Kilgetty end. We could see the light ahead was green but knew that, if we slowed down to observe the 40 mph speed limit, it would change to red just as we got there. Someone should write in to the local newsletter about it!

22

Anywhere but Here

"Where shall we go?"

"You say if you want to go here, and we'll go there," came back the response from Deborah.

That sounded like dissension in the ranks to me. A quick glance over revealed that Debs was not challenging my position as top dog, but rather just pointing to different places on the map.

I still didn't like the sound of this though. This was holiday time, and I didn't want to have to make decisions on holiday.

It had been easy when Paul was about as I had acknowledged his position as leader and was happy to drift about, doing what I was told as long as it didn't involve the washing up. Debs was right to recognise my status as top dog in our pack, but this was my holiday from the daily grind of decision making which I was forced to face in everyday life. Every single day, I had to make important choices like when to have a cup of tea, when to play with Barney, when to stare aimlessly out of the window. I needed a break.

I toyed with the idea of sticking a pin in the map, but I remembered the poor downhearted Chinese takeaway owners who had ended up cursing their days away, running a shop in Scunthorpe or Staines.

I looked into the back seat of the car. Not for the first time during the holiday, Barney just sat there with a stupid, vacant expression on his face. Being the lowest of the low had its perks. A quick glance at Deborah revealed her sporting a similar expression.

I was on my own. "Ross-on-Wye," I said to myself. I mulled it over for a bit and then reluctantly agreed. Ross–on-Wye it would be.

。 ° 。 ° 。 °

The borderland between Wales and England around Hereford and Ross-on-Wye, if you ignore the busy A40 and M50 motorway, is a county of unspoilt beauty, market towns and ruined Marcher Castles - evidence of centuries of border battles and disputes. National Trust houses, historic cities and fascinating villages on the edge of the Forest of Dean complete the scene. Turning off the A40 felt like escaping into a different world, where real life 'Postman Pats' and 'Windy Millers' might actually still exist.

Be warned though, as it is also a place of hidden evil. I was enticed by the enchanting siren call of the local cider but, if there is one lesson you can take away from this tale – remember, cider is bad.

After calling in at Tourist Information in Ross, we decided on a pleasant looking campsite at Symonds Yat. I remember visits as a child and what a fantastic place it was. I excitedly told Deborah and Barney how wonderful it would be, spending a few days camped there on the riverbank. The River Wye is one of the longest in England and, as it meanders through this beautiful county, it provides excellent salmon fishing, as well as being perfect for canoeing and swimming. There is a castle round every bend and twist in the river, with hawks soaring over the fields and forests, and secret places along every stream. Many artists, poets and writers have sought to capture its tranquil charm and elusive beauty. This was where we were heading for.

We arrived at our destination, which seemed to be at the back of a fun fair car park. The car park attendant stood there, his hands thrust in his pockets, looking like he was feeling a little cocky, and demanded to know what we were doing.

"None of your business, old man – I am the top dog in search of tranquillity. I need not answer to the village monkey," I replied. Actually, I didn't. I just said that I was looking for the campsite, and he pointed a stubby finger to the corner of the car park.

We drove in and drove straight back out again. This was 'Craggy Island meets Alton Towers'. Not at all what I had expected. Surely some mistake?

A strange feeling of déjà vu came over me as I sheepishly looked over towards Deborah. She said nothing, but I knew she was thinking something along the lines of "Symonds Yat? Symonds Shat more like!"

。°。°。°

I was relieved when Deborah said she would choose the next location and, after a ponder over the map, we set off for a site on the banks of the Wye, closer to Hereford. I had been relegated to the passenger seat and, as I sat there in disgrace, I toyed with my mobile phone.

I had only recently learnt what LOL and LMAO meant in text language, but the continual use of abbreviations was difficult for a Luddite like me to grasp. They made things much quicker though, and I liked that. Despite the worry that my thumbs might be wearing out, I had embraced this new system of communication and I had even invented my own titanic text abbreviation language for the things that I would probably be saying most during the summer with friends and family.

ORTI stands for, 'Oh really? That's interesting.'

ITIJSAT stands for, 'I think I've just seen a Thylacine.'

YIVVVH stands for, 'Yes, it's very, very, very hot.'

TWIWGTS stands for, 'That's what I was going to say!'

IDUYLSCYE means, 'I don't understand your last sentence, can you explain?'

O means 'Oh!'

SIYRSM means, 'Stop it, you are scaring me.'

LMAY*I means, 'Leave me alone you * Idiot.'

NIFIBGCOTL2DATGBRWYCIHHIWWWWIANT means, 'No, in fact it's been getting cooler over the last two days and that's good, because really, wow, you can't imagine how hot it was when we were in Amroth near Tenby.'

When we arrived at the site, Barney just looked on, not lifting a paw to erect the tent. I had come to the conclusion that he was taking advantage of my good nature.

° ° ° ° ° °

The next day, I went round Goodrich Castle on my own, without Deborah, because a big sign outside the castle read 'No Dogs Allowed'. Let me re-phrase that. I went round Goodrich Castle on my own without Deborah because a big sign outside the castle read 'No Dogs Allowed' and Deborah volunteered to stay behind and look after the 'forbidden one' whilst I pottered round the ruins.

Superbly sited, high above the River Wye, Goodrich Castle was a fortified baronial palace and was first recorded in a document dated 1101, when it was probably just a timber palisade on top of an earth bank. It was likely that the stone tower was added during the reign of King Steven, around 1150, and subsequent generations modified the castle to suit their own particular requirements. Its medieval buildings are still largely intact, although they took a hammering during the English Civil War when both the Royalist and Parliamentarian forces occupied the castle at different times. Eventually, a massive mortar was cast, capable of throwing a two hundred pound shot, which served to hasten the garrison inside to surrender.

In case you were wondering, I'm not a gifted historian, making snap judgements, or a computer-based reconstruction of a Dark Age settlement, based on someone finding a broken piece of napkin ring with a picture of Blackpool Tower on it like they seem to do on those archaeology programmes ("…and from this pile of old chicken bones in this Hessian sack, we can just imagine King Arthur riding out pillaging and killing people in his quest for the Holy Grail… or maybe just for fun"). No – this was all written in the guidebook I had bought. History to some may just be the thing that they hastily delete off their computer when they hear their girlfriend coming up the stairs, but not to me. Oh no, I had even invested some of my cider money in my quest for knowledge.

I had also hired a tape that talked me through the different areas within the stronghold, although for some strange reason it neglected to mention that probably the easiest way into any castle is through its weakest defended position – normally the gift shop. I had enjoyed a fantastic morning but I'm not sure how Deborah felt, having to sit in the car park because of the English Heritage prejudice towards Barney.

I remember telling her how I had read about 'the perfect crime'. The killer had stabbed the victim in the heart with an icicle and once the icicle had melted, both the murder weapon and any fingerprints were lost in a pool of water next to the body. By the look of it, Deborah wasn't too angry, just a little bit pissed off, as I caught her on my return, poking my four-legged friend in the belly with the 'Fab' ice-lolly she was eating. I had come back in the nick of time!

I decided that she was in need of a treat and I told her as much. Her little face lit up but, as I informed her that I was taking her to Symonds Yat, her little face went out again.

There must have been some kind of terrible mistake earlier. The Symonds Yat I knew was a glorious place. Surely it couldn't have changed that much in my absence of twenty years?

Checking the map seemed to indicate a Symonds Yat East and a Symonds Yat West. My continued holiday harmony depended on East being the total opposite of West. It normally was. As we set off, I displayed a cheery confident exterior to my travelling companions but, beneath my boyish good looks, I was a seething mass of nerves, and butterflies were fluttering about where my 'Fab' ice lolly should have been slowly digesting away.

The road we were following gave way to a steepish single track leading down to the river. The sign read 'Symonds Yat East'.

⁘

It was like listening to the audience at a firework display, hearing the "Ooohs" and "Aaaahs" emanating from Deborah, and these were good "Ooohs" and "Aaaahs."

Arriving at the river's edge at Symonds Yat East was like entering a different world. Teashops and an ancient pub that could best be described as 'olde worlde' huddled together on the banks of the river. This was truly an area of outstanding natural beauty, with the Wye cutting a swathe through a wooded gorge on the edge of the spectacular Royal Forest of Dean. Further along the river's edge stood the old hunting lodge, built in the 1870s, which had now been converted into a hotel, where terraced gardens of magnolia trees and well-established wisteria overlooked the river.

A hand-pulled ferry operated across to the other side and boats carried passengers along this lovely stretch of water. Rare wild Peregrine falcons could sometimes be glimpsed flying overhead. The plaintive cries of buzzards could also be heard as they circled about the valley along with a variety of kestrels, sparrow hawks, ospreys and red kites.

I had redeemed myself and felt confident once more to leave Barney alone in Deborah's care.

I felt happy and bought an ice cream from the booth on the quayside. I asked for a '99'. The vendor must have misinterpreted my smiling face as that of someone who was brimming with the milk of human kindness. "Would you like hundreds and thousands?" he asked. I paused as I looked around me at the crowds of families milling about on the riverfront. I wasn't feeling *that* generous. "No, just two," I replied.

We chose a river cruise on which to enjoy our cones and, afterwards, walked the couple of miles to the 'Biblins'. The name alone was worth a trip and, on our arrival, we were delighted to find out that this was a lovely campsite, situated on a strip between the river and forest, complete with Indiana Jones-type suspension bridge.

We had also bought some local cider which can be pretty strong stuff. I had once bought a gallon of it in a plastic jerry can and foolishly left it in a kitchen cupboard for a week or so. When I eventually remembered it was there, I found the container all misshapen and distorted as if the still-living cider was trying to suck its way out. Anyway, not one to learn from my previous experiences, we bought some more and, when we got back to the campsite, drank too much of it and felt ill.

° ° ° ° ° °

As campsites go, it was a very well-organised one – maybe a little too organised. A sign near the toilet block told of some unspecified 'horseplay' that certain children had got up to the previous season. If 'it', whatever 'it' was, was repeated, children would be banned from the site.

The showers were a 'twenty pence for three minutes' type affair. No 'thirty seconds to go' warning, just a clunk as the water cut out. Believe me, there is no feeling more vulnerable than being a naked bloke, covered in foamy shower gel, when the water cuts out and you find you spent your last twenty pence on sweets an hour before. *Now* who was guilty of horseplay?

Deborah said it hardly gave her time to get her whole hair wet. I didn't check on the spelling but, either way, it was more information than I needed.

The next morning, we made the journey back up to the North East and reality.

When we arrived back and I pushed open the front door, a pile of letters on the floor greeted me. I looked through them. Bills mostly. I don't know why I had them as Bill lived next door, or at least his replacement did. Also in my absence, I appeared to have missed out on a special rate of five per cent on a ten-year loan, a miss-spelt personal invitation to a champagne reception at the Sofa King showroom, and the chance to meet with some kitchen sales reps who just happened to be in my area. I was gutted.

Not as gutted as Barney was going to be in a couple of days' time. He was booked in to be castrated so, in an effort to cheer both Barney and myself up, it was decided to press on with Project X.

23

Pictures from a Confiscated Camera

The recce to Snitter had yielded some valuable information. The village appeared small, prosperous and humourless, inasmuch as a village can look humourless. The signs leading into the place were written in block capitals to negate the possibility of a 'black masking tape' incident and an efficient local neighbourhood watch system provided a network of prying eyes against anybody trying to do anything funny. I had the feeling that any amusing alteration of their sign would be about as welcome as a fart in a spacesuit. Oh, how these sensible locals must have cursed their place name.

Their Achilles heel was a crossroads about four hundred yards from the village. Here, a small lower case 'Snitter' indicated where cars should tootle off to, to reach 'Party Town'. In fact, even 'tootle' seemed too fun a word. No, cars driving to Snitter would proceed soberly to their destination. This crossroads road sign would be the site of our dastardly abomination.

Despite the fact that the place was in the middle of nowhere, there seemed an inordinately high volume of traffic passing our potential crime scene. The only explanation was that these were some kind of anti-masking tape patrols, funded by the local neighbourhood watch Czar.

Once parked up, we would alert the residents to our wrongdoing, so we had to act fast. Deborah would be camera operator, I would wield the masking tape and Barney would pose by the sign. We synchronised watches, wished each other good luck, rubbed the lucky rabbit's foot which had been very lucky for us, but less so for the rabbit, and we were off. With a screech of brakes, we pulled up alongside the sign. I was out, the sign was amended, Barney was hoisted into position and Deborah took aim with the camera.

Suddenly, out of nowhere, a Snitter patrol came into view. Debs hid the gear, I leant on the sign to obscure our handiwork and we pretended to talk about the weather, while Barney clung on to me for dear life. The patrol passed and we waited in silence for a few seconds, listening for the peal of the village church bells that would signify that we had been detected. Nothing. We quickly posed again, the picture was taken, then we all bundled back into the vehicle and sped off in a cloud of dust and gravel. The 'Shitter' photo was in the bag!

Goodness knows how their nerve held out in the old days when such a jape would have involved the photographer crouching under a black cloak, the apparatus balancing on a tripod and the animal hoister standing next to the sign for a full minute while the Snitter patrolman ambled ever closer on his patrol donkey.

We also managed to locate the sign for Wark not too far away and with a bit of black electrical tape, this was quickly amended to Wank, although this sadly wouldn't make the finished calendar (it's a family show!), but it made me smile. Whilst I'm on the subject, there's the River Uck in Sussex, but the sign is tightly cropped around the word Uck specifically to deter such puerile behaviour. Spoilsports. Wasn't it Henry Ward Beecher, the nineteenth century American reformer, who said that the art of being happy lies in the power of extracting happiness from common things? Well, it seems that not everyone agrees.

₀ ° ₀ ° ₀ °

On a sugar high, due to our success at Snitter and possibly due to the two bottles of Panda Pop we had just consumed by way of celebration, we decided to push our luck. We set course for Once Brewed and the mysterious Twice Brewed, which didn't actually exist on our map, but which I was confident did exist in reality. Why else would you say something was Once Brewed, unless you were going to follow it with 'Twice Brewed'? Otherwise, you would just call something 'Brewed', wouldn't you?

Once Brewed lay close to Hadrian's Wall in Northumbria, about an hour's drive from Snitter, along winding country lanes.

Hadrian's Wall fascinated me. Once the frontier of a mighty empire that covered most of the known world, here was a seventy-three mile long wall, built across the country from coast to coast. Two thousand years ago, Roman soldiers had built this fifteen-foot high wall, complete with turrets, forts and mile castles, to keep the civilised apart from the barbarians. In its heyday, the wall was even whitewashed to make it seem more imposing and impressive to the heathen hordes on the other side. As luck would have it, it ended up on the eastern side in a place called Wallsend. On the 'right' side of the wall, the soldiers of the Empire could enjoy Roman baths, accommodating ladies and worship at the temples they had constructed. Even so, a posting here, in this spectacular yet bleak, cold and windy countryside, would have seemed like a right bummer. Hmmm, a mandatory tour in Tunisia (complete with sparrows) or Hadrian's Wall? Which should I choose? I can just imagine them now. "...in THESE sandals?"

If I had been here, I would have wanted something a little stronger than 'Once Brewed' to take my mind off things. I had total confidence in myself, which is more than my driving companions had in me.

 ° ° ° ° ° °

Once Brewed was easily bagged for the calendar. The sign we photographed indicated the place a full fifteen miles away. The problem now was that everyone else wanted to turn back for home, but I cleverly resolved the mutiny problem by pretending to be deaf as I drove on to our next destination. As we pressed on, we passed a dead deer on the side of the road.

"Looks like Santa's lost his temper again," I commented, which, in hindsight, I don't think added one bit to the already awkward atmosphere in the vehicle.

Even as we pulled into Once Brewed, there was no sign indicating the existence of a Twice Brewed anywhere. To say that Once Brewed was a one-horse town would be a bit of an exaggeration. It consisted of a tourist information office and, in all my travels, I have often come across towns without tourist information offices, but never a tourist information office without a town.

I asked the old woman at the desk if she knew where Twice Brewed was.

"Why do you want to go there?"

"I just do."

"Who do you want to see there?"

I was beginning to think that I had stumbled onto something that I wasn't meant to. I couldn't be sure, but I suspected she might be pressing some button under the desk as we spoke and I was now probably being projected onto some massive screen in an underground bunker, whilst simultaneously being x-rayed to see if I was packing a piece. A young woman at the other side of the room was now glancing over the top of her guidebook at me. I couldn't be sure, but she could have had a pair of .38s on her.

"I just want to pop there."

"Who told you about Twice Brewed?"

I was too embarrassed to tell her that I was doing a crappy little calendar project and I thought it would be fun to take a picture of odd place names, and that this would probably be March or April.

"I know all about Twice Brewed. Just tell me where it is," I replied in a mock confident tone. It appeared to work, and she crumbled. Clearly, she now saw me as a senior official in whatever sinister organisation she worked for.

"Out of the car park, left and left again. You can't miss it, Sir." She didn't actually say, "Sir" but I mentally added it onto the end of her apology. Oh, and I made it sound like an apology in my mind. Did I forget to mention that?

I couldn't miss Twice Brewed because it began before Once Brewed had ended. They overlapped and, for about ten yards, I was in the mystical realm of Thrice Brewed. Twice Brewed proper then took over and continued on for another hundred yards before it too ended. All that Twice Brewed consisted of was a pub. I took my photo of the sign and was off.

I don't know what the pub was a front for, and I didn't stay to find out as I thought I had pushed my luck too much already that day. Snitter neighbourhood watch vehicles would already be scouring the countryside for me and, sooner or later, the old woman would cotton on to the realisation that I wasn't 'one of them'. Besides, I had driven too many miles to have someone pulling the film out of my camera, especially since it was a digital one. Time to go home.

24

Goodbye to All That

The term 'the dog's bollocks' would only be used in the past tense by Barney by the time the day was over.

I had thought long and hard about the subject of his apparel in a responsible owner-type way, as opposed to some kind of sick, perverted type way. I had bought Barney to be my obedient companion, not for me to be the hapless bloke who would have to fund his canine playboy life of debauchery. Also, being lulled to sleep to the sound of him licking his own genitals wasn't the perfect way to relax.

I had heard that when dogs with the full equipment had got the whiff of some brazen hussy bitch in heat, all other thoughts would be ejected from their mind to the exclusion of having their dirty, filthy way with her. They could do all this too without having seven or eight pints first. They would run off, ignoring all the lessons they had ever learnt and camp outside the bitch's home for days until she came off heat. Fifteen minutes had been *my* limit, before I became bored and pottered off. I'm talking about a lady here and not a canine, I hasten to add.

He was to be castrated, have his knackers chopped off, become a 'Jaffa' or however else you wish to put it. I had tried to persuade Deborah to take him to the vet so that Barney would associate *her* with the deed and not me, but she was unavailable. I drove him to the surgery and stayed with him until the anaesthetic took effect. His tail kept on wagging, as he grew drowsier and drowsier. When the nurse led him off, his little legs wobbled as if he was pissed, and she had to pick him up and carry him to his fate.

I received the call to pick him up about three in the afternoon. I had been warned that he might be a little sulky, which seemed like a bit of an understatement to me. I was also told that he would be very fragile for a day or so, and the nurse told me I should make sure he drank plenty of fluids, which is lucky as it's literally the only thing he does drink. She also suggested that I should make scrambled egg for tea, which seemed like a splendid idea. I love scrambled egg. Goodness knows what poor Barney would be eating.

She opened the door and Barney bounded in to greet me, which wasn't what I had been led to expect at all. He bounced and leapt about, wearing a big 'buster collar' which, basically, resembled a large lampshade. The nurse said it was to stop him from licking himself. If she meant his balls, she was crediting him with more intelligence than he actually had. I don't think it had ever occurred to him to drive the ten miles back to the vet's, pick the lock on the surgery and rummage through the dustbins to find them. To be honest, as he bounded about as if nothing had happened, I began to wonder if the vet had charged me a hundred pounds just to tie the cone on his bonce.

What I like about Barney is that he seems to think everything is just meant to be. He didn't try to get the cone off because, in his little mind, it was meant to be. He just blundered away, bumping into chairs, doorways and legs because, like the departure of his knackers, it was just meant to be. He looked funny and I laughed as he crashed into everything with his over-sized lampshade. Out of sadness would come joy. Sadness for him and joy for me, admittedly, but sadness and joy all the same.

° ° ° ° ° °

That evening we were returning to Snitter territory. Mick Thomas, the acclaimed singer-songwriter, was playing at a pub in Rothbury. The 'acclaimed' bit, and the 'Well *I've* never heard of him' thoughts occur in the same sentence because he is acclaimed in his native Australia but, tragically, pretty much unknown in the UK.

He was a founding member of 'Weddings, Parties, Anything', who had a cult following in Oz before he split the band and re-formed as, 'Mick Thomas and the Sure Thing' and 'Mick Thomas and various other incarnations'. His single 'Father's Day', about a divorced dad seeing his kid each weekend, was voted 'Single of the Year' when it was released.

I was excited about seeing him live again and had a chat with him at the bar before the show. When I took my seat, I told Deborah that I had arranged for a dedication and her little face lit up. A couple of songs in, Mick told us about one of the new songs from his latest CD. At the time of the success of Father's Day, his record label had asked him to make another one like that. The result was a sort of joke song that he hadn't released until now.

He told us the story of how, in Australia, dog sharing is the latest thing between divorced couples. He then related how he had been approached by a guy before the show (me!), asking if he would dedicate the song to his dog.

When Mick had asked why, the guy (still me) had explained how, on that morning, his dog had been castrated. "Poor Barney," said Mick as he started into his song, 'Half a Dog'. I was chuffed. I turned towards Deborah with a big smile on my face to see her reaction, but a small black cloud hung over her. She obviously didn't like the song as much as I did.

She must have been tired too because she didn't chat much on the journey home.

Never mind, the next day was to be a cracker. As part of the calendar project, we would be heading for the small village that, according to the map, went by the name of Low Bell End.

° ° ° ° ° °

There was no time for a full walk that morning, so I just let Barney out into the back yard to do his business. A matter of minutes later, I went out to check on him and it was like Shit Central Station. Turds abounded. I led him to the front garden, went back, cleared his mess, and then went to bring him back through. In the short space of time he was in the front garden, he had managed to uproot a lavender plant and overturn a tub of flowers. He either didn't appreciate the irony of going to Low Bell End, or Deborah had been stirring things with him. The realisation that I had put my pants on back to front completed the abysmal start to the day.

According to our map, we would be heading into the heart of the North Yorkshire National Park. As we journeyed through the picturesque villages that were dotted throughout the moorland, my spirits started to lift. The shit shovelling that had marred the morning was forgotten as the calendar took shape in my mind. The purples of the heather, the wandering sheep, the gurgling of the streams – maybe with the right angle, I could convey all this in the photo. We laughed as we drove on, and then we turned the corner.

I couldn't believe my eyes at what I saw. More to the point, I couldn't believe my eyes at what I didn't see. It was there on the map and we were here on the ground, but there was no road sign. This was a big shock. On the plus side, it did cure my hiccups but, on the negative side, there was no photo opportunity. I felt conned. What was going on? Twice Brewed hadn't been on the map, but was there, whilst Low Bell End had been on the map, but wasn't there. I had the feeling that someone was toying with me.

There was a farm where the village should have been, with the sinister name of 'Bell End Farm'. All sorts of bizarre images were conjured up in my head – even more bizarre than the puppy farm images. This was a bad place and I wanted to leave. If I was going to be toyed with anywhere, I certainly didn't want to be toyed with here.

It's surprising how fast you can travel on those moorland roads.

。°。°。°

Scotland seems to have more than its fair share of Twatts. There is a Twatt on the Shetland Islands and another on the Orkneys. There are also places called Muckle Flugga, Lamb Head, Chicken Head, Papa Little, Holm of Papa, Sound of Papa and, following close behind, Butt of Lewis. My God, there is a calendar in the making just on the Scottish Islands themselves.

When I was a Midshipman in the Royal Navy, we had used the rugged West Coast of Scotland for our navigational training. The coastline, with its multitude of inlets, was ideal to take bearings on and every small fishing village seemed to have a church with a massive spire to line up on. We were all a long way from home, except for 'Worm'. Worm was one of our fellow Midshipmen who came from this part of the world. He was called Worm because someone had discovered that he pronounced the word worm as, "Wurrrrrm". So, in the early days of our training, when everybody was trying to establish where they stood in the group, this hasty and clumsy moniker was given to our Scottish friend. Now with *him* telling the tale, the 'Lambton Wurrrrrm' *does* sound scary!

Worm and I, along with the boys from the Mersey, Thames and the Tyne, were all given orders to attend elocution lessons at the Naval College to make us talk proper. Ballroom dancing lessons were also mandatory at Dartmouth and I had considered myself pretty shrewd when I managed to move fast and 'nab' the College Librarian's teenage daughter as my dancing partner, as opposed to one of the gaggle of shrews that was wheeled in for such occasions.

As much as I would have liked a 'Twatt' now, I was playing by the rules – that is, our self-imposed rules, which dictated that the place names for the calendar had to be local to the North East.

Hence, we were now headed for Swaledale to capture a couple of home-grown calendar girls. Both were clearly marked on the map – in as much as a tiny square can be clearly marked but, moreover, they were tiny squares with a name – funny names. Today we were off to Crackpot and Booze.

I'm not sure if we actually found Crackpot. We followed the map, turned off the main drag and onto a twisting single lane road, where we followed the sign for Crackpot and drove past a big house and onwards into a dead end in the courtyard of a hill farm. But that's not important. The important thing was that we had found somewhere, which *could* have been the place and, more importantly, the sign. We retraced our tracks back to the pointer. Barney and 'Barry the mask' were taken out of the vehicle, whilst Debs got the camera set up. Barney finished the apple core he was eating and, as he was propped up in 'Barry's' arms, he poked his tongue out for the camera in a dog-type 'Say cheese' moment. 'Dog poking out tongue' antics in an oversized-lampshade next to a scary looking Barry – Crackpot indeed. Perfect.

Booze was only a short drive away. This was turning into a very productive day.

Deborah followed our progress on the map as I drove. Turning off the B2670 at Reeth, we took an un-named road through Arkle Town and kept on driving until we got to Whaw. Too far. We must have missed it. The excitement in the car was mounting as we headed back down into Langthwaite. "*The excitement was mounting?*" What was I saying? What had we been reduced to, being excited about finding a sign for Booze? Still, we were excited all the same. Deborah told me to take a left turn. "This is it!" she exclaimed. She remained silent as I did an eight-point turn to try and get the car out of the small churchyard. By the time we had extricated ourselves I'm sure we were on at least five different Facebook neighbourhood watch groups.

After we had both examined the map, we agreed that it must be the *next* left. I turned down the lane and drove until the road petered out before parking up. We looked at what lay ahead of us, looked at each other, and then back at the map, then at what was ahead, then each other again, then back to the map once more. This was map-making at its laziest. No sign, no nothing. Just a pub.

I decided to cheer myself up with a 'Wetwang'.

。 ° 。 ° 。 °

Maybe I was pushing it slightly to get Wetwang in, as it was roughly a hundred miles to the south of me but, what the hell, it was *my* calendar idea. I relied on my assumption that, despite my repeated requests for visitation rights (for my family to visit me, that is), not many would bother to make the journey in the end. It wasn't as if I was taking the piss by travelling way off-area and visiting the brewery where they made 'Piddle Beer' not far from 'Wyre Piddle' (which sounds more like the symptoms of a rather unpleasant STD than a picturesque village). Neither would I be taking in 'Lord Hereford's Knob' or indeed 'Lickey End', (on the Welsh border and Worcestershire respectively). Likewise, I also respected the fact that 'Pratt's Bottom' and 'Brown Tongue' were out of bounds, (the Deep South and the Lake District). 'Ham' and 'Sandwich' sounded appealing (Kent) but with my luck I'd get there and find it 'Peasedown' (Somerset). Anyway, who would know of this deviation? My dark, seedy secret would be safe.

I think they felt that travelling to fifty-five degrees North was something Shackleton or Scott could aspire to, but not them. Soon afterwards, I received a phone call from my sister, Kate. Woody was going through his midlife crisis, she informed me, and they were moving to open a beach bar in Thailand. They too would need a servant, but would look for one who sounded a bit more oriental than Neil's maid. I suggested 'Minjeeeta'. *She* certainly wouldn't want to visit Wetwang (but could probably easily win me another goldfish with her extensive ping pong ball skills).

The people of Wetwang seem very proud of their village name, and a large sign welcomes careful motorists. We stopped and had fish and chips at the Wetwang chippy.

As I found a massive chip and we imagined how big that potato must have been, I reminded Debs of the great chip shortage, which had closely followed the great potato shortage. It was a dark time because, as we all know, a life without potatoes is no life at all. When I was a youngster, buying chips on their own was banned. It had to be chips and fish, or chips and sausage, or chips and something else, all in a bid to deter reckless chip purchases. Chip prices had virtually doubled overnight − a perfect example of the supply and demand theory model at work. This precedent sort of stuck after that, as the prices never came down, even when the potatoes started flowing again. As she looked at me blankly, I began to doubt myself and wondered if it was a bizarre phenomenon that had only affected the Colchester Avenue chippy.

Other events lost to history include the 'great baked bean war', where prices of beans tumbled to as low as a penny, as rival factions tried to corner the baked bean market. At the time, I had considered bulk buying penny tins of beans to hang onto and then sell on when the bean market stabilised − a rather tame version of playing the stock market. I literally shelved the idea when I discovered that the penny tins consisted of little more than a slack handful of beans, floating in a veritable sea of bean juice. The whole thing almost got out of hand and there had been a dreadful stink about it all.

Sufficiently sated, we photographed the 'Wetwang welcomes careful drivers' sign, which had recently replaced the 'drive like your cat lives here' placard, and continued on our journey to Scarborough, the seaside resort that had died.

Once majestic hotels had become shabby, once grand theatres now hosted shows by unfunny comedians, and even the donkeys on the beach looked knackered. There was, however, a daily naval battle, held in the municipal park. The resident organist, who was located in a little gazebo on a small island, played on as the warships and planes fought their daily duel. He would be merrily bashing away on his organ as all around him the ships, some over twenty feet in length and manned by council employees, would fight it out, with the RAF planes screeching overhead on wires, dropping bombs; there would be explosions, smoke and fire, towers of water erupting from the hit vessels, some keeling over, some sinking. Actually, perhaps I'd been a bit harsh on the town; this sounded magnificent!

Alas, when we got there, we discovered we had missed it. Curse those Wetwang chips!

Deborah, meanwhile, still seemed to be harbouring some strange sort of bad feeling toward me following the Mick Thomas gig. She told me that her friend Jane was coming to her house that night to cheer her up - they were going to stay in, have a bottle of wine and enjoy a chick flick.

Is it me or are women just that much more brazen nowadays?

25

I Alone Am Best

Is it just me, or does every other ex-squaddie I meet seem to have served in the Special Forces or shot some terrorist? It makes me feel that my time was just spent drinking brews in the NAAFI by comparison.

In hindsight, I tend to think that war stories and their tellers follow the same rule of thumb as pepper grinders and food. As you may know, the rule of thumb states that the quality of food in a restaurant is inversely proportional to the size of the pepper grinder. In the same way, the actual deeds of 'derring-do' are inversely proportional to the number of tales told about 'derring-dos'. In such cases, it normally turns out that the Walter Mitty plagiarising Andy McNab, or Ernest Hemingway, had probably served in the Pay Corps all his life and the full extent of his adventures involved a nasty incident with a rogue stapler.

I was normally too busy asking inane questions between brews to pull up a sandbag and swing the lamp. Where was it that the Navy bred those strange mutant chickens they fed us that had one hundred and ninety legs but no breast? (and how did they catch the distorted little fuckers? - they must run fast). What was the difference in the Army ration packs in the eighties between a bacon burger and bacon grill? Why were the Spangles soft? Why was there Arabic writing on the Mars bars? And why did they give us tracing paper style-toilet paper that just served to spread stuff around? It was like wiping your bottom with an inside out crisp packet.

I could never work out either how the human digestive system takes about twenty four hours to change food into shit, yet the Army Catering Corps could do it in just two. Fair play though, the chef's course is reputed to be the hardest course in the military... at least I don't know anyone who's passed it.

I could no more find the answers to those questions, than the reason why the old women who were invited for dancing practice at Dartmouth plucked off their perfectly good eyebrows only to re-draw them back on (badly) with eyeliner. You know that we know, don't you? One of the women had drawn hers on too high, and she just looked mildly surprised at everything that was going on.

Some of my questions were answered by experience. I found out what a monkey bath was when I lowered myself into an over hot bath, emitting 'Ooh ooh ooh aah aah aah,' as I did so. 'Donkey Shite' was a mystery to me as well until I found out that was the soldier's version of 'thank you' in German. Meanwhile, a nine coiler was normally what was produced when you loosened up after a week on compo rations.

Other phrases peculiar to the forces seemed to get right to the point far more succinctly than the standard Queen's English ever could. If a piece of machinery onboard ship 'failed under continuous testing', it was marked as 'FUCT' (much to the annoyance of the Engineering Officer).

The Devil dodger would be the Padre, just in the

same way as a salad dodger is a fat person in civilian life. The Turdis is, in my view, a much better name for a Portaloo, whilst a Hitler Piss is the sort you have when you are drunk, and you need to place one hand against the wall in front of you to retain balance as you stand over the urinal.

An ex-wife was often referred to as a hurricane – starts with a gentle blow and ends up taking your house away. A very ugly person would be called a baby eater, with 'a face that would scare a police horse'. And, if you were running around everywhere like a maniac, you were running around 'from arsehole to breakfast'.

But I digress.

The reason stress levels were running high was that my dad was due to visit at the weekend and, as a result, I was running around from arsehole to breakfast, trying to get things sorted.

Debs had lit the fuse under the 'powder keg' weekend by announcing that I was like my dad. It was a particularly hurtful thing to say that neither my dad nor I appreciated. Susan had then topped up the keg with more powder when she said that Bethan was just like me. I was initially delighted by this comparison until I realised from her expression that this only related to any negative traits my daughter might have.

Things could either go swimmingly or blow-up big style. I could see myself now, staggering back under a hail of friendly fire, whilst someone else's heart fell off their sleeve because someone else was speaking off the cuff. Just a mess of chicken wire and fertiliser would remain. I shivered at the thought.

I had always tried to live by the 'six Ps' – Prior Preparation Prevents Piss Poor Performance. As a result, over the next three days, the history of my life was effectively re-written in a frenzy of planning, cleaning, falling-out, tidying, hiding things and ethnic cleansing.

My dad was only coming for slightly less than two days, but the explosives in the keg were unstable and could be set off just by a wrong word. I was taking no chances.

To mark the occasion of the visit, Barney's cone of shame following the removal of his testicles was officially taken off. He pottered off into his kennel to continue with some private business and then emerged, seconds later, with a puzzled expression on his face. He then slowly and carefully retraced his steps, looking and sniffing everywhere as he went as if he was trying to find where he had left his balls. I swallowed hard and mentally retracted my previously optimistic claim that I would have nothing to worry about if dogs suddenly took over the world.

。 。 。 。 。 。

My dad and Ann arrived earlier than expected, while I was still wearing my 'Jesus is coming, look busy' T-shirt. Barney ran around, excitedly jumping and weeing at the same time, while I hid my favourite stripper coffee mug and dubious magazine that someone must have left at my house by mistake. The cavalry arrived moments later in the form of Deborah and Tess and, as my dad looked in disbelief at his photo, stuck onto the 'Iraq Most Wanted' poster, I scuttled away to change.

On the basis of the 'idle hands/devil' theory, I reasoned that we should be kept as busy as was practicable. Therefore, all of us were soon on our way to wonder at the structure that was Hadrian's Wall. Minor disagreements about whether Hadrian had a beard or not were quickly put to bed when I was proved right (as well as the first Roman Emperor to have a beard, Hadrian was also considered by many to be a very wise and just leader... and he probably had more time on his hands than other Emperors to do this as the average person spends about 3,350 hours shaving during their life. I only had a beard for a few months in the Arctic... so that's my excuse – too much time shaving to be very wise... or just). Four hours into the visit and no major arguments. Things were going well.

The evening's serial was a trip to the Italian restaurant opposite. Bethan joined us, and her constant chit-chat contributed to an excellent evening without incident. When my dad offered to pay, I remembered the warning I had received from Deborah about not being argumentative so, naturally, although against my better judgement, I agreed that he should indeed settle the bill.

Sunday morning and the five of us squashed into the car. To avoid involuntarily igniting any of the powder keggers, Deborah sat in the back in the middle so that Bethan could have the window seat. Fair play to her, powder keg Bethan had already given up her seat in the front for her powder keg Grandpa. Ann had the audacity to suggest, mid-journey, that maybe it was a bit uncomfortable for Debs sitting there. She should try sitting curled up, wedged on the bump on the floor, being repeatedly kicked in the back for eight hours! I remained calm and pretended I hadn't heard. We were off to Alnwick Castle to see the new water gardens, the pride and joy of the Duchess of Northumberland.

As we drove on, I pondered on whether the undercurrent of tension, which prevailed during the weekend was because it was perhaps one big challenge to see who could be top dog? No, that was ridiculous. Surely everyone knew *I* was top dog here.

The castle itself has been in such films as 'Robin Hood,

Prince of Thieves' and, more recently, was used in the Harry Potter films as Hogwarts. This is also the location of the famous Poison Garden where, hidden behind ominous black iron gates, are around one hundred toxic plants. Sadly, they don't have a gift shop, which is a shame as I wanted to be prepared in case Ann complained about the seating arrangements again on the way back.

Inside the castle, as in most stately homes, the rooms were furnished, fires were burning, 'Country Life' magazines lay open on tables and photos stood in their frames as if the family had just quickly abandoned the place in true Mary Celeste style. In fact, there were so many little photos in frames everywhere that I wondered if they were all real family members or had other visitors to the castle beaten me to it, and already indulged in one of my favourite hobbies – Mantelpiecing.

For the uninitiated, to quote from the Urban Dictionary:

Mantelpiecing: *verb: To bring a photo of yourself (preferably pre-framed) to a party at someone's house, then place the photo amongst other photos of host's family on such as mantle or dresser.*

It goes without saying that you don't tell your hosts what you're up to. Most people have photos on their mantelpieces that have been there forever, and they never really look at them anymore – they are just things that they dust now and again. Your grinning photo may sit there for months before anyone notices and when they do, you can just imagine the confusion as they scramble through their minds wondering who the idiot on their shelf is. I'm sure some of my photos of me grinning like a loon are still sitting next to grandparents and distinguished uncles in front rooms across the nation. I may have even initiated a few domestics when a husband has discovered my smiling countenance resting happily on his wife's bedside table.

Indeed, don't just limit it to party invites – I don't! Today, I would be joining the ranks of the great and good at a castle, of all places. These places usually have pretty good security to stop people stealing anything but leaving something behind was a much easier task. You know the setting; the reading room is all laid out as if the family are in residence, and you are allowed to venture a couple of yards into the room before your progress is impeded by a luxurious thick burgundy rope suspended between two metal posts. About an arm's reach away is usually an antique occasional table with numerous framed photographs of family members. To give your photo the best chance of being undetected, it's worth investing in a decent frame so that your picture blends in with the others. For somewhere quite as grand as Alnwick Castle, I was to be wearing my full Royal Military Police mess uniform and sporting a rather fine Clark Gable moustache. When the attendant was looking away, or asleep on his chair, a quick stretch and the dirty deed was done. Captain John Donoghue RMP was now in situ amongst the other official family members. I'm not sure how long I lasted until I was detected, but next time you visit there, have a look and drop me a line if I'm still there, grinning away.

We perhaps lingered a little too long, walking the ramparts, admiring the wonderful water gardens, playing in the magnificent tree house (there's even a restaurant in the branches) and looking for a suitable spot to mantelpiece, as there was a real danger on the return journey of an outbreak of hostilities induced by tiredness. Deborah was ready to pour oil on the water if needed, but the whole episode passed off without event.

Two thirds into the trip and all's well.

That evening, the operational HQ for the visit was re-located twenty five miles south, to Deborah's cottage. I offered to make everyone a hot beverage on arrival and then realised my mistake. It can be quite nerve wracking making other people hot drinks. You know the dilemma; have I left the tea bag in long enough, have I left it in too long, have I put enough milk in, have I put too much milk in, have I put the right amount of sugar in? Clearly, it was easier to make tea for Catholics as the sugar dilemma wasn't an issue, but both Ann and Debs were Protestants. Brew making may be scary, but it has its rewards - nothing compares to the proud glow of satisfaction you get when you're officially informed that you make a good cup of tea... well, I expect is. As it turned out, no trophies were awarded. It seems that no one was either overwhelmed nor underwhelmed by their beverage... just whelmed.

As the evening progressed, things almost kicked off during the cheese course at dinner when Ann enquired if Barney was my only pet.

"I've just got the one dog, that's under two."

"Don't patronise me," she replied, "I know how many one is!"

Things remained tense while I quickly explained I was just saying how old he was, and as order was restored, Debs silently re-pocketed the electric cattle prod she had covertly got out ready to quell any insurrection.

Bedtime. Unless there was an unfortunate sleep-walking incident, only breakfast remained. How stressful could *that* be?

I hadn't bargained for my morning pee routine being disrupted by a queue for the bathroom and, as I hopped from foot to foot, making pleasant small talk, I released my weapon. Barney was brought in from the confines of the garden and, as he rampaged around the house, jumping up in his excitement and almost knocking people over, I made best use of the confusion to queue jump. Aha, I alone am best.

My dad and Ann departed, thanking me for a good weekend. I had gone from the black sheep to the prodigal son in the space of a couple of days.

I don't think there was any real argument as to who was top dog and, against all the odds, the visit had been a success. Paul and Kate both rang, hoping to hear tales of pandemonium and were both obviously disappointed when I informed them that the whole thing had gone off without incident. I felt like Joseph – he of the amazing Technicolor Dream Coat. I had the feeling that, in future, people would look at me differently and maybe even come to me for advice or maybe to interpret the odd dream. The one with Miss Tucker in it had been very odd. She had been dressed immaculately in a kimono and wearing mad professor glasses.

Kate rang me again later, still deliberating whether she should go to Thailand. She had heard that there were both Sun bears and Asian black bears over there and was feeling a bit worried. I tried to comfort her by telling her that if she happened across one in the wild, she should play with its cubs to show that she wasn't a threat. She seemed happy with that, but it was only after I put the phone down that I wondered to myself if I'd got that right. Well, what's the worst that could happen?

26

Super Furry Animal

Somehow, Sparky and GoGo were still living with me. Susan always seemed to be in too much of a hurry to take them with her and I was seriously thinking of charging them board and rent. To be honest, I think she was just a bit fed up with them. After all, they didn't seem that exciting and had clearly outstayed their welcome at her house. I actually felt a bit sorry for them, just swimming endlessly around their little tank, past their ornamental sunken castle, until someone told me that goldfish only have a six-second memory. I felt sorry no more. What a fantastic life they must have! Every six seconds they were having a new adventure and what could be better than discovering a sunken castle?

"Look GoGo, a sunken castle!"

"Wow Sparky, that's amazing!"

"Look GoGo, a sunken castle!"

"Wow Sparky, that's amazing!"

"Look GoGo, a sunken castle!"

"Wow Sparky, that's amazing!"

Here I was, feeling bored with their apparent lack of

amusing antics, whilst they were having the time of their lives. I thought about putting a little deep sea diver man next to the castle, but they would probably overdose with excitement and, by the time Sparky had finished telling GoGo about the castle and the diver, he would have forgotten what he had started talking about; it would be unfair.

"Look GoGo, a sunken castle … and what's that … Oh, my God … a deep-sea diver! I wonder if he's dived… No, no, hang on, I've lost the thread … what was I on about again?"

I had also been joined by Hammy the hamster. Hammy was no trouble really and spent most of the day driving about in his small toy car. He was meant to be the classroom pet at Deborah's school, but she had lent him to me in case I grew bored whilst Barney was away.

Oh, and in case I forgot to mention it, Barney was away.

If you suddenly become overwhelmed by a strong sense of déjà vu at this point, rest assured that you are not a fish. This is where the book started for some bizarre reason.

If you don't remember reading that part before, either the pages of the book are very wet, or you'll start to do sit-ups on the floor at any moment.

Anyway, Barney was *still* away.

With a heavy week of work commitments, which meant I could be popping all over the country at short notice, it had been agreed that Barney should be put into kennels during that time. I was missing him, and going for walks without him just wasn't the same. Even with the benefit of his car, Hammy was too slow to keep up, and so I was left to stroll around the circuit on my own.

The effect of the tidal flow on the river made for some

strange sights. For a period of about three weeks, a fridge had floated back and forth downstream, then upstream until it became snagged in the moorings of a boat at Cox Green. Bethan and I had seen a duvet once, heading downstream with a water rat lying basking in the sun on top of it. Ratty must have alighted somewhere downstream because he was gone when the duvet made the return leg. And now, following the annual bath race down the river, an abandoned tub was making the daily trip up and down, outside my house. *"Barney would like to have seen that,"* I told myself. Deborah had even called the kennels to ask how he was getting on.

Then, the next morning a card arrived. It was from Barney!

When I had taken him to the kennels, I had mentioned about the jumping up and the guy in charge said he would see if he could teach Barney some things. I never once thought that he would teach him to write. I read it to Deborah.

> *"Hello Dad,*
> *Just a quickie to let you know how life is at Stalag 17.*
> *It's a bit 'ruff' really. Someone mentioned digging a tunnel but when a 'spayed' was mentioned we gave it a miss.*
> *I told everyone your Shih Tzu joke but they all thought it was crap.*
> *It's lights out so I'll have to go. I'll have a 'tail' or two to tell when I get home.*
> *Barney*
> *PS. It's great here, really."*

It was the *"It's great here really,"* phrase that gave it away. Barney would never use language like that. He was a perennial ingrate, and he would never let on that he enjoyed something I did for him. I concluded that the kennel owner must have had a hand in this.

We replied in a similar vein to the kennel owner, marking it for the attention of Barney. We told him that we were sorry for having him castrated before he went away, but that Deborah loved her new earrings and we also hoped that the change of dog food hadn't had him shitting through the eye of a needle.

。 ° 。 ° 。 °

If anyone is going to call Deborah a freak, it's going to be me. Not that I would, you understand. I'm not that brave, although I do concede that her hair does go a little frizzy in the rain.

If anyone dared call her a freak, it would cost them. At the electrical superstore that rhymes with 'Ruby Murray's', which apparently can't be beaten on price, it would cost them a tenner. Deborah had the audacity to ask a gaggle of five assistants, chatting together by the cookers, if anyone could help us with the vacuum cleaners. She was abruptly informed, in no uncertain terms, that they were 'cooker' assistants only, and was called a freak for asking such an impertinent question. The management explained later that these staff were relatively new to Ruby Murray's. I guess this meant that they hadn't yet attended the 'Don't call customers Freaks' induction course. She was subsequently offered a tenner off the Dyson cleaner that I wanted by way of hush money. I tried to persuade her to go over to the girls again and ask which colours the cleaners came in, and if could they be used on laminate floors, in the hope of inducing a frenzied outburst on their part and maybe halving the cost of the vacuum cleaner in the process, but she refused.

If only I had brought John Merrick, the Elephant Man, with me. After the assistants had finished their pointing and jeering, Ruby Murray's would be paying *me* to take a Dyson home.

Me: "Do you want to hear the cruel things they're saying about you?"

Elephant Man: "I'm all ears."

Me: "Yes, that's one of them."

His luck probably wouldn't be all out, though as I'm sure one of them would suggest he'd like a little head.

Bethan had come over at the time and witnessed Deborah's humiliation first-hand. Still, out of sorrow came joy. Deborah's sorrow and my joy admittedly, but sorrow and joy all the same.

Bethan was quite excited that day as she had just learnt that she had been chosen to play Beauty in a forthcoming production of 'Beauty and the Beast'. I didn't like to say too much to Debs at this stage in case she thought I was implying that she should play the beast after the freak 'freak' incident. This was a dancing school production and followed on the success of the previous year's 'Snow White' show. Unfortunately, big business has its greedy paws everywhere and the dwarfs had to be called slightly different names to avoid a legal battle with the Corporation who has an over-sized rodent as their mascot. Even *I* am having to run scared of the big mouse! It took the shine off it slightly for the children, but at least the greedy shareholders were happy (or 'smiley' as the dwarf had to be re-named). I'd like to think the head of Disney would one day come to his senses and question what kind of Mickey Mouse operation he was running... if that is his actual name. It sounds like a made up one to me. You never hear of a person called 'Harry Human'.

Anyway, I digress. Bethan had also found out that a

piece she had written about Hadrian's Wall had won first prize in a tourist competition about Northumbria. It was written on the theme of 'The Spirit of Northumbria; strength of the past and vision for the future' (I have had to leave the actual piece by Bethan out of this book for two reasons. Copyright now lies with the Tourist Board, and Bethan didn't want her masterpiece to be in any way associated with this drivel. And fair play to her, she's not a performing monkey… that's my sister Kate's job).

We tried the Dyson when we got back and then all stood round the clear Perspex cylinder, marvelling at the amount of dirt and Barney hair that was sucked off the apparently clean carpet, along with something that sounded as if it might have been important. I then tried to put to the back of my mind the state of filth that I had unwittingly been living in, before Bethan and Freaky had come with me to buy the miracle cleaner. Prior to then I had always kept a few 'Get Well Soon' cards on the television so people would think I was recovering from some illness if they had just 'popped round', and that's why the house was a mess.

It was probably clean enough for me to get an actual cleaning lady in now. The Dyson was a modern-day marvel, but it was a shame that it didn't have a light at the front like vacuum cleaners of old; not that I planned on hoovering in the dark, but I thought it might be fun to wake Barney up thinking he was about to be hit by a train. Mind you, the way he acts when the hoover is about you'd think that his whole family had been murdered by one.

As Hammy drove around on the super clean carpet highway, I looked at the mass of Barney hair in the cylinder. I was surprised that my pup wasn't walking around naked! I must admit, the 'no fur coats' lobby had made me a little embarrassed about being seen out with him sometimes as he flaunted his furriness but, despite that, I was missing his little grimacing face. Still, he was due home soon.

* * * * * *

If anyone *was* a freak around here, it was Hammy. And I wasn't about to stump up for saying so. He was as happy as Larry when he was driving round in his car but, if I picked him up, he would scream his little head off until I put him down again, when he would promptly clamber back into his vehicle and drive off at high speed.

Worst of all though was his fitness regime. He would sleep most of the day like the lazy layabout that he was, until it was time for *my* bedtime. Then, as I lay in my bed, waiting to be taken into the land of nod, he would start his gym training and the house would reverberate to the sound of his treadmill spinning around and around and around and around and around. I think he knew very well what he was doing.

I hadn't meant to drop him on the kitchen floor when he had first arrived here, but clearly, he took it personally. OK, I did snatch him back off the floor pretty quickly too, but that was only because I didn't want him disappearing behind the cupboards. I had a vision of him emerging several weeks later, with a scrawny body and bloated deformed head, after feasting on the various rotting flotsam and jetsam that had found their way behind the units over the years. I had been well-intentioned in all my actions towards him, but obviously Hammy thought otherwise.

Our relationship just wasn't working out. I would tell him that it wasn't really him, it was me. I was still missing Barney and wasn't ready to move on. Yes, it had been fun in the early days and I still wanted to be friends with him, but that was all.

Little things that I would normally let go just started to really get on my nerves – the way he would climb into his food bowl to eat his dinner, or the way he just left his little poops lying where they had fallen.

I toyed with the idea of annoying him so much that he would want to finish with me, so that, when we parted, I would still have a clear conscience and maybe even leave it open for me to return if I ever grew bored with Barney. Maybe I should tell him that we just needed some time apart. That way, I could play with Barney and *still* be able to play with Hammy later. Maybe we should just have a clean break. That would probably be the fairest way for both parties, but it had the disadvantage that it didn't really leave me with a safety net in case things went wrong elsewhere. Or maybe I should just get up at six in the morning and smash the little door to his house in with a cocktail sausage on a stick and tell him it was a police raid.

Sparky and GoGo had to go go too. I was sick of looking at their happy little faces as they kept on rediscovering the castle, while I was pining over Barney. I made the decision that, if Susan didn't pick them up at the weekend, I was going to get nasty and buy that deep-sea diver.

It was late and I was tired. As I set the alarm and turned the lights off, ready to go upstairs, I could just about make out a shadowy figure climbing into his wheel.

27

Salesmen, Cheats and Liars

Red sky at night, shepherd's house on fire. The summer had been persuaded to stay on for a few more days, and it was on a lovely warm, balmy, evening that the chilling discovery was made. It was Bethan who noticed first. Something wasn't quite right. Something was missing. The hand of a thief was afoot.

I would have suspected a cat burglar except that it was a theft from a dog. While Barney had been away in kennels, someone, or something, had crept into my back yard and stolen his toys. How low can someone get? Stealing the toys from a dog. I'll tell you what's lower, stealing toys from a six-month-old puppy!

Just to clarify, I feel quite happy switching from dog years to actual time where Barney is concerned. Whichever gives best dramatic effect will be wheeled out and blatantly exploited. It's no different to the tactic that old people employ – the one where, in one breath they elicit sympathy when they tell you that, in their day, they only earned ten shillings a week and then, in the next breath, they tell you how stupid you are, paying so much for things and how cheap things were when they were young. "Aye lad, in them days you could go to the pub with tuppence, drink until your kidneys failed, get a fish supper from the girl in the chippy, wear an over-sized flat cap, buy a tortoise from the market and still have thruppence change." Ah, old people, you can't beat them. Shame.

Barney's 'denty bone' for healthy teeth, two hard plastic bones, a food ball that he would push along with his nose to make the treats fall out, a three-pointed rubber thingy that wouldn't look out of place in an Ann Summers shop, a rubber Kong that you could stuff with food and he would spend all day getting it out again, cuddly toy… the list goes on. They were all missing, but no 'Brucie bonus' for Barney. He didn't do well; he did very badly. I wasn't looking forward to telling him and seeing his little face drop. Even the 'lowest of the low' sign that Bethan had made for his kennel had been stolen. I guess the crook knew that this accolade rightly belonged to them now.

They clearly needed help and obviously had psychological problems. I pondered on what I would do if I caught them. Would I talk the issue through with them? Would I invite them to a self-help workshop? Maybe I could persuade the government to give them an all-expenses paid trip to Alton Towers? Would I employ them in various menial tasks so they could earn some money to buy an iPhone, which would clearly help them out of their desperate state and allow them get some much needed self-respect back? No. I wouldn't even bother to beat them senseless with a large stick, bind their feet and stuff them into a Hessian sack. Instead, I decided if I ever caught them, I would just get Barney to piss on their troubled head.

°°°°°°

When Barney returned from the kennels, he was a different dog – literally. A mistake had been made somewhere along the line and they brought a Dalmatian out. Confusion was resolved and, soon after, Barney was waving goodbye out of the rear window to his new found chums as we drove homewards.

It wasn't only Barney though that had undergone a change. I was regularly being told that I was changing and, what is more, changing for the better. I wasn't aware that I was *that* bad before, but I am sure there will be a steady stream of women ready to testify that they knew my evil twin. I'm not sure how much I buy into this 'adult changeling' theory as it means acceptance of 'bad John', but even *I* felt much more relaxed and easy going than I had done for a long while. Much more than I had been since I left the military and entered 'the wilderness years', if truth be known. Deborah had even started to tell me how I was different until I interrupted with, "Don't," and then, "Stop." I had actually meant to say, "Don't stop," but in between getting the two words out, I did one of those little burps where a bit of sick comes up too, which had put me off my stroke slightly. By the time I had re-composed myself, she had wandered back into the kitchen. On the rare occasion that someone is saying something kind about me I like to make sure they speak at full volume and switch off the television.

However, now I would therefore have to try and interpret how and why these changes were taking place. I know it's not very British to accept praise and even less so to tell everyone about it, but may I remind you of the old maxim,

"If you don't blow your own trumpet, someone else will use it as a pisspot."

Certainly, having a daughter had made me a shadow of my former selfishness and, more recently, the arrival of Barney had given me a renewed sense of responsibility.

He certainly had a lot to do with it and, if I was the great dictator, I'd have all the shorthand typists in the land typing out compulsory orders for everyone to own a pet. Apart from fish, which just make me jealous, a good majority of the other pets love you unreservedly, just for being there. Now, that has to have a positive effect on anyone. And, since I had long ago stopped believing that cats were Catholic and dogs were Protestant, either variety would do. I mean, how good do you feel in those few brief seconds when your Bonzo or Puss comes over to greet you, wanting you to stroke them because they love you so much, and they want to see that you love them too? OK, I appreciate that a cat might be waiting to reprimand you if you've come in late, but you get the idea. As secretaries across the UK turned all those seconds into minutes, we would be reading about thousands upon thousands of feelgood factors. A dog is basically just a funny little buddy who always wants to hang out with you. How can that not make you happy?

I realised how my idea, during the Foot and Mouth epidemic, of using all the sick cows and sheep to clear landmines in former war zones was bad too. I had become more humane.

I appreciate now how sending flowers to my neighbour's wife on the first of every month, just so I could hear the big argument between them was cruel.

I also spent far too much time worrying about small trivial things instead of appreciating that there are people with a lot more to worry about than me. On the eve of the new millennium, with all the talk about the potential havoc caused by the millennium bug, there was me worrying that my toaster might not work, or that I might have to reset the central heating timer, when poor old Stephen Hawking must have been shitting himself.

However, probably none of us were shitting ourselves as much as a certain gentleman from Brighton. I had read somewhere that he commuted up to London every day, and to pass the time, he had started reading The Exorcist on the train. He said he thought it was the most evil book he'd ever read, in fact, so evil that he couldn't even finish it. So, at the weekend, he had gone to the end of Brighton pier and thrown it as far as he could into the sea. His big mistake in all this, however, was telling this to his colleagues, because later that day, one of them went to a bookshop, bought another copy, ran it under a tap and left it in the guy's desk drawer for him to find. I can just imagine the thoughts that ran through his head when he discovered it.

I've never really thought of it before, but maybe that's why there's always been a slight look of horror on Barney's face whenever I've replaced his toy monkey he's just ripped to shreds, with an identical one the next day.

Anyway, we're back in the room. The other thing is that I've never been much of a diplomat, and office politics has always been beyond me. I'd much rather sit at the back of a meeting and play 'bullshit bingo'. (If you have never played before, all you need to do is write in a grid all the pseudo-intellectual business-speak words these highly paid consultant gurus spout. Things like 'think out of the box', 'wow factor', 'etched in stone', 'walk the talk', 'playing hardball', 'mind share', 'strategic fit, 'touch base', 'synergy', 'win-win' etc. As your boss, or some highly paid consultant, sits with his legs apart as if he's got two prickly pears for testicles, and regurgitates these magic words of wisdom as part of his spiel, you cross them off your grid. When you have crossed them all off, you jump up waving your piece of paper and shout "Bullshit!").

I've also never been one for sucking up to the big nobs in the company either. It just leaves a bad taste in your mouth and, anyway I wasn't very good at disguising the fact that I only respected those people who I felt deserved it. It seems that the great and good in business were gradually being replaced by the greedy and mean. Too many hands in pockets and not enough hands on hearts. There are too many people who would be quite willing to betray you with a Judas kiss if they thought they could get some benefit out of it. I didn't really want to be a part of that.

At our last annual conference in some swanky hotel, my boss had boasted, "I'm a country member". I remember alright. In fact, some of the women there gave him the nickname 'The Thrush' because they said he was such an irritating fanny.

Later on, after she eventually finished with the important people in the company, informing them all no doubt that she loved the consultants' talk, but personally preferred to avoid clichés like the plague, the Human Resources Manager wandered over in my direction. If an unenthusiastic hand job had a face… She took a moment to look me up and down and then greeted me with the same sort of kiss that had brought Him down at Gethsemane. I guessed that this could only mean one thing - she had got the course report back.

Six months ago, I had obviously been identified as someone who was in need of 'warm fuzziness' training as I had been selected to go on an external training course. According to Human Resources this was to – 'make me a more balanced individual'. I suspect they were implying that after my time in the forces I might be lacking in tact and finesse. I'd show them they were wrong!

The course was at a conference centre in the Cotswolds in an old stately home, where the radiators rattled like a skeleton having a wank in a biscuit tin. To show I was keen I had arrived early, placed my pad and pencil on the desk next to a particularly attractive young lady and joined her and the others for coffee at the back of the room. She looked full of warm fuzziness. Maybe her warm fuzziness might rub off on me later if I was lucky.

We were then told to move our chairs into a circle. Shit! – I found myself next to a geeky looking librarian type and a bloke who looked like a geography teacher. Still, I could see my potential new friend (or Lindsey, as deduced from her name-badge) sitting almost opposite in her pale-coloured dress (Virgin Mary blue, I do believe).

This clearly wasn't going to be the usual type of presentation that I was used to in the military - where you sit through a slide show of enemy tanks, battleships and fighter planes, and just when you are getting bored, the instructor slips in a slide of a naked woman pretending that he had left it in by mistake. That always got a good laugh.

I wondered if Hugh Hefner did the same when he was trying to decide the Playboy Bunny of the year. Halfway through a show of all the bunnies, would he suddenly slip in a slide of the Russian T-90 battle tank, complete with the 1A4GT integrated fire control system? I'm sure that, after the initial shock, the sweeties would be laughing their little ears off!

Anyway, PowerPoint had spoilt that bit of fun for a whole new generation. Sorry again, that was a digression of a digression. Half of you reading this book are probably wondering what the hell I'm on about. I know how you feel. It's OK for you though, you've just got to read it... I've got to live it!

Back to the course.

We were sitting in a circle and our 'mentor' explained that we would start with an ice breaker. "List the two worst sounds known to mankind". I sat back smugly whilst the others chewed on their pencils and looked deeply engrossed in some internal dilemma.

This was easy! I knew my hours spent making various lists of things hadn't gone to waste!

My three favourite CDs: *Donkey Serenade* by Weddings, Parties, Anything, *Shakespeare My Butt* by The Lowest of the Low and *Get Happy* by Elvis Costello and the Attractions. Favourite song: *What's so funny 'bout peace, love and understanding?* by Nick Lowe, performed by Elvis Costello and the Attractions. Book: *A Mouthful of Rocks* – Christian Jennings. Film: *Dogma* or maybe *School of Rock,* and so on. I could go on, so I will. Ten places to keep a torch, ways to tell if everyone else is an alien except for you, three ways to humiliate ants, where I would visit if I was invisible, signals I would make if I came back as a dog to let people know it was me, which one would I go out with if they both asked me out at the same time – Cameron Diaz or Miss Tucker (I'd probably come down on the side of Miss Tucker) - and a late entry, but an obviously inspired choice - sounds that I don't like.

When our mentor asked for a volunteer to start the session, I was the first on my feet. I looked over at Lindsey and then formally addressed the group.

"The two worst sounds known to mankind are:

1. The sound of metal coat-hangers clanking together.

2. The sound of the washing machine sloshing away."

I even had a spare up my sleeve: the noise of a toilet seat falling down in the middle of the night, but I don't think I really needed that as, I think you'd agree, I'd already nailed it.

I sat back down waiting for the nods of acknowledgement and murmurs of approval from my colleagues – particularly Lindsey. Except everyone just stared at me. Someone coughed, but other than that, just silent stares. I don't know if you can have good silent stares, but even if you can, these weren't. I wondered what had happened. Had they thought I had farted when I sat down? Those chairs sometimes make it sound like that. I hadn't though. I was on my best behaviour.

The mentor spoke. "Lindsey, maybe you would like to tell us what you think are the two worst sounds known to mankind?"

The Virgin Lindsey then arose and told us she believed the first was the sound of a baby crying whilst the rest of the world ignored the plight of poverty in the Third World. There was clapping, some stood up, I could hear people scribbling on their pads. The place was buzzing with, "So true" and, "Oh, yes," comments of appreciation. I just sat there looking down at my pad, felt very red and warm and thought "Fuck". I don't know what they thought the second worst sound was – probably the sound of me spontaneously combusting. Actually, they'd have probably thought that was good. On their turn, someone said silence was the worst sound. That's like saying bald is a hair colour! These people just seemed to be on a different wavelength to me and, to be honest, I'm not sure if I wanted to join them. I felt like I'd been dropped off in a different world and the aliens hadn't briefed me properly.

By the time that something worthy of noting down did eventually come up, I'd taken my pen apart and lost the spring. To add insult to injury, I also discovered later that morning that I apparently suffer from sleep apnoea. At lunch, I thought I'd console myself at the buffet, but there wasn't a pork pie or cheese sandwich to be seen; instead, it was all strange looking healthy options. I reluctantly got myself a humous and chickpea dip along with a coconut water. And by the way, if you've haven't tried coconut water – don't. It tastes like what I would imagine a monkey ejaculating in your mouth would taste like. And I had another two days of this to go!

"So, what did you think of the course?" the lady from HR asked, although I think she already knew the answer.

"Stella, my friend," I replied, "I haven't learnt a thing. If fact, if I came home to find a big, hollow wooden horse outside my house, I'd probably wheel it straight into my front room."

"So where do you see yourself in five years' time?"

"Is that a Tuesday?" I queried.

"Remember what happened to Shakespeare's Yorick," she sighed whilst picking some imaginary lint from her cuff. I told her that as far as I was aware, after Hamlet, he was used to keep pencils in. After this, I think she felt that she had wasted enough of her valuable time on me, since I was failing to catch the pearls of wisdom she was casually discarding, and finished by informing me that it was only a matter of time before someone added the word 'syndrome' after my name. What the hell was that supposed to mean?

OK, I admit I wasn't totally 'a new man' but I was improving and was beginning to see what was important in life, and I think Barney had a lot to do with that.

Most possessions we purchase, we get to make our lives easier, but getting a dog actually makes your life harder. We have to get up to take it for walks, make its food, take care of its welfare and so on. Yet we do all this willingly (most of the time!). What's more, we go out of our way to make our new possession happy by getting it presents, taking it to new places we think it would enjoy, introducing it to new friends etc. I strongly believe that having a dog, or any pet for that matter, causes a paradigm shift in how we behave.

Nothing loves you as unreservedly as a dog. They make your bad days good and your good days better, and having Barney was making me reassess what was really important to me, not least of which was the need to open a packet of biscuits really quietly.

I didn't need a list of all those I was apparently superior to, just to feel good about myself. My dog thinks I'm the best, why should I need a second opinion? Mind you, last night he did bark for hours at a goth butterfly, as he called it (or moth, as you and I and any sensible person would call it), trapped in the porch light, so maybe I shouldn't rely too much on his infallible judgement.

Regardless, I was now a much more relaxed and contented individual.

I know that growing old is unhealthy, but I guess that worldly wisdom had also contributed to why I was much more tolerant. Again, I was just taking a leaf out of Barney's book. Everybody loves him because he doesn't judge people. He just treats all human beings as equals, whether they be grey, grey, grey or grey.

I used to be pretty bitter about some things when I was young, to the extent that, if I bit a lemon, the lemon would make a face, but now I know that all the pent-up grievances in the world won't change anything. What's the point? Don't get me wrong, I'm not saying that I'm going around committing random acts of kindness or senseless acts of beauty, and I'm not exactly dancing like nobody's watching – the last time I did that someone stabbed me with an epi pen - but I am more open-minded. You can never make good wine out of grapes of wrath anyway. Generally, I only get bitter now when I go down the pub.

I was also being told that I was more approachable and listened more. It probably just seemed that way because it takes me a bit longer nowadays to think of a witty one liner to come back with. I normally think of a fantastic one after the other person has just left the room. Still, if people thought I was a nicer guy because of my slow reactions, so be it.

The milkman of human kindness must have visited one morning and left an extra pinta. I had developed 'Socialism of the heart' and it felt good.

"Hello, reader, you are looking good today. Have you done your hair differently? Of course, I love everyone who has bought my book. But you... you're my favourite! I'd never do that thing to your toothbrush where you've got to throw it away as soon as you find out about it. Read on, you splendid thing."

I was learning how to enjoy life more stupidly, and it felt good. T'ai Chi, self-discovery workshops, hugging trees, colonic irrigation? You can shove them up your arse. Just get a daughter, a dog, and some hobbies; get older and get over it.

I looked at my horoscope and, apparently, the moon was in my seventh house. What the hell was that supposed to mean?

。˚。˚。˚

Barney was in his third house so far that week – the kennels, a sleepover at Deborah's and now back to his own home, sweet home.

The work that John, the kennel owner, had put into Barney seemed to have tipped the balance. As he explained, any dog only understands two things: pleasant and unpleasant experiences. If the owner can cause the dog to experience these two totally opposite sensations, then dog training is easy.

When the dog understands you are top dog, the leader of the pack, the worst punishment that a trained dog should suffer is the word, "No," uttered from his master's lips. Praise was at the other end of the spectrum.

When I picked Barney up, we had chatted some more about how to assert yourself as the top dog, before John showed me how theory had become reality. As Barney pottered away to sniff at something or other, John delivered a sharp, "No!" The black one looked up from his sniffery with a devastated, "What have I done wrong now?" face. He genuinely meant it too. It wasn't the sarcastic, "What have I done wrong now?" that Deborah gives me if I am brave enough to tell her off – the one with the long emphasis on the word "now". No, this was genuine concern that he was doing something that he shouldn't be. It was an "Oh My God, what can I do to please the Boss to make up for my wrongdoing?"

John gave him the opportunity with a "Good Boy" and Barney came running to his side, delighted with the fact that he could make up for his misdemeanour. It was like the final piece of the jigsaw, the one that always seems to be missing.

John finished off by saying that Barney had had a blast… I wasn't sure whether he meant that my dog had really enjoyed his training or that he'd had diarrhoea. I thought it best not to delve too deeply.

His first evening's walk round the circuit, after returning home, was a delight and, even with the lead off, Barney never left my side. It was like walking with an invisible lead, as opposed to the old days when I would be walking with an invisible dog. I was keen to apply the lesson to his jumping up too, and was slightly disappointed that he wasn't doing anything wrong for me to correct!

The one thing that hadn't changed though, was his chewing capacity and, by the end of his first day back, the front door 'map' had changed from the outline of Australia to resemble one of Tasmania. And, as my Australian friend Digger will tell you, that is one place Barney would have no desire to visit, following his op.

28

How Long Will Breakfast Be?

Doctor Shit was on the phone. He had gone camping.

It was a weekend trip, and the six of them - his wife Linda, along with their children, Ceri, Gethin, Rebecca and Joseph - had set out, pitching the tent on the Friday evening, looking forward to a lovely weekend in the Welsh hills.

Linda had gone out on the Saturday morning and come back with bacon, sausages, beans and eggs that were arranged carefully around the frying pans. The children sat round expectantly with a knife and fork in each hand.

When Paul starts a story like that, you know it's not going to have the happy ending it should. It's not going to be a funny, "How Long will Breakfast be?" – "Four inches – it's a sausage" type tale. No, this was going to be something else altogether.

Meanwhile, back at the campsite, Paul turned on the gas bottle. 'PSSSsssst' – the gas had run out.

No worries. Paul then hopped in the car to get a refill from any of the seven local garages. Paul returned half an hour later, reporting that none of the seven garages had any gas.

All six then got in the car to make the seventeen mile trip to Brecon where there *must* be somewhere that had gas.

Sixteen miles into the trip, BRRRrrrrrrrr, the car conked out.

The RAC were called; the RAC arrived and looked at the car; the RAC went away and came back with a low loader to put the car on, because the car was totally dead. The RAC then took Paul to the campsite; RAC man waited patiently whilst Paul took the tent down, emptied the portable toilet and chucked the uncooked breakfast away, and hoisted trailer onto back of low loader. The RAC then took Paul and family home – hungry.

Not a good weekend so far. The car was taken to the local garage, and they rang him on the Monday to say it would cost £1,100 to repair. I asked if he'd have to pay for that out of his savings. After a few minutes of maniacal laughter, Paul reminded me that he had four children, and that the term 'savings' had left his vocabulary many years earlier. Fair point.

It hadn't been a good start to the week for him. As for me, it was the start of what should be an excellent week. I was off to the circus, and by circus, I mean work.

It was an important day. After the bad course incident, I had been in the doghouse. Here was an opportunity to show that I could be a team player and make up for the course debacle.

I had arranged to meet my boss, the Security Services Director, to discuss an imminent security operation. First though, I got up extra early to take Barney for a full leisurely ramble around the circuit. I was getting a bit concerned that the only thing that my pup associated with going outside was having fun, walks and playing. He didn't understand the concept of work, so did he just think I was leaving him each day just to have fun elsewhere with some other dogs? And whilst I'm on, I was never sure whether he thought I was using him as bait to catch an owl when I took him out for his night-time wee, but that's another matter. In fact, just forget I mentioned it.

I planned to sit down and talk through it with him soon, but in the meantime, I was hoping that the extra effort I'd put in this morning would tide me over. However, the judgemental look he gave me when we returned made me question my timing.

After this sticky-up haired morning walk, I planned to clear the car of the assorted Barney debris and accoutrements (as I was going to be driving the boss), before getting ready for our meeting. With Barney ensconced in the house, I ethnically cleansed the vehicle and was going back into the house to get ready. This is the point at which I started to doubt Barney's new-found angelic status. He had locked me out!

He hadn't yet mastered the mortice key operation, but his little paws had managed to push the bolt across. I stood and pondered on my predicament. As a good security professional, all the windows were closed, of course, so climbing through one was not an option, and calling a locksmith would be no good as the locks were fine; it was an internal bolt that was the problem. Barney obviously hadn't thought this through properly as I hadn't prepared his breakfast yet, and his little pea-like brain wasn't able to link the *"Unlock bolt,"* and *"Have breakfast,"* thoughts that were pottering around aimlessly somewhere within. I fetched Bethan's folding hairbrush with a mirror on the handle from the car and, going down on my knees, pushed it through the letterbox. I could see the bolt and the big knob that Barney had pushed across while all the time, an excited dog was leaping up to lick my fingers and grab the new toy that, in his mind, I was clearly pushing through just for him.

They say a good way to catch a monkey is to put a monkey nut in a bottle. The monkey can fit his hand in but, when his fist is clenched around the nut, he can't get his hand back out and, being a stupid greedy fellow, he gets stuck. So it was that I was stuck. I couldn't get my hand back out with the brush held tight and, if I loosened my grip, Barney would grab it and run off. Worse still if the mirror dropped and broke, it would be seven years bad luck for me and forty nine years bad luck for Barney. The musical sit competition that Barney had won a month earlier suddenly inspired me, so I sang the song that had instigated the original zoo trip and then, just as suddenly, stopped.

"The bushes dance, and the world outside just makes you tense,
So once a year you stick you head out to see if the coast is clear,
Thylacine, the way they treated you was a tragedy,
And I don't know the things you must have seen,
You're a 10,000-year-old has been

In another place, on a school excursion I first saw your face,
Through a glass case
And I had a million questions and the least of which was ...
Why?
But I knelt down and saw no answer in your marble for an eye.

You're famous...
The Marsupial Elvis
You've been seen in places I know you've never been
SIT!"

As he sat, the brush was quickly withdrawn. After a rummage through the shed, I returned with a bungee rope. I couldn't fit the brush/mirror in as well, so the bungee was left to go it alone. I fed it through the letterbox in the general direction of the knob but, as I imagined the hook to be in about the right place, the rope went limp and floppy. This was an experience that I was unfamiliar with, and if any girl tells you otherwise, she's a bloody liar. This was a job for a wire coat hanger!

I don't know if you have any wire coat hangers in your house, but it seems they are now an object of derision, and their plastic moulded counterparts have all but driven them into extinction. The traditional old hangers that left a nice line across the place where your trousers were folded over are not welcome anymore in polite society, it seems. I tried next door, but 'Bill's replacement' didn't have any either and things were starting to look bleak.

Then, into the breach, strode Jack. Jack lives two doors down and is the type of guy you would want as an uncle. He always seems to know the right thing to do and, in the case of the door-locking dog, he was not going to disappoint. He too had succumbed to the lure of the moulded hanger but, being Jack, he had a wire one squirrelled away in his own shed for just such a 'dog locking door' occasion. Equipped with the hanger, converted into a knob-hooking device, we returned to my house. I must admit, as I knelt there, peering through the letter box at the brush/mirror and then poking my hook device through and scraping it about, I felt more like a back street abortionist than a dog rescuer but, within seconds, the dirty deed was done, and breakfast and dog were once again reunited.

Meanwhile, I quickly hurried upstairs and got ready to leave. I've got to say that The Bangles made a Manic

Monday sound a lot more fun than it actually is. As I drove down, I rang my boss to let him know I was running late. Barney had become a Shenanigator – one who instigates shenanigans. However, as I explained, I felt like a schoolboy, saying that the dog had eaten his homework and I sensed that my boss felt the same way. When I eventually arrived, Karen, his secretary, greeted me with a Machiavellian smile and asked what else the 'dog' had done. Had he deleted the week's itinerary I was supposed to have sent the previous Friday, or maybe he had persuaded me not to action the things I should have done after the last meeting? Had he deleted the operational risk report off my computer or been sending emails pretending to be me again? Once! It was only the once that I had sent an email to her starting, "Hello, I know you are busty". It was a typo because, as it happens, I was busy too, and I didn't try and blame it on Barney, and I thought we had cleared all this up in the disciplinary, anyway. The irony of the irony being lost on me wasn't lost on me.

Anyway, call me intuitive, but I suspect she was not being altogether straight with me, and it even led me to question her sincerity some time ago when she had complimented me, saying that I made a good cup of tea. I told her that I was going to turn over a new leaf, but she told me that I didn't need to turn over a new leaf so much as uproot a whole forest. The room then went silent, but I'm sure that if I listened really carefully, I could just about hear the sound of my employment contract being torn up in the office next door.

29

Project X - A Place Oddity

The sky was filled with birds flying south and the windscreen wipers on the cars seemed to be waving them goodbye. It was as if the weather had realised that it was being too nice for that time of year and felt that it had to make an extra effort to be cold and wet, just to make up for it. The rain was torrential, and I was expecting to see two of every animal wandering down the road at any moment. Perfect!

I rang Deborah and arranged a rendezvous at Pity Me. The original shoot hadn't quite captured the 'pitiful' element but now, with the rain and cold, a snap of me shivering beneath the sign would be ideal. If we weren't miserable enough in the first picture, we had certainly made up for it now. Things were definitely a bit strained between us and I'm sure the 'half a dog' dedication had kicked off this whole episode.

As the rain came down, with the cold wind biting into me, I stood below the sign as if it were some type of strange, old-fashioned advisory caption to explain away the situation to anyone who was in any doubt about how I was feeling. I tried to think what the opposite was of 'saying cheese'. I guess it must be chalk. I decided against saying it out loud as it might look as if I was pouting at the camera. Instead, I just thought it. I thought about the scary man we had seen the first time round too and I was scared, thinking of chalk, cold, wet and miserable. This is what they must mean by suffering for your art. Excellent!

Deborah had brought her teddy bear along to the shoot and that could only mean one thing – a trip to Bearpark was on the cards. As we drove on through the rainy streets to Beau Repair, it looked anything but a beautiful retreat. I'm sure, if the Normans had seen it like this, we would be converting 'Merde' into an unusual, Anglicised place name now, but they didn't, so we're not.

We found an old rusty sign for Bearpark Colliery, the type with a hand on the end pointing the way. Barney stayed behind to guard the car as we hurried over to the sign. The area looked a bit dodgy but, even though he wasn't much of a barker, I'm sure he would put up a decent fight if anyone tried to break in. I'm not so sure what he would be like at putting fires out though. As Debs poked Teddy's head over the top of our pointing signpost, I took the photo. I suppose, as a model for the calendar, Teddy should have been covered in body oil so he would glisten in the light of the flickering orange streetlamp, but it would only have become matted in his fur.

It would have slowed us down too. We wanted to be in, get the job done and out, before any locals saw us. That's the thing about these places with funny or strange names. The locals seem to be overly protective and take any mockery of the name of their hometown personally. Goodness knows what the Twats, (or whatever you call the locals from Twatt) would do if they caught you sniggering as you photographed their sign. They seem exceedingly proud of their hometown and even have a Twatt web site which lists, amongst other things, Twatt Celebrities and Twatt eating places. My kinda place.

۰ ۰ ۰ ۰ ۰ ۰

We were on a roll. Well, I was anyway. Deborah didn't seem to share my enthusiasm and I spent the rest of the evening persuading her that the sooner we could get the calendar finished, the sooner life could go back to normal although, as she pointed out, I would probably just embark on another stupid quest as soon as life became *too* normal. I think she liked it best when it was just an idea. I told her of my new name for Project X – 'A Place Oddity' in an effort to cheer her up but that didn't work. In the end, I agreed that we would do one more sign tomorrow and that would be it for the rest of the weekend.

۰ ۰ ۰ ۰ ۰ ۰

The next day was bright, dry and fresh as we set off – destination Cockfield. The name literally means a field full of cocks. It was a lovely village, with a well-tended war memorial, a couple of nice-looking pubs and wide, clean streets. There were a number of wriggly tin buildings on the outskirts of the place that looked as if they could have been garages once upon a time. They were covered in black pitch and some had small windows, obscured with cobwebs. In contrast to the orderliness of the Cockfield streets, the garages seemed to have been plonked, in a haphazard fashion, on the outskirts. What I would have given to have one of my very own – my own big shed. Surely, that's every man's dream. I would have an old desk in there, with a vice attached to the end of it. There would be a pile of old papers on the floor, tied up with string, along with some old copies of *National Geographic*. There would probably be some copies of *Look and Learn* too and an old encyclopaedia. I'd have lots of jam jars on a shelf, containing bits of screws and nails and a couple of bottles of fortified wine on the end. An old piece of carpet would do for the floor and an oil heater, with one leg missing, would warm the place up. I would have all the gear as well, in case anyone wanted any wood planing or the chain putting back on their bike.

The seating would consist of an old armchair and an old wooden school chair, in case I wanted to do a bit of writing in there. There would be lots of other stuff too. It would be cluttered, but not messy, and have the pleasant smell of an empty tin of biscuits. An old clear glass bulb, without a shade, would hang from the roof, with that sort of woven material covering the wires. Barney would just curl up on the piece of carpet while a stray cat, that seemed to have come with the big shed, would sleep in an old cardboard box, lined with a blanket, next to some useful bits of spare wood. Barney and the unnamed cat would just ignore each other, and an old, half-used tin of pitch would sit by the door.

The sign welcoming us to Cockfield was yellow and blue, on a stone plinth. To make it more amusing, I decided to get my cock out and have it photographed next to the sign. Technically, it wasn't a cockerel but a rubber chicken, but I doubt whether anyone would look that closely. Again, like the teddy, it was decided not to oil it up. It was a prop for one of my magic tricks and I didn't fancy cleaning the slippery thing afterwards. Shots were then taken from several angles, with the chicken in various poses.

Once the shooting was over, I bid goodbye to the big sheds, and we drove over the cattle grid and away. I liked Cockfield and, although she wasn't saying much, I think Deborah did too.

30

The Secret of My Excess

Concurrent Activity: that was what was always drilled into me in the armed forces. While you are at your orders briefing, the soldiers can be getting their weapons prepared or kit organised. A lot of armed forces life is spent waiting, so there was lots of concurrent activity opportunity. Getting a brew on was a particular favourite of mine.

I had a problem and it needed sorting fast. Deborah was not in the happiest, or indeed erudite, frames of mind I've ever found her in. Apparently, I was becoming (expletives deleted) obsessed by this project and, as is normally the case, I think she was probably right – it was taking a toll on our friendship. The word 'autistic' had been used. I am not sure if that particular word can be used in a complimentary way but, even if it can be, it was not being used as such in this instance. Even Bethan agreed, and told me I was fixated. They were right too. If I'm involved in a project, I usually focus on that and everything else goes out the window. With me, things that start as hobbies usually become obsessions and eventually end up as grounds for divorce. This was the secret of my excess. I needed to complete Project X and try and get things back to normal as soon as possible.

As a consequence, morning walks were no longer mindless meanderings and had, instead, transformed into brainstorming sessions as I racked my brain for other place names that could grace the calendar. We were only three months short, but those three months were proving elusive, although Deborah hadn't helped things by (rather selfishly, in my opinion) putting the veto on my photo suggestion for 'Wide Open'. To be quite honest, the maps were not being at all helpful either.

As a sailor, when navigating across the Atlantic, by day we took sun sightings, and by night, we established our position by moon and star observation. Global positioning was in its infancy and, anyway, in case of war, the Russians would probably target the satellites. I would use a sextant that hadn't changed that much from the one developed back in 1757. If it was a celestial sighting, first I would establish where particular stars in the sky were, using complex astronomical tables, then, after using the sextant to calculate the angle of the star from the horizon, another series of calculations would allow me to draw a line of position on the chart. After a few more sightings of specific stars, the chart would have a number of lines of position, criss-crossing. Where these lines intercepted represented the position of the ship, which in this case was HMS Fearless.

In mitigation, it is a complex and lengthy process, compounded by the fact that the ship was constantly steaming towards the Americas, as well as being buffeted by the Atlantic swell as the sightings were taken. My lines of position would normally criss-cross to resemble a cocked hat type of affair, and I could reasonably assume that we were within five to ten miles of the middle of the hat. That sort of give in our actual position was fine as we were in the middle of the ocean on a big blue chart, but it can also be reasonably assumed that celestial navigation was not my forte. However, compared to the people who drew up my road atlas, I felt like a new age Vasco da Gama.

After a study of our map, we had set off into North Yorkshire to capture such beauties as Blubberhouses, Kettlesing Bottom and an even smaller New York than its Tyneside namesake. It was a fresh, bright autumn morning and the light at the end of the tunnel seemed very bright too. Three months to go, and three places to visit. I had considered driving over to Wham on the way but decided against it after what happened last Christmas.

My mind was full of thoughts and questions as we drove into the low September sun. Blubberhouses was a sort of 'Octobery' month, or it may even be given the coveted December spot. I could understand a Blubberhouses near the coast too, but in the middle of land-locked Yorkshire? My investigations hadn't even managed to find an origin for this strange name and what would the hamlet or village look like? Wobbly?

After passing the massive golf balls that formed the not-so-secret American Menwith Hill Listening Station, we saw the sign for Blubberhouses seven miles ahead. We drove on excitedly and I asked Deborah to keep an eye out for signs as we got closer. But that was the problem; there were no more signs. There were signs for Dacre, West End and Pateley Bridge, but nothing for Blubberhouses. We scoured the area, leaving no dodgy B road or lane unscathed in our search – it had just vanished. We drove up past fields with sheep in, past fields *without* sheep in, past what looked like a graveyard for trees, with their little wooden posts as headstones, past tumbledown barns, but not once past Blubberhouses.

Deborah finally piped up saying that, when she had lived in Doncaster, she went to the Lake District via 'Blubberhouses Way'. And I think that's all Blubberhouses was – an 'over there, somewhere' type place; a 'Blubberhouses Way' type direction, only to be taken seriously by non-Yorkshire folk like me. I'm sure it was their little in-joke that even the council had bought into by erecting signs – not a 'Blubberhouses Way' sign but a specific, 'Blubberhouses – 7 miles' sign. I couldn't just have the sign in the calendar without having set foot in the village. It would be a betrayal of everything that the Place Oddity stood for. I wasn't quite sure *what* it stood for actually, but a sign to nowhere just didn't seem right (although a sign to No Place, of course, was fine).

Anyway, I knew my target audience. If I told them there were three billion stars in the sky, they would believe me but, if I told them the bench had just been painted and the paint was still wet, they would have to touch it, just to make sure. Also, if they ever did make the journey North, visiting Blubberhouses would definitely be on their list of things to do. It wasn't a good start to the day. Disaster number one. I refused to let it get to me; we still had another two to knock off.

° ° ° ° ° °

I wasn't convinced that New York was all that funny. After all, there was the actual York itself just down the road, but I suppose, if I could get the photograph to include a rural sleepy village instead of a city metropolis, it might raise a wry smile. It looked tiny on the map and that was ideal.

There is a mill in New York. I knew that because, as we entered the place, a big sign told us that we couldn't turn down that way to it. There is an industrial estate in New York too, and I know that because I saw a big sign for it as I left the place. In between the mill and the industrial estate, which is a distance of about a hundred yards, there is a fire station. It has the sort of neon sign outside that you would normally see outside a dodgy gambling bar (the type where the girls would wear T-shirts saying things like 'Liquor in the front and poker in the rear'). It also has a bus stop with a rather impressive shelter made of stone, with 'New York' chiselled into the side so the bus drivers know where they are. I guess they need it because, search as I might (and I know I search pretty well as, on more than one occasion, Deborah has told me that I have eyes like a shithouse rat), I could find no conventional sign for the spot. No sign, no photo, no month, no smiles all round. Disaster number two.

Still, we had Kettlesing Bottom to finish the day with. The 'Kettlesing' bit was alright, I suppose but, being puerile, I thought the 'Bottom' bit might crack a smile. We found Kettlesing easily enough (and a lovely village it is too), by following the well-posted signs for the village. At last, some order seemed to have been restored. The 'Bottom' must be close, and we even found a sign for Kettlesing Head, which was strange because there wasn't a 'Head' on the map. In my experience though, the 'Bottom' was never that far from the 'Head' so the search continued. More signs instead of fewer appeared, which was a novelty. We smiled and we searched and searched and searched. All to no avail – here was disaster number three.

The audacity to have a 'Kettlesing Head' sign, but no

'Kettlesing Bottom'. It's on the map! Have the sign people never thought to look at the map? What did they think they were playing at?

Still, I didn't have to let it spoil my day, but I decided I would. And why, oh why, did the bastards invariably put the places we wanted to find in the crack between two pages?!!

Great Cock Up is rumoured to be in Cumbria. The 'Up' means valley and this valley was apparently occupied by a cock, a woodcock probably. But can I find it? The place I mean, not the woodcock, although I can't find that either.

It's becoming an epidemic. I live near Shiney Row, where we have the Shiney Row Cobbler, Shiney Row College and we even have 'Shiney New Appliances' – a shop that sells shiny new appliances, as luck would have it, but there is no 'Shiney Row – You are here' sign. I know because we looked for one that night.

As I was getting increasingly wound up, Deborah tried to calm me down by telling me that everyone was just doing their best, but then I remembered that I mostly do things half-heartedly, so how do I know that everyone else isn't just doing the same? Then I became even more angry because of their deception.

How those Frenchies, with their 'In' and 'Out' signs to their towns must be laughing their berets off, as they weave all over the road, trying to control their onion-laden bikes, shrugging and making a "Haw he haw he haw," sound. Two can play at this game. That's the last time I buy any of *their* letters.

* * * * * *

My mood didn't improve at all the next day. It was a leaving do for someone from work. Sadly, not mine, but some lucky fucker who had managed to tunnel out of the organisation. I was standing at the bar with the others, coiled like a spring waiting for the drift towards the dining table. It always ended up the same. If I wasn't quick enough, I'd end up sitting on the boring end of the table with people talking about year-end results, margins and strategic business plans. At the other end of the table, people would be laughing and misbehaving, talking about all kinds of dirty, depraved stuff... that was where I should be! Worst case scenario would be a whole evening sitting next to a guy they called 'Shit Crack' because his banter was so rubbish.

Then the age-old dilemma. Have I got time to pop for a piss before it all starts? No, no, hang on, John, as soon as you go, they'll all meander over to the table and you'll be left with the reject seats next to the blokes with the humour by-pass. Good thinking John... I'll wait.

So, I wait, and wait... and everyone is still milling about and chatting at the bar. Damn... I've wasted the opportunity... I could have gone and dropped the kids off while they were all chatting. Fuck it, let's go for it, John. If you walk out the door, and then run down the corridor to the toilets, you can still get a quick piss, run back and wander nonchalantly back in through the door, exchange some pleasantries and still be in pole position for the move to the dining table.

GO! Big steps to door smiling and nodding at colleagues, out of the door into corridor, sprint down corridor, concurrent activity... unzip as push bog door open, member out ready, ignore shocked look from bloke coming out of bog, urinals busy, quick think... push into trap, Hitler piss (you're a genius John... this is working like clockwork!... even time to make little joke to fellow pissers; "This water's cold!"), finish, unexplained little shudder, shake, zip, wash hands, no time to dry, run up corridor, walk into room triumphantly. SHIT!

Curse you, Donoghue - you and your stupid plans!

Everyone was seated happily, breaking their bread rolls and discovering that the hardness of the butter is inversely proportional to the softness of the bread. Above it all, a big finger, invisible to everyone else but sadly only too visible to me, was pointing at the only remaining seat. To the left of the big finger was seated Shit Crack, to the right was the Thrush. I slowly did the walk of shame and took my seat, whilst managing a feeble and unconvincing grin.

Gradually, as the evening wore on, I began to lose the will to live. As the Thrush talked to me, I could see his lips move but he was prattling on like a lonely person at a bus stop, and all I could hear was a 'blah blah blah' as I strained to catch the fun at the other end of the table. I could just about overhear someone describing how they had taken a laxative and a sleeping tablet on the same night and woke, to find he was covered in paste. Through the raucous laughter I could just about make out someone else telling the tale of when his girlfriend went to the... then suddenly, oh shit! The Thrush's lips stopped moving. I've got to say something now. Was it a sad tale or happy tale? Will a laugh and a nod suffice? Is he expecting a response?

The Thrush looked at me expectantly. I glanced over at Shit Crack. He had his eyebrows raised in a sort of 'What do you think about that then?' type expression. Why-o-why didn't I take up smoking a pipe? This would have been the ideal time to look pensive and buy some time by puffing away for a minute or so. Instead, I sat like a teabag for a few seconds before I decided to resort to my tactic of choice – change the subject entirely.

"Do you know what the two worst sounds known to mankind are..?"

By the end of the evening, I had convinced myself that it would be perfectly acceptable to use violence to get a decent seat next time.

31

Blubberhouses Revisited

I had calmed down sufficiently by the following Wednesday to reconsider my rashness in writing off the Blubbery one. I was due at Leeds/Bradford Airport and I thought a quick detour wouldn't do any harm.

I approached the area from a different direction to last time, and eventually picked up a sign for Blubberhouses. 'Blubberhouses 7' it read. I drove in the direction indicated for half a mile until I reached the next sign. For some bizarre reason, it read 'Blubberhouses $5\frac{1}{2}$'. I drove on until I reached the next one, which indicated 'Blubberhouses 6'. Clearly the blubbery nature of the place meant that even the council couldn't pinpoint where it was. I continued along the road until I came to 'Blubberhouses 3' but then, at the next junction, ten yards further down the road, we had apparently gone backwards as the sign indicated 'Blubberhouses $3\frac{1}{4}$'. As I proceeded, I found 'Blubberhouses 3' again. This was the last time the council were prepared to commit themselves because, after that, it was just general 'Blubberhouses – This Way' type signs. I set the mileometer to measure the distance from the last specific indicator and duly stopped three miles on. There was no Blubberhouses village, not even a single Blubbery house. I had gone 'Blubberhouses Way'. At least, if you are sent to Coventry, there is somewhere you can call home.

As sad a confession as it may be, I considered myself something of an expert on signing. In wartime, one of the prime functions of the Military Police (not to be confused with the Regimental Police, whose main duty is to beat you up) is to get the troops and supplies to and from the front line, and we spend a lot of time practising signing routes. You may have noticed them as you drive around. The signs are normally attached to posts about headlight height by the side of the road, or attached to existing road signs. Basically, an arrow indicates the direction to the front, whilst an arrow with a line at the end indicates the way back. There is also a name on each sign, like 'Dog' or 'Crab', so soldiers know they are following 'dog' route instead of various road numbers. The point I'm making is that all the routes lead somewhere and, when you get there, you have a sign informing you that you have arrived. So far, Project X had been plagued by either roads to nowhere or places that existed on maps, but with no signs to them at all.

I might be a confused man, but I was also a man without pride when it came to finishing the Place Oddity. I needed to fill in three more months on the calendar, with a depleting supply of odd place names. I quickly got out of the car, photographed the sign and drove off before security at Menwith Hill reported me to the police.

* * * * *

I like to know the history of the places I visit and how the village acquired its name, especially if it is an unusual one.

That morning, we were off to Quaking Houses, a small mining village near Stanley in County Durham but, as much as I tried, I couldn't discover why it was called that. Maybe one of the houses has fallen down because the ground became unstable with the mining works. Perhaps it was on the Durham equivalent of the San Andreas Fault, except there was no Mexican to blame over here. Maybe it was something religious to do with Quakers. Perhaps, once upon a time, a Mr Quaking had lived there. There were a number of villages called '*Something* Houses' in the vicinity. Obviously, we have the 'Scarlet Pimpernel' that is Blubberhouses but, not too far away, there is also a Halfpenny Houses, with Burnthouses only a few miles away from that. They were starting to sound like places the three little piggies would build.

Quaking Houses is on top of a hill and seemed to consist of a number of busy back-to-back streets, with beautifully tended fronts. The backs all had low walls, where a blackboard would have been hung out when the mine was still going. The miners living in the houses would write down what time they wanted to be up for their shift, and the colliery would send a man to wake them up at the designated hour – a sort of human alarm clock. This was done by a person called a 'knocker-upper'. Sometimes they used a big stick to bang on your bedroom window, or occasionally they had a pea shooter, and would shoot peas at your window until you got up. Who knocked the knocker-upper up though, remains a mystery.

I'm not sure if the term 'knocked up' meaning that someone is pregnant also comes from the knocker-upper. Maybe a lonely housewife invited him in for tea and crumpets after her husband had gone to work and the rest is history.

Quaking Houses was a logical sort of place, with street names like First, Second, Third and Fourth Street. There was a colliery wheel embedded in the village green, along with two coal carts, to commemorate the mining heritage. At the bottom of the hill was a park, dedicated in memory of the dead from both World Wars, along with a couple of churches, one of which had the shiniest Jesus I have ever seen on a large wooden cross. It came over as the sort of place that would have a strong sense of community. Sadly though, it wasn't a Thankful Village.

A Thankful Village was one where all those who volunteered to fight in The Great War survived. Of the tens of thousands of villages and towns in England and Wales there are only fifty three parishes identified where all the serving personnel came back home. There are only fourteen 'Doubly Thankful' villages which lost no one in the First or Second World Wars.

We took the photograph to get in both the road sign and the coal carts. This would be November.

I looked around to see if there was anything that would give an indication of how the place got its name, but drew a blank. I guess it just evolved over the decades.

Evolution amazes me, although it generally happens too slowly to be a true spectator sport.

All dogs started as wolves, I guess, from pretty amiable ones like Barney, through to real nutcases who would tear your head off as soon as look at you. You have big, sturdy beasts through to ones that look like a long sausage. You can clearly see the proud-looking dogs with a strong work ethic who have been bred to assist man, while others must frankly be ashamed of themselves, being raised just to travel around in a handbag. Mind you, if evolution was all it was cracked up to be, they would have grown an extra pair of arms by now. A dog that can run really fast, open his own tins of food and, more importantly, shovel up his own poop – now that's what I'd call proper evolution! And instead of all that woofing, they should learn to speak. Haven't they noticed how useful it is for us humans? I keep telling Barney that if he could only say one word, we'd be rich... as long as it wasn't 'sausages'. That's been done before. And what's this about dogs only seeing in black and white? Even if they did ever learn to drive, it would be chaos at the traffic lights. "Do I stop when the light turns grey, or do I go when it turns grey?"

Despite all this though, you can see how humans have had a controlling interest in the way the species has developed.

Plant evolution is another thing altogether. It seems to me that plants were set up from the get-go, ready to take advantage of their environment. In my garden alone, there are a variety of species, all with different characteristics. It's almost like they had a list of qualities to choose from when they were setting out. If they chose some particular characteristic, there were pros and cons.

Plant: "I want to be a quick grower so I can spread quickly."

God: "OK, but you'll have to have shallow roots, which means that you can be cleared easily."

Plant: "Oh, how about me being really pretty then, with flowers and things so people want to cultivate me?"

God: "OK, but that means people will want to pick you too, you realise?"

Plant: "How about me being poisonous or thorny so that people won't want to pick me?"

God: "OK, but they won't want to cultivate you in

their gardens, will they? Fair's fair now, plant – you can't have it all ways."

Plant: "What about the Rose?"

God: "Doh! That happened on my day off. It's the last time I let one of those bloody Scraphim stand in for me! Last week he let through a bendy yellow fruit and the week before that it was a platypus. Jesus Christ, no wonder people think I move in mysterious ways!"

32

Victim of Geography

For some reason, Barney had turned on the ones he loved most. His blanket bed, which he seemed to love to the extent that he would try to hump it, had big chunks bitten out of it. I also came down to find that my walking shoes and trainers had been strategically chewed to render them useless. Perhaps he had seen the state I was in when I returned from my run and wanted none of it.

He must have had some dark secret to hide as well because the bank statement in that morning's post had been shredded. Was he ordering stuff on the phone or online that he didn't want me to know about? Maybe it was a surprise for me for Christmas? Actually, that thought only came to me later. At the time, I was convinced that he must be up to no good. In fact, it's a good bet that he *was* up to no good.

I pondered on what might have caused this. The previous evening, I had given him some left-over vegetables with his dinner, which must have been the four vegetables of the apocalypse as far as he was concerned. If Bethan drinks cheap fizzy pop, she gets hyperactive on some kind of sugar high. I should have remembered that giving children too much sugar voids the warranty. Barney must have had the vegetable equivalent as it had driven his existing chewing habit into overdrive.

He clearly knew that what he had done was wrong, as he made a special effort to be my friend on that morning's walk. Even when I threw the ball and it bounced off his head by accident (yes, it was an accident) before landing in the stingy nettles, he made three valiant attempts to retrieve it. He eventually emerged, with the ball and so many 'stingies' in his mouth that I was stung when I took it off him, but I gave him the benefit of the doubt on this. Ball bouncing on head and hidden stingies were both accidents. No specialist personal injury solicitors were summoned. He seemed happy enough now, sitting there looking pleased with himself because he had just caught an airborne currant. I didn't have the heart to tell him that he'd just eaten a fly.

Regardless, maybe he was becoming frustrated with Project X too, but there was only one remaining month to fill.

We had both been amused by the legendary newspaper headline 'East Fife 4, Forfar 5', but we had now discovered our very own place name headline, 'Nasty man weds Ugley woman'. Apparently, there is a village called Nasty down in Essex, with Ugley not that far away. They even have an Ugley Women's Institute. Just to balance the issue, in the village of Idle in Yorkshire they have the splendidly named Idle Working Men's Club. It's had thousands of requests for affiliate membership and even the club logo - a man leaning on a shovel - helps to give the impression that the Idle Working Men's Club is just that.

It's a shame, of course, that this isn't a sports book as sporting quotes are ten a penny. Take 'The bowler's

Holding, the batsman's Willey'. In case you're not aware, Michael Holding was one of the best fast bowlers to have ever played Test Cricket, nicknamed 'Whispering Death' due to his silent light-footed run up to the bowling crease, and Peter Willey was an English batsman.

My own particular favourite is 'Kournikova has given us a semi to remember.' She always does.

Crime can also generate some decent headlines. A budding tabloid writer more than a century ahead of his time penned the headline 'Bastard stole my horse' in an 1866 copy of the Shields Daily News. The report actually referred to John Bastard, a notorious horse thief who was up to his shenanigans again. More recently the Worcester Observer's 'Drunken man threw crisps in dry cleaners and shook fist in bakers' is vying with 'Woman in sumo wrestler suit assaulted her ex-girlfriend in gay pub after she waved at man dressed as Snickers bar' to demonstrate how the country is falling apart.

Perhaps the most British headline of all time is 'Sex festival in Tunbridge Wells sparks concerns about parking' whilst the Somerset Gazette's 'Drive-by yoghurt attack on crochet teacher's haberdashery leaves her shaken' wouldn't be amiss in Notes from the East Williamston Scene.

Still, place names do have their own potential. How about Pennycomequick with Brown Willy? That's two places by the way, the first in Devon, the other in Cornwall. Westward Ho! is the only place I could find that is named after a book and has an exclamation mark as part of the place name, and Deborah noted that some places we had been looking for were difficult to find and that most men find it hard to locate Clitheroe. Oh, I see what she's made me write. I feel dirty, telling you that now.

Elton John said sorry was the hardest word, but he had clearly never been to Llanfairpwllgwyngyllgogerychwyrndrobwllllantysiliogogogoch in Anglesey, which couldn't be included on two counts. Firstly, it was out of our area and, secondly, I didn't have a wide-angle lens. Muff would be easier to fit in but was, unfortunately, beyond our catchment area. However, it does boast Ireland's oldest scuba diving group, the Muff Diving Club.

Occasionally, people who live in some of these places do actually have a sense of humour and take the mickey out of themselves. Dull in Perthshire, for example, is twinned with Boring in Oregon and Bland in New South Wales, whilst Climax in the USA has "more than just a feeling" as their town slogan and may, or may not, be twinned with Spunk Creek in Minnesota.

Elsewhere, in Norway, Hell does actually freeze over, Dildo in Canada has a bit of a buzz about it (although squatters are frowned upon), whilst Anus in France is the back of beyond. Germany has a Wank (and you can even get a Wank Pass for the cable car). If you close your eyes and think of England, there is the Hole of Horcum in Yorkshire, and Wilsford cum Lake is in Wiltshire, but before you visit, if you want to be extra careful, France has a Condom.

Austria, though, doesn't find it amusing in the least when you mess with their Fucking signs. In fact, they got so unhappy that the angry Fuckers (or whatever you call the residents of Fucking) recently voted to change the name of their village from Fucking to Fugging, even though the place has a proud history dating back to the eleventh century. That'll Fugging teach us!

"What's the big Fucking joke?" railed the mayor. "It's puerile. Every American seems to care only about The Sound of Music (the 1965 film shot around nearby Salzburg) and the Japanese want to see Hitler's birthplace in Braunau, but for you British, it's all about Fucking!"

Apart from the obvious strange names, the scary thing about living in Great Britain is that a lot of names don't seem strange until an outsider points them out. It's that non-barking dog thing.

Crook in County Durham is just another ex-mining town, with nothing strange about it until you apply for a job with the police and tell them that you attended Crook School. Try to be taken seriously when you live in Derbyshire and tell people that you went to Clowne School.

"Did you have to wear big shoes and an orange wig?"

Maybe, though, we have got it easy. How do people react in America when you say that you come from Wanker's Corner in Oregon, Horneytown in North Carolina, or Monkey's Eyebrow in Kentucky?

They might laugh at us for needing a licence to be able watch the telly, but I think they drew the short straw (yes, foreign readers, unbelievable as it may sound, just as you may need a licence to own a shotgun or to drive a car, you also need a licence just to watch the telly in this country!).

Then again, there are short straws and there are shorter straws. I would guess that, if you come from the tranquil isolated retreat for outdoor enthusiasts in the foothills of Ohio, you may be used to people being a bit tongue in cheek, when they talk about where you come from. What did you really think they would say when they know you come from Gobbler's Knob?

。°。°。°

Somewhere in rural America, two Jehovah's Witness women call on an unsuspecting household.

"Knock, knock."

"Hello, can I help you?"

"Howdy, there should have been three of us gals calling on you but Rubella from Horneytown is laid up. Let me introduce ourselves. I'm Latrine from Wanker's Corner and I've got Chlamydia from Gobbler's Knob. If we pray together, we can save our souls."

"It's OK thanks. You can save some other arseholes; I'm already signed up for the Catholic Deathbed Repentance Scheme."

33

We Should Have Gone
Swimming

Me: "I'd like the Welsh Rabbit, please."

Waitress: "One Welsh Rarebit?"

Me: "No, I want the Welsh Rabbit, not the bloody Welsh Rarebit!"

It's a touchy subject for me. I haven't been a big fan of this sort of political correctness but haven't made too much of a fuss about it either, as I've always wanted to keep my job.

Welsh Rabbit is cheese on toast, just as Bombay Duck is a type of curried fish; a Yarmouth Capon is a herring, and a Scotch Woodcock is egg on toast. Let's just leave things as they are instead of insisting on making everything politically correct, because otherwise, before too long I can just see my friend Guy Chapman becoming officially known as Person Person Person.

In ye olde worlde days when poor Welsh folk couldn't afford meat, some English wag ridiculed them by calling their meagre toasty snack 'Welsh Rabbit'. It's no good trying to make amends now.

Actually, I'd probably just mutter, "Yes please," and

that would be the end of it. I have always made it a practice to stay in with the cooks and serving staff, wherever I've been, even when the waitress asked if I wanted any Ball Sack vinegar, when I assume, actually, make that hope, she meant Balsamic. I politely refused, just in case she had got it right, and it was just the chef's little joke. The thing is, you just never know what they might be doing to your food before it reaches your table. My sister Kate confirmed this with some horror stories. I suppose it was best summed up for me by the cartoon where the nasty food critic who, for ease, we shall call 'Mr W', is eating in a fictional establishment.

Waiter: "Mr W would like another bowl of your lovely tart-tasting soup?"

Chef: "Duz ze think zat I am *made* of piss?"

Note: the consistency of soup and bodily function involved can be mixed and matched to suit the appropriate audience. Oh, and it's a French chef. It's the Ball Sack thing all over again!

As for the cheese on toast thing, I guess the correct course of action would be to run back into the restaurant, after you've finished your meal and shout your objection to the use of the 'rarebit' word and then rush out again, but I've never really felt *that* passionate about the whole rabbit thing, especially when I've got a full belly.

There are more important things in the world to become irate about, like asking someone if they want a bag of chips too, because you're getting one, and they reply that it's OK, as they'll just have some of yours. There are other things too, of course, besides food-related topics that get me going.

Tim: "Did you get my last e-mail?"

Me: "For feck's sake. How am I supposed to know?"

Another touchy one. How am I supposed to know if the last one I received was the last one he sent?

"Don't forget to remind me to take the holiday photos to work tomorrow".

Why? Why me? Why should I remind you?

You have just the one thing to remember – the photos. I, on the other hand, have two things. To remember something that I have absolutely no interest in, *and* I then need to remember to tell you about it! *Plus,* by agreeing to remind you, I have then taken on the mantle of blame for when *you* forget. And you will forget, because I will forget!

No. I will not remember for you. Get a reminding bear or something (for those blue-chip retailers reading, a reminding bear is *my* idea, so no stealing it and making loads of money out of it while I sit here with my puncture repair kit mending my Wellingtons). After years of 'Don't forget to remind me' episodes, I invented the 'John Donoghue Patent Pending Reminding Bear'. OK, so it's just a teddy bear I gave to Deborah to prop on the doorknob on the inside of the front door, but the idea is, as you go to leave the house you will see the reminding bear sitting there. 'Aha,' you will think. 'What did I leave the reminding bear there for?' You will then think ...and think ...and think ...and eventually remember what you needed to remember before you left the house.

So, no blame for Johnny. Bear feels as if he has done a good job. Everyone happy! (Well, except for the poor hapless workmates who then have to sit through someone else's holiday snaps, which are only ever fun if someone has left in some photos that should have been taken out. Are you listening, Mr Hefner?).

Since this book was written, I have since discovered that Hugh Hefner, founder of the Playboy empire has sadly passed away. Some say he's in a better place now, but, no offence, I sincerely doubt anywhere could be better than sitting in a mansion, in your PJs, surrounded by Playboy bunnies all day.

My other million-dollar idea is an alarm clock that sounds like a dog's pre-puke warning grunts. That'll get you out of bed and down the stairs in a flash!

Back to irritating things, and how about when your expectations are raised and then crushed in the cruellest way? Like when a girl rings and tells you she is bringing over a DVD to watch – and tells you to have a box of tissues ready. Then when she arrives you find out she has actually brought over a girly weepie movie!

And what about the annoying know-it-all who pipes up in the middle of some amusing anecdote to inform everyone that, "actually you'll find that Frankenstein was the name of the man who created the monster and *not* the monster itself". Was he? Was he really? Thank you very much, Professor killjoy clever dick. Tell me, are you able to suck the enjoyment out of *every* situation or did you just want me to look a twat specifically today?

…or when your boss suggests that you should really get back to work instead of laughing and joking with your colleagues.

…or those people who look at you disapprovingly because you're sniggering when someone suggests that the answer is 'Miss Peacock in the library with the candlestick'.

…or what about those bloody lights at Kilgetty?

The 'Barney eating my running trainers incident', it turns out, and if you can remember that far back, was just his way of showing me he loves me. I would have been happy with a box of Milk Tray, but he had to go just that bit too far. It's the sort of love gesture that kind of backfired.

"I'm Spartacus."

"No, I'm Spartacus."

"No, I'm Spartacus."

"No, I'm Spartacus," and so on.

That was a joke that backfired if ever one did!

A Place Oddity was in danger of disintegrating from a joyous romp through the summer countryside into an onerous trawl along the B roads of Britain, in the wet and windy cold winter evenings, unless we got a wiggle on. It was all so tantalisingly within our grasp too, with just one month to fill.

I decided that New York was the 'I'm Spartacus,' of place names. After my disappointment in the Yorkshire New York, the whole appeal of small Big Apples had gone. There was one in Newcastle, one in Lancashire and, hell, we even had the original York. Another place name had to be sourced.

。 * 。 * 。 *

During my life, my travels have taken me from the Gulf of Mexico to the Arabian Sea, and from the Arctic Circle down to North Africa. For the most part, the British Government paid me to go there.

I have been on patrol with the French Foreign Legion in Djibouti and waded through swamps with American Marines in Puerto Rico. The Russians caused me to split my head open in the Barents Sea, and I have played football with our former enemies in an old Red Army camp in Poland. I have swapped various items from the ship's supplies to buy some presents in India and got embarrassingly drunk on Sangria on every visit to Spain. In New Orleans, I tried to sell my blood for beer money and have ferried gold back to Britain from Qatar. Our ship was almost wrecked on rocks near the Eddystone lighthouse, and sailors were washed overboard on manoeuvres in the Bay of Biscay. I could go on, so I will. I almost went mad through lack of sleep in Germany and have climbed through the internal passages of a pyramid in Egypt. I've seen a desert night sky fall and roll the whole day over, and I've experienced the majesty of the Northern Lights. I've felt the sun beating down hard on me and felt the bitter Arctic chill. Hell, in Oman I had even eaten sweets after I had brushed my teeth one night.

The point is that all these experiences were special to me. I have enjoyed all the places I visited and love the thrill of discovering new ones with their unique experiences. But I didn't want to go to Quebec.

Quebec is a small village in the County Durham countryside. It is a lovely village and no doubt full of lovely people too, and its only failing was that this would be the place that would complete the calendar. Once Quebec was in the bag, 'A Place Oddity' would be complete. My personal project would be concluded. Finished. Over.

Deborah and Bethan would be over the moon that life could revert back to normal but, for me, the chase is always better than the kill. I wanted to keep them happy, but I also wanted to continue my quest. I didn't want it to be over. I was in a quandary.

Between the deep blue sea and the devil, that was me.

° * ° * ° *

There was Barney, the sign and John; there was just the sign and John and, sometimes, there was just the sign. Since the 'Happy Pity Me' had been replaced by the 'Sad Pity Me' photo, something was missing.

The calendar had started with the idea of making sure people remembered Bethan's birthday. Subsequently, it had also developed into a romp through the outlandish place names of the North East, with the intention of persuading the family to come and see what they were missing out on. All those places that we had taken photos of, for sure, but, more importantly, I was trying to encourage them to visit my daughter.

What was missing from A Place Oddity was Bethan!

So it was that, on a cold and windy October afternoon, Bethan accompanied Deborah and me to Quebec.

Quebec was apparently named as such because the fields in the area were enclosed in 1759, the year General Wolfe captured Quebec from the French in Canada. It was not unusual for fields to be named after foreign towns and places and, often occurred where they were situated at a considerable distance from their home farm. Fields might be given names like Botany Bay or Nova Scotia, playing on their remoteness from the farm. As settlements grew up around the fields, they often adopted the field's name.

You could go on a virtual world tour, without leaving the North East, as you travelled from New York near Whitley Bay; onto Toronto near Bishop Auckland; Philadelphia and Columbia in Washington and finally Canada, which is part of Chester-le-Street. Battles in foreign lands also provided a plethora of places, such as Bloemfontein near Stanley; Portobello near Birtley, from a Battle of 1739, and Inkerman near Tow Law, named after the battle of the same name during the Crimean War.

When we arrived, I could see the sign in front of me, the low winter sun-bathing it in shades of doubt. Bethan and I adopted a shivery pose next to it as if we were freezing in the middle of a cold, unforgiving Canadian winter. Once the photograph was taken, Deborah and Bethan resisted the temptation to do a little victory jig, but it was over all the same.

I was cold and sad and, to cap it all, I had sore, dry lips. Deborah handed me a ChapStick and I duly sorted myself out.

"Maybe we could go for a coffee or something…" she suggested. I knew she was going to say 'to celebrate' but her voice just trailed off.

"I don't know, I'm not really in the mood."

"I'm buying," she added enthusiastically.

"C'mon Daddy, we can have some cake too!"

With Bethan joining in how could I refuse? We all climbed back into the car and set off for a little teashop that I'd seen on the way. When we arrived, the girls told me to go ahead and find a table and order as they had to get their things together, so I set off without them fearing the worst; that this was a trap and I'd end up footing the bill again.

"You'll have to pull!" shouted the woman inside as I tried to push the door open. What did she think I was going to do next? Start lifting it from the bottom?

As I got inside, the few customers looked up and started to giggle. What? Have you never tried a door wrong before? Some people!

I hung my coat over a seat at an unoccupied table in the window to stake my claim and went up to order.

"Circus in town, is it?" the waitress enquired with a smile, before turning away. I could see her shoulders rising and falling. What was wrong with this place?

"I've literally no idea," I responded.

I ordered two coffees, a Coca Cola and three pieces of chocolate cake which I proceeded to carry on a tray back to the table where the Bethan and Deborah were now sitting, moving at a snail's pace for fear of spilling anything. A couple looked up and chuckled as I passed them. What, have you never tried to walk whilst precariously balancing a fully laden tray? Pathetic!

When I arrived at the table, the girls looked up, smirking. I shook my head and sat down before whispering that I thought we'd found a mad house here. It was all too much for Bethan and she collapsed in a fit of giggles whilst Deborah bit her lip in a bid to keep herself together. Well at least some people were entertained. I looked around and noticed more customers were surreptitiously glancing over in our direction before quickly looking away. What was all that about? Had word quickly spread? Was everyone rejoicing in my misery at the end of Project X?

"Can we take some photos?" queried Bethan. "You know, so we can remember what we've been up to?"

Of course we could. And so the snaps began; me and Bethan; me and Debs; me, Bethan and Debs... the staff even joined in with the waitress asking if she could have a picture taken with me. Well, it would be churlish to refuse so I happily posed with her. I started to feel like a bit of a celebrity when they even called the girl from out the back who was making the sandwiches to have her photo taken next to me. The day was looking up; maybe I should be celebrating the end of the calendar instead of being miserable about it.

I don't mind telling you that I had lost some faith in humanity after some of the things that I'd seen in the military, how badly people can treat each other, the lack of compassion. However, my belief in human nature was being restored today. They didn't have to do this; nobody had to cheer me up, but here were just nice, kind-hearted and supportive people who obviously sensed I was feeling down and who were making the effort to make me feel better about myself. This was just fantastic. It lifted my heart, and I made a mental note to never think the worst of people ever again.

As I popped to the washroom before we left, I was walking on air, grinning from ear to ear, and high fiving the other patrons as I passed (I thought it better to do that on the way there rather than the way back!).

I laughed to myself, shaking my head as I stood at the urinal. You never know where you'll experience your Eureka moment. Did it really take half a lifetime and Project X for me to realise people are inherently good?

As I washed my hands I looked into the mirror and saw a changed man looking back at me. No, literally, I was a changed man – I looked like the bloody Joker! Deborah must have given me her lipstick instead of a ChapStick and what's more, the way it was liberally smeared over my lips made it look like I'd been putting it on whilst someone had been driving over some speed bumps. So THAT'S why everyone was so full of bonhomie and wanted their photos taken with me!

I quickly made for the door and swung it open before poking my head around the corner looking like some sad curious clown scanning to see where the culprits were but, unsurprisingly, neither Bethan nor Deborah were anywhere to be seen. I re-entered the tearoom trying to look nonchalant but inside my chalant was off the scale. I quickly walked purposefully through, not making any eye contact and pulled the door to get out.

"You have to…"

"ALRIGHT, ALRIGHT, ALRIGHT!" I replied curtly.

I could just about hear someone mutter something along the lines of, "Steady on, OutKast," before the door slammed behind me.

I knew then that we should have gone swimming instead!

34

The Thirteenth Month

Sometimes I don't believe that women *can't* read maps, I think it's that they don't *want* to read maps.

Maybe Deborah knows that, like any man, I hate to ask the way and, if she pretends that she can't follow the route on the page, she will witness a demonstration of how men are different from women. It's not just me. Moses, it is said, wandered in the desert for forty years because he refused to ask for directions.

She watches me turn the music off so that I can concentrate better as we reach a series of complex junctions. She also hears me request that both Bethan and Deborah stop chatting and look out for the signs which, apparently, confuses them as they feel that, as women, they can both talk and look for signs simultaneously.

When we arrive at wherever we are going to, the two girls may then disappear to the rest room together. Why? I don't know. I've never shouted over to Tim that I was off to the toilet and asked if he wanted join me. Maybe I should next time, to check I didn't look like some bizarre jester.

And what is it with women and sharp knives? I've seen Deborah digging stuck toast out of a plugged-in toaster with one, using another as a screwdriver and generally using a knife for any task that a normal person might use an adjustable spanner for. As a result, I've felt compelled to doctor the knives in my house to the extent that they are now so blunt that I could ride bare-arsed to London on them, just in case Deborah arrives and decides she fancies loosening a jar lid or opening a tin with one.

Mind you, I admit that when I go shopping with Bethan, and go to the cash point, as the money emerges I have an overwhelming urge to punch the air and shout, "I've won! I've won!" Poor Bethan then glances around hoping that no one she knows is within hearing distance and desperately tries to pretend that she's not with me. Also, as we get to the counter to pay for her new top or shoes, I have an overwhelming compulsion to say to the young girl serving, "I'm not sure if it'll fit me, though!" As Bethan hangs her head in embarrassment, their response is to either shoot Bethan a, "Don't worry, my dad does the same" sort of look, or else they will think I'm serious and give me a, "Hey, it's a free world, I'm not judging you" look, to which *I* then hang my head in embarrassment. I tell Bethan that I don't mean to embarrass her, I just can't help it; it's a dad illness!

Mind you, I confess as a man that if someone tells me something is really hot, I've got to touch it to make sure – and in the process lose the skin off whatever part of my body I decide to poke it with.

Sniffing – that's another male thing. If I find a bottle in a garage marked 'Do not inhale' and marked with a skull and crossbones, I, along with 80% of the male population, feel compelled to have a sniff, 'just to check', before reeling back croaking 'Jesus Christ!' and waiting to black out.

Deborah also knows that, like a lot of men, I also suffer from a strange form of butter blindness. As much as I search, I can swear that the butter is nowhere in the fridge, only for her to come over and find it instantly.

It was probably a fair deal. We were different. I couldn't find the butter and Deborah couldn't find Kirkby Overblow.

What can be more frustrating than reaching December and wanting to plan some dates in January? You don't want to bin last year's calendar because you're still using it, but you haven't got the space for two calendars on the wall.

Solution? The thirteen-month calendar. Patents pending, that was where Kirkby Overblow came in.

It might not have the funniest name, and it might not boast the most exciting history ('Kirkby' means church village, whilst 'Overblow' is a reference to smelters who presumably worked there), but it was a good reason to go and do another shoot.

I had become a place name junkie and needed one more fix.

∘ ° ∘ ° ∘ °

Barney was bundled into the car and the journey was made to our final photoshoot. We drove at a sedate pace – I say 'we' but mean 'me'. I drove and Barney just lay in the back and at one stage he began to sigh melodramatically. I knew he wanted me to ask him what was wrong, but I wasn't falling for it. Eventually he fell asleep, with his puppy snoring punctuated by the occasional fart.

I thought about turning the radio on to try and drown him out. *"...and now a request for his daughter who is 111 today. My goodness, that's a wonderful age. Oh ... no, sorry, she's ill".* Or maybe not. I'd stick with the snoring and sighing for now.

We drove down an autumnal tree-lined lane with the low sun behind, accentuating the russets and browns of the leaves. We eventually pulled over onto the grass verge, next to the sign alongside the Kirkby Overblow cemetery, at the dead centre of the village. It was a delightful place and one that I took an instant liking to, and the fact that it had two pubs helped immensely. I fetched the camera from the back of the vehicle and, a few minutes later, the dirty deed was done. The thirteenth month now joined Bearpark, Once Brewed, Twice Brewed, Crackpot, Wetwang, No Place, Shitter, Cockfield, Pity Me, Quaking Houses, Quebec and Blubberhouses.

The project was over. I allowed myself a moment to stand in quiet contemplation.

About thirty seconds was enough. I was glad when it was finished. To be honest, I'm not really sure what you are supposed to be thinking of when you do meditate. I usually find my mind wandering and thinking things like, *"What if the Hokey Cokey is REALLY what it's all about?"*

Mind you, it's the same when, after some romantic interlude (delicately put – even if I say so myself), your girlfriend rolls over to you and says those words every man dreads – "What are you thinking about?" You know what you *should* answer – what she *wants* to hear. Tales about chasing a dream, skipping barefoot hand in hand through poppy fields, the both of you having a picnic in the park, feeding each other strawberries, laughing together on sunny days... maybe a puppy is in there somewhere as well. The trouble is, what I'm normally thinking (and I think I speak for most men here) is something like, *'How do flies land on the ceiling upside-down?', 'What's on telly?'* or *'Where did all the change go to that dropped out of my pocket when I took my trousers off? I'm sure I saw a couple of one pound coins rolling under the bed.'* I know, though, what the reaction will be if I share my true innermost thoughts at that point in time. After years of bitter experience, I have finally learnt my lesson. I find it best to lie.

Anyway, Project X – A Place Oddity was over. It was time to think of something else to do. I'm not sure what Deborah and Bethan's reactions might be but, hell, if they have a blacklist, put me on it.

"My name is John... and I'm in love with my addiction."

I need to have my own hobby, stupid boy project, pointless quest – call it what you will. If Deborah and Bethan think that this is a crime, then I'm a self-confessed recidivist.

A penguin, swan, goose, emu, scorpion, baby crocodile, dog, cat and sheep have all bitten me, and I almost had my finger taken off by a piglet. Maybe I could get bitten by the A-Z of animals?

I've eaten Pontefract cakes, Eccles cakes and Cheddar cheese. Perhaps I could eat all the foods named after places, in the actual place that bears their name.

Maybe I could start talking in the third person. Could John manage a whole twelve months? What would John do when he actually *needed* to talk in the third person, but he was already doing it because of his stupid project?

It might even be fun to watch every episode of Sgt Bilko in succession, with only a cup of tea and a packet of chocolate Hobnobs for company.

Then again, I was almost forty and Bethan's first decade was almost over. Maybe I should do something to mark the occasion. Maybe I could write a book.

35

This Is My Kingdom Now

I met up with a girl once after I had come back off military exercise and was suffering from sleep deprivation. She said I talked a load of rubbish. I met her a week later after I had a decent night's sleep and she said I spoke a load of rubbish then too. Apologies if you feel you've just had to sit through the written equivalent. Although maybe one day we'll look back on those times and call them the good old days.

Anyway, a year has passed since I completed Project X and I thought it best to have a debrief. Make yourself a cup of tea and I'll see you back here in five minutes.

Ready? Well, I suppose we should start with what I've missed out. It's like when you've had an argument and later on you think that you should have said this or that. Well, writing a book is no different.

Anyway, you'll not find out about the women I've kissed in places I'd better not mention, nor will you find my list of things that should be invented anywhere in print. You will not read about how I was abducted by aliens, nor will you find out what would be banned or made law if I were king of my own island. How annoyed I become by students in coffee shops in Durham, hogging the tables as they nurse a single cup of 'Mocha Latte' for three hours, as they work on their dissertations, will not be fully explored either. If you are going to sit there for hours, do something useful. How about designing the perfect pet? I've already started on it and it's coming along pretty well. Obviously, it would have to have dog-like features and instincts, but also include some cat elements to balance the Catholic/Protestant angle. I had solved the arsehole showing off problem relatively simply (this was both a multi-denominational issue, facing cats as well as dogs). My solution? A stiff tail.

Finally, my pet needed some sort of conveyance device to bring the paper back or carry around a few tins of beer. A pouch, maybe? In fact, my perfect pet was starting to look something along the lines of a Thylacine. I think I'll put in a call to the JML people tomorrow. Maybe I could even start a rumour that I had spotted one to drum up a bit of publicity. Where better for a phantom sighting of my elusive marsupial Elvis than No Place? I could send out a text 'ITISATINP'. On second thoughts, I think that girl was right – I do talk a load of rubbish.

I also digress far too much, it seems (but not as much as the taxi driver in London who made me realise that from the train station to Neil's house isn't the mere three miles that it shows on the map, but rather a whole hefty seven miles).

I know it's good to be there on the bad days as well as the good ones. It's supposed to be character building, and I am probably in need of some. I haven't forgotten the bad things – it's just that it's more fun to remember the good times. So, the bad stuff is not here either.

As for Deborah, she eventually moved to Turkey, into

another time zone. I'd been clock blocked. I guess I should have realised the signs were there when she started referring to our 'relationship' in air quotes. Mind you, I'll admit that I perhaps wasn't the best partner she could have had:

Me: "Pick a card, any card, memorise it and now put it back."

Alas, I wasn't doing a magic trick, we were in the card shop on Valentine's Day.

I asked her once if I had any annoying little habits and was frankly taken aback when she surprised me with a full PowerPoint presentation.

When the final moment came it was as if she was working for Personnel, as she wished me well in all my future endeavours, gave me a pat on the back and told me to clear out my hypothetical desk. I left her house looking like I'd just been fired in a film, carrying an old cardboard box with all my stuff, including a potted plant and framed photograph poking out the top (Japanese Peace Lily and a mounted photo of me and Abi Titmuss). It seems that all that time I spent on the nights before recycling day, pondering whether to keep a cardboard box because it was a 'really good one' hadn't been wasted after all.

You can have ex-wives and ex-girlfriends, but you can never have ex-children. I am pleased to report that Bethan is going from strength to strength. She's a beautiful young girl and I'm very proud of her. She's started back up with my education, although I regret to say that she hasn't yet brought in the big TV on the stand that we all used to love seeing being wheeled into the classroom as kids. She is going to grow up into a smart young woman and make an excellent teacher one day. Just thinking about her makes me smile.

And Project X worked. We were inundated with a

steady stream of visitors coming to visit me, Bethan and Barney, and to see some of the nonsense-named places. Too many people, in fact. I'm starting to think I may be anti-social after all, but still just want people to visit so I don't feel like I'm missing out. I've finally made the transition and realised who is the better company – it seems I'm not a people person anymore, I'm a fully-fledged dog person.

Barney and I, meanwhile, have moved to a little cottage in the country. We live at the very end of the village, and on one side I have cows for neighbours and a very pleasant lady on the other side, although I don't think she watches porn. She asked me round to fix her sink last week, and twenty minutes later I was *still* fixing the sink. She has a cat named Colonel Mustard, and actually, that reminds me, I must tell Barney that when a cat wags its tail, it doesn't mean the same thing as when a dog does. We don't want another awkward misunderstanding.

Speaking of Barney, he now looks longingly at the fields next to us where the cows meander and the sheep potter and munch the grass all day. He doesn't want to chase any of them, but I think instead he remembers that we lost a tennis ball somewhere in there.

He's grown into a lovely dog and I often find myself shouting forlornly, "Don't worry, he's super friendly!" as he charges at full speed towards a terrified group of toddlers, intent on licking them to death and discovering if they have a biscuit, just for him. With other dogs, he is ever hopeful that they want to play chase with him, and he'll bark hello as they go past. He has a new best friend too, Ben, a lovely dog from up the road, and they love to go on walks together as well as playing the 'chase me but don't quite catch me' game. As for any other four-legged creature – he just refuses point blank to acknowledge them.

I tried to point out a hedgehog on the path to him the other day, but he just pretended that he couldn't see it, looking everywhere except directly in front of him where our spiky friend was waiting expectantly. Indeed, ever since the horny toad episode, Barney has had a 'live and let live' attitude to life. So much so that he now only chooses to recognise other dogs and humans. It's the same with the farmyard felines who wander by – to Barney they just don't exist. There'll be no cat calls in this dog-eared village.

There are some lovely country walks near our cottage and on one such meander he once found half a pie that someone threw away, and so now, until the end of time, we will forever have to stop at the magic pie bush for a sniff. He has also developed an intricate pooping ritual which he seems to put into practice mainly when he knows I'm running late for work. I'll take him up the lane to do his dirty, sinful business before I can rush back and get ready to leave. However, Barney's sixth sense clicks in at this stage and he'll try and wind me up. In the middle of our walk his little brake light will come on to show poop time is imminent (well that's what it looks like), but then he'll potter around and around his desired patch of grass looking for the ideal place to lay to rest his doings. He'll just continue to potter away, back and forth, back and forth, back and forth over the same little patch of ground until he knows I'm ready to shout in desperation, "JUST POOP, YOU FOOL!". He takes more time finding the perfect place to poo that I do on most of my life-altering decisions. All in all, I actually think he's cleverer than me nowadays as he understands quite a few human words, but I still don't know any dog barks. But the most important thing is that he seems a very contented and happy dog with a tail in a near state of perpetual wag. And that's all I ever wanted for him.

As for me, since getting Barney, I've realised that it's never too late to restart your life, to create a new Year Zero. Perhaps one of the main things he taught me was that you don't need money to be happy. There's no point staying in a job if you don't enjoy it, even if the pay is excellent – life is too short for that. Money isn't worth your soul. In fact, sometimes, when you're in a dark place and you think you've been buried, you've actually been planted and it's time to grow again. Maybe Barney was sent to water me... hang on, I'm taking this analogy thing foo far, aren't I?

To tell the truth, I missed the camaraderie of the military. I'd been a sailor and a soldier, and I thought it was time for some new adventures. So, I joined the police. I'd watched enough TV programmes to know what to expect and, in true Donoghue fashion, I'd even drawn up the top ten things I could expect based on what I'd seen:

1. Most crime is solved by a Chief Inspector with his sergeant sidekick.
2. During all police investigations, it will be necessary to visit a strip club at least once.
3. The job entails lots of action and no filling out of reports or file prep.
4. It takes minutes to run any DNA or forensics test, and a million to one DNA match comes up 99% of the time.
5. If DNA says that someone has an airtight alibi, there is always an identical twin nobody knew about.
6. If you see a suspect you need to arrest, don't grab them, just shout "Oi" at them from over the road giving them a chance to run off.
7. Anyone with a crucial piece of information to

solve the crime won't divulge it over the phone but insist on meeting in person… but when you turn up, they'll be dead.

8. If you hear a noise in a basement, you'll go and investigate it on your own.
9. When a cop investigating a crime has an idea, they'll just say, "I've just thought of something," and rush out of the room without telling anyone what it was.
10. Printers always work.

Not long after joining I soon found out that that little glowing box in the corner of the room that tells me stories had been lying to me. It was like another world that I could never have imagined. Maybe I should write some books about what it's *really* like in the police.

Well, that's us all up to date except for that final question, the one I asked myself after seeing Billy the Bush Dog at Edinburgh Zoo. Was I able to be the Top Dog – the leader of the pack?

As I looked over at Barney, he was just sitting there, scratching his head with his foot. I finished making him his dinner, put some fresh water out for him, and then donned my coat before I ventured outside into the dark, cold, wind and rain to clean out his kennel and pick up his turds. As I glanced back through the window into the cottage, the roaring fire making it look warm and inviting, I could just make him out, having a big stretch, before climbing up onto the sofa and letting out the biggest yawn in dog history.

Yes, I think we all knew who was the boss alright.

Acknowledgements

I just want to clarify from the start that if anyone reads this book who knows me, please understand that I'm a different person just with the same name. Anyway, if you wanted me to write fondly about you, maybe you should have been nicer to me.

In particular, thanks go to Nancy, Dave, Poppy and Seth for their help, and if anyone else thinks I owe them a debt of gratitude for their assistance, support, inspiration, supply of biscuits (delete applicable) – then you are probably right.

If you're American and reading this book, what you call 'sprinkles', we call 'hundreds and thousands'. It'll make sense later.

Finally, I may get some common expressions mixed up in the book, but that's neither there nor here, but be warned, if you criticise my grammar, I shall think fewer of you.

John Donoghue

About the author

John Donoghue has served Queen and Country in the Royal Navy, British Army and the Police. He also has a dog.

Twitter: @johndonoghue64
www.policecrime999.com

Other books by John Donoghue

Police, Crime & 999 ASIN: B00570B6YW

Police, Lies & Alibis ASIN: B00E4QVNLG

Police, Arrests & Suspects ASIN: B016E1IO9C

Sample from: '*Police, Crime & 999*'

(The True Story of a Front Line Officer)

There is a tale of two police officers who went to the
house of an elderly lady to take a statement from her.
She made them both a cup of tea and ushered them into
the front room where they all sat, discussing the purpose
of the call. As they talked, the door was nudged open,
and a German Shepherd dog pottered into the middle
of the room. The dog looked around and then
proceeded to squat down and, with his back legs all a-
quiver, deposited a fresh steaming turd onto the lounge
room carpet. The police officers exchanged sideways
glances but didn't say anything. After all, it was the
woman's house, and everyone has different standards – it
wasn't up to them to admonish the hound. They looked
over at the house owner, but she just acted as if nothing
had happened. Instead, she avoided looking at the dirty
beast and his doings, picked up her cup of tea, took a sip
and continued to politely chat to the officers. Meanwhile,
the dog, having completed his ablutions, sauntered back
out of the room.

Twenty minutes later and ready to leave, the officer's
curiosity had finally got the better of them. As they
thanked the lady for the tea, one of them felt compelled

to enquire why she hadn't said anything when her dog had come into the room and pooped on the floor.

"*My* dog?" replied the old woman. "I thought it was *your* dog!"

Printed in Great Britain
by Amazon